CAPITAL STREETCARS

CAPITAL STREETCARS

EARLY MASS TRANSIT IN WASHINGTON, D.C.

JOHN DEFERRARI | Foreword by Ken Rucker

Published by The History Press
Charleston, SC 29403
www.historypress.net

Copyright © 2015 by John DeFerrari
All rights reserved

First published 2015

ISBN 978-1-5402-0291-8

Library of Congress Control Number: 2015945064

Notice: The information in this book is true and complete to the best of our knowledge. It is offered without guarantee on the part of the author or The History Press. The author and The History Press disclaim all liability in connection with the use of this book.

All rights reserved. No part of this book may be reproduced or transmitted in any form whatsoever without prior written permission from the publisher except in the case of brief quotations embodied in critical articles and reviews.

This book, once again, is for Sue.

Contents

Foreword, by Ken Rucker — 9
Preface — 11

Chapter 1. The City of Magnificent Distances:
 Transit in Washington Before Streetcars, 1800–1862 — 15
Chapter 2. Horses in the Mud:
 The Early Horse-Drawn Streetcar Era, 1862–1888 — 28
Chapter 3. Close Quarters: Riding the Cars, 1862–1888 — 44
Chapter 4. Hard Choices:
 Modernizing the Streetcar System, 1888–1897 — 61
Chapter 5. Grid-Ironing the City:
 The Rise of Streetcar Suburbs, 1868–1899 — 76
Chapter 6. Bigger Crowds and Bigger Cars:
 The New Century's Challenges, 1900–1918 — 108
Chapter 7. A Vast Amount of Harm:
 The Struggle to Maintain Equal Access, 1900–1920 — 133
Chapter 8. Yesterday's Technology:
 Competition with Automobiles and Buses, 1920–1940 — 143
Chapter 9. War and Peace:
 The World War II Years and Afterward, 1940–1950 — 160
Chapter 10. Endgame:
 Washington's Streetcars Disappear, 1950–1962 — 181

Contents

Chapter 11. Lost and Found:
    Nostalgia for the Streetcar Era, 1962–2015   200

Notes   215
Selected Bibliography   225
Index   231
About the Author   237

FOREWORD

There was a time when folks rode the rails through the streets of Washington. Beginning during the Lincoln administration in 1862, streetcars carried people around the city. For one hundred years, from Lincoln to Kennedy, streetcars connected the communities of the federal city and enabled the development of communities in the county of Washington. First with horse traction, then cable traction and, lastly, electric traction, the streetcars provided what a 1902 census report called "an imperative social need" by spreading growing urban populations over a much wider area than would have been possible without ever-faster and cleaner street railways. By the 1930s, gasoline-powered buses were providing more flexible transit services, and the automobile beckoned commuters with private, on-demand transportation. After World War II, prosperity accelerated the abandonment of street railways and the expansion of the suburbs served by massive highway development. Sixty years on, many people are looking to urban areas for homes to relieve themselves from long commutes on crowded highways, and revitalization of older communities is welcoming the return of streetcars as symbols of urban renaissance.

Prior histories have chronicled the era of street railways in the nation's capital for the traction or railway fan. Now, *Capital Streetcars: Early Mass Transit in Washington, D.C.* addresses a larger audience as it explores the economic and social needs met by these railways as well. With vignettes establishing the social and political contexts influencing the actions of the characters who made the development decisions, as well as carefully selected images,

Foreword

this work expands the scholarship available beyond the nuts and bolts of railway construction and management to include the social fabric of life in Washington through the streetcar era.

Ken Rucker
President, National Capital Trolley Museum
May 2015

Preface

*The streetcar decided where we could live and where we would shop.
It gave shape to the city.*
—*Jack Eisen,* Washington Post, *January 28, 1962*

Streetcars had a powerful hold on Washingtonians during their one-hundred-year reign, profoundly shaping the patterns of our lives and the city around us. Where the streetcar went, so went the city's residents. Along with them came the neighborhood groceries, the dress shops and hardware stores, the mom and pop cafés and restaurants—all the fixtures of our urban existence, strung out along the lengths of their routes. And it was on the streetcars that so many lives intersected. In their heyday, virtually everyone rode them. From day laborers to Supreme Court justices, the cars brought Washingtonians together like nothing else ever had.

At times, they could be tremendous fun. Several generations of small boys delighted in stealing rides downtown or in causing mischief by setting blasting caps on the rails or jamming the slot rail in the center of the tracks. As one of the capital city's cheapest forms of entertainment, the much-loved open-air cars of the early twentieth century took thousands of riders on airy jaunts to see baseball games at Griffith Stadium or out across the countryside of Maryland and upper Northwest D.C. To this day, many Washingtonians recall with special fondness riding the Cabin John streetcar out to Glen Echo Park on pleasant summer weekends. Those were experiences of a time and place that will never return.

Preface

Most of the time streetcar rides were far from thrilling. For thousands of commuters, they were merely a practical means of getting from point A to point B. They were often crowded, poorly timed and frustratingly slow. Although integrated by federal law since 1864, streetcars were also a flashpoint in the struggle against discrimination in the early twentieth century. During the dark days of the 1919 riots, African Americans, who depended on the streetcars for transportation as much as everyone else, might have feared for their very lives when stepping aboard.

The cars had an impact on almost everyone's life, and much of the drama of their story comes from all the change they brought. In the mid-nineteenth century, when streetcars were first proposed, many older Washingtonians were upset at the idea of laying railroad tracks down the middle of Pennsylvania Avenue, splitting the north half of the street from the south. It seemed an outrage. More angst came with the arrival of cars powered by overhead trolley wires, a technology so offensive that it was banned in the downtown part of the city. And not long after that controversy was finally settled, the whole concept of a railed streetcar system was questioned again when automobiles and buses arrived. Technological change fed constant upheaval.

And yet the transportation wants and needs of most people changed little during this time. They wanted streetcars to be easy to access from their homes, to run on convenient schedules, to be reasonably comfortable to ride, to take passengers to their destinations quickly and efficiently and to be inexpensive to use on a daily basis. In many ways, the history of Washington's mass transit system, like that of others across the country, is the story of an unending struggle to achieve these confounding, elusive goals. It is also the story of the owners and operators, a long line of local transit barons who were all convinced that they could wring profits from the system one way or another. Few of them ever fully succeeded.

The trials and tribulations of streetcars, and the joys and frustrations of riding them, were part of everyday life for hometown Washingtonians of the past. My hope is that this book can help readers paint for themselves a fuller picture of that past life.

What This Book Isn't

Capital Streetcars is not the first book about the history of streetcars in the District of Columbia. Two impressive, lavishly illustrated books on the same

Preface

subject have previously been published: LeRoy O. King's Jr.'s *100 Years of Capital Traction: The Story of Streetcars in the Nation's Capital* (1972) and Peter C. Kohler's *Capital Transit: Washington's Street Cars: The Final Era, 1933–1962* (2001). These two encyclopedic reference works provide a wealth of detail about the city's vast streetcar infrastructure and how it was managed and operated, including precise route locations, schedules and the numbers and types of rolling stock that served them. King, whose father worked for the Capital Traction Company, amassed an extraordinary collection of images and documentation that detailed the operations of the city's many historic streetcar companies. Kohler's book offers an extensive year-by-year review of all the important events that occurred in the Capital Transit Company's history, from its inception in 1933 to the last streetcar trip in 1962. I highly recommend both books and certainly do not aim to compete with either.

A Note on Terminology

These days, the terms *trolley* and *streetcar* are considered interchangeable, but that wasn't always the case. Washingtonians who were here in the days of streetcars know that they were never called trolleys in those days. Trolleys were specifically the kind of streetcar that drew electric power from overhead wires through a trolley pole, and Washington's streetcars did this only outside the central part of the city. For that reason, I've used the term *trolley* only when referring to cars drawing power from overhead wires. Otherwise, I have used the term *streetcar* or just *car*. I have used these terms interchangeably because that was how they were used historically. To avoid confusion, I have tried to consistently use the term *automobile* to refer to private motor vehicles. In general, I have attempted to limit the amount of industry jargon, although a certain amount is unavoidable—and even, at times, entertaining!

Acknowledgements

I could never complete a book of this scope without the help of many people, and I am grateful for the tremendous assistance I received from many quarters. Laura Barry and Anne McDonough of the Historical Society of Washington, D.C., provided valuable assistance in locating and

Preface

examining records of the Capital Traction Company, as well as identifying key historical photographs. The entire staff of the Washingtoniana Division of the D.C. Public Library provided critical assistance, as they always do, in accessing a variety of newspaper clippings and other key source materials. Matthew Gilmore prepared an excellent custom set of detailed maps of historical streetcar routes. John Muller located and shared several valuable and little-known sources of information. I also received help from Garrett Peck, Bill Rice, Robert Ellis of the National Archives and Records Administration and Kim Williams of the D.C. Historic Preservation Office. In addition to these, others helped me specifically to locate and use a wide range of great historical photographs, including Katie Crabb of the D.C. Department of Transportation and Sharon Knecht of the Oblate Sisters of Providence. Clark Frazier and Charles Houser graciously allowed me to use photographs they had taken. Derek Gray and Michele Casto of the DCPL Washingtoniana Division assisted with photos from the *Washington Star* collection, as well as the library's historical image collection. Jerry McCoy, who always has something new and interesting to contribute, shared his set of streetcar photographs originally collected by Bob Truax and provided scans of several images. Charles Plantholt, treasurer of the Baltimore Chapter of the National Railway Historical Society and archivist of the Maryland Rail Heritage Library, and Alexander D. Mitchell IV, president of the Baltimore Chapter of the National Railway Historical Society, offered enthusiastic assistance in tracking down several unique photos from the collections of the Maryland Rail Heritage Library.

I am particularly indebted to Ken Rucker of the National Capital Trolley Museum, who assisted me in several vital ways, including writing the foreword to this book, providing a number of historic photographs and painstakingly reviewing the draft text. Zachary Schrag and Fran White also read the text or portions of it and provided many useful and incisive comments. The book is far better as a result of their gracious and generous assistance.

Chapter 1

The City of Magnificent Distances

TRANSIT IN WASHINGTON BEFORE STREETCARS, 1800–1862

In early Washington, everything was very far from everything else. The ten-mile-square District of Columbia, as laid out by George Washington, began as mostly farmland and wilderness, with two small port towns—Alexandria and Georgetown—to the south and west. Washington City was envisioned as a separate settlement in the middle, on the relatively flat stretch of land where the Potomac and Anacostia (then known as the Eastern Branch) Rivers met, an area largely devoid of any previous development.

In 1791, George Washington commissioned talented French-born architect Peter Charles L'Enfant (1754–1825) to design the layout for the new city. L'Enfant's plan, which would be revered by succeeding generations for its commodious public squares and grand diagonal avenues, foresaw development growing not from a single downtown focal point but from several different simultaneous centers of activity.[1] Wharves on the banks of the Eastern Branch (where the Navy Yard would be established in 1799) were to serve as the easternmost focal point. This site, one of the earliest centers of employment in Washington, was about one mile to the southeast of where the U.S. Capitol was to be built on Jenkins Hill. The White House was to be sited more than one mile in the opposite direction, to the northwest. And Georgetown, already a separate, well-established town, was about that same distance again northwest of the White House. Thus, the city's early focal points were spread out over a stretch of several miles. If ever there were a town in need of efficient public transportation, it was this one.

CAPITAL STREETCARS

This circa 1800 watercolor by William Birch of the unfinished Capitol gives a sense of the emptiness of the early city. *Library of Congress.*

José Correia da Serra (1750–1823), Portugal's minister-plenipotentiary to Washington from 1816 to 1820, has been credited with first calling Washington the "City of Magnificent Distances," a name that elegantly conveys both admiration for the grandly conceived spaces of the L'Enfant Plan and subtle criticism of their emptiness and dispersion.[2] The title clearly resonated with the city's early residents and visitors, many of whom were skeptical of the yawning boulevards, especially Pennsylvania Avenue, which seemed to stretch for such unnecessary and presumptuous lengths.

There were no easy answers to the problem of transportation in the nascent capital. The vast majority of city residents owned no horses, and still fewer owned carriages. Within Washington City, they mostly lived in houses along Pennsylvania Avenue between the Capitol and the White House or on nearby F Street, with a scattering of dwellings on other streets. More buildings were scattered over the stretch of Pennsylvania Avenue between the White House and Georgetown, as were houses clustered on Capitol Hill and near the Navy Yard. In 1800, there were just 6,203 people living in Washington City and Georgetown, about half in each town. As in other major cities, these early urban dwellers simply walked everywhere they needed to go. Places that were beyond a comfortable walking distance were not easily accessible. The resulting gaps in the city's physical development persisted for decades, with the city growing slowly. The 1840 census registered a population of

Early Mass Transit in Washington, D.C.

30,676 for Washington and Georgetown—a big increase over 1800 but still less than one-third of the population of major cities like Baltimore (102,313) or Philadelphia (93,665). When Charles Dickens visited the capital in 1842 and found that the great planned spaces were still largely empty, he penned this famous description:

> *It is sometimes called the City of Magnificent Distances, but it might with greater propriety be termed the City of Magnificent Intentions; for it is only on taking a bird's-eye view of it from the top of the Capitol, that one can at all comprehend the vast designs of its projector, an aspiring Frenchman. Spacious avenues, that begin in nothing, and lead nowhere; streets, mile-long, that only want houses, roads and inhabitants; public buildings that need but a public to be complete; and ornaments of great thoroughfares, which only lack great thoroughfares to ornament—are its leading features.*[3]

The earliest attempt to offer a system of public transportation across this vast city-to-be was a twice-a-day stagecoach service begun in May 1800 that ran from the center of Georgetown (at what is now the intersection of M Street and Wisconsin Avenue) to William Tunnicliff's hotel on Capitol Hill, just east of the Capitol building. That business quickly failed; service was too infrequent and too pricey. For another thirty years, Washingtonians who could not afford to hire private hackney cabs, which were expensive, had few transportation options.

What we now think of as a city bus—a vehicle traveling a set route and carrying multiple passengers for a low fare—didn't appear until the 1820s. The first such conveyances went into operation in London and Paris. In short order they were dubbed "omnibuses," from a term originally coined by the French philosopher Blaise Pascal (1623–1662) and derived from the Latin word meaning "for everyone." (It wasn't until the twentieth century that the term would be shortened to just "bus.")

Abraham Brower, a New York businessman, is generally credited with introducing omnibuses in America. In 1827, he ran his first public coach along Broadway. Called an "accommodation," it was an open, two-horse carriage featuring four rows of seats facing one another in two pairs. It was an immediate success, and in 1831, Brower commissioned a young Irish-born coachbuilder named John Stephenson (1809–1893) to construct the first true American omnibus.

Stephenson's omnibus went into service on Broadway in 1832. It featured a single enclosed passenger compartment with a row of seats lining each side,

John Stephenson's first omnibus, built in 1832. *From* World on Wheels *(1878)*.

a design that would become standard in later nineteenth-century streetcars. Passengers climbed rickety steps to enter a door at the rear. Stephenson soon began making important innovations, such as setting the passenger seats lower—close to the tops of the wheels—and locating the floor space between them in drop wells between the wheels. This resulted in a car that sat about a foot closer to the ground and was much easier to board than earlier coaches. Stephenson received a patent for this invention—signed by President Andrew Jackson—in 1833. His company would go on to become one of the most prominent nineteenth-century makers of streetcars, reportedly producing more than twenty-five thousand vehicles for street railways both in the United States and around the world.

As for Washington, the first omnibuses began operating in early 1830, almost as soon as they appeared in New York. The first line ran along Pennsylvania Avenue from Georgetown to the Navy Yard. The *Daily National Intelligencer*, Washington's principal newspaper at the time, ran a letter to the editor in March 1830 praising the new coaches:

> *Gentlemen:—I am not aware that any notice has as yet been taken on the new Stage which has just been established to ply between Washington and Georgetown, a convenience to the inhabitants of this portion of the District, which cannot fail to make itself felt. The proprietor, whoever he may be, of this useful enterprize, is certainly entitled to the thanks of the community… In the Stage, of which we are speaking, we may ride from the Capitol to*

Early Mass Transit in Washington, D.C.

> *the upper end of Georgetown, a distance of more than three miles, for the small sum of twelve and a half cents, when we have hitherto been paying from twenty five to fifty* [for a private cab]. *It runs at all hours, and is constantly taking up and putting down passengers on the way.*[4]

The new omnibus line was a great success, and soon additional lines competed with it. North–south routes along Seventh Street and Eleventh Street were added, running from the Southwest waterfront to around L Street Northwest. Omnibuses became a common sight, rattling their way along Washington's muddy, rutted streets, often with some hapless soul standing on the rear step and hanging on for dear life. Many were individually named for famous people or events, and some had elegant paintings of sailing ships or early steam-powered vessels on their sides. Keeping them clean must have been a nightmare.

Discomforts, Inconveniences and Annoyances

However happy Washington residents were to gain omnibus service, they, like the inhabitants of other major cities, soon grew weary of the limitations of these spindly coaches. They were cramped, dirty, hard to get in and out of and often late. Overcrowding—a problem that would continue into the modern era—was hard on the horses that pulled the coaches and unpleasant for the riders inside. The layout of the omnibuses also made paying one's fare a challenging task. One was supposed to pay the driver, who sat on an open bench on top of the passenger compartment, stagecoach-style. A small hole, called the strap hole, was used to pass one's fare up, and the driver was supposed to make change, if needed, and pass it back down. Unless the omnibus was empty, it was difficult to make one's way up to the front to pay. And if change was expected, it was a matter of luck whether the right amount would be supplied. The driver, who was out in the elements and busy tending to the horses, might nastily harangue passengers who felt they had been slighted. Fellow passengers, constantly being jostled and jolted by the bumpy ride, were rarely sympathetic. It could all be rather unpleasant.

And that was just for the lucky travelers who managed to get onboard. A young Samuel L. Clemons, visiting Washington for the first time in 1854, complained that

> *if you should be seized with a desire to go to the Capitol, or somewhere else, you may stand in a puddle of water, with the snow driving in your face for fifteen minutes or more, before an omnibus rolls lazily by; and when one does come, ten to one there are nineteen passengers inside and fourteen outside, and while the driver casts on you a look of commiseration, you have the inexpressible satisfaction of knowing that you closely resemble a very moist dishrag (and feel so, too) at the same time that you are unable to discover what benefit you have derived from your fifteen minutes' soaking; and so, driving your fists into the inmost recesses of your breeches pockets, you stride away in despair, with a step and a grimace that would make the fortune of a tragedy actor, while your "onery" appearance is greeted with "screams of laftur" from a pack of vagabond boys over the way. Such is life, and such is Washington!*[5]

Competing omnibus drivers could become quite reckless in trying to beat one another to the next fare-paying customer. The city council took up a bill in 1850 to "prohibit racing and several other improper and dangerous practices, which generally result from the rivalry of different lines," according to the *National Intelligencer*. Eventually, omnibus drivers were subjected to five-dollar fines for "passing ahead of or in front of, or in any other way to annoy the passengers or drivers of any other omnibus," but not before an alarming incident occurred in June 1855:

> *A respectable citizen tells us that in the afternoon of the day before yesterday the driver of the Georgetown omnibus, No. 25, at a point on Fifteenth street, opposite the Treasury Department, drove up to the side of the lead-horse of a three-horse stage, and commenced beating that horse most unmercifully, causing in the melee the running off of both teams, a wheel horse of each to fall, both being dragged some distance. The omnibus was crowded with ladies, who left it. The conduct of the driver was most reprehensible, and endangered the lives not only of the horses, but of the passengers—men, women, and children—in both vehicles.*[6]

Most city dwellers of the early nineteenth century had been raised in rural settings and were accustomed to the quiet civilities of an earlier era. In contrast, all manner of humanity was crammed together in alarmingly tight spaces on the omnibuses, and social niceties quickly fell by the wayside, as it were. The newspapers, for example, ran letters from women distressed at the unsavoriness of riding cheek by jowl with uncouth strangers. One pleaded with the *Evening Star*'s editors to "intercede with the proprietor of the Washington omnibuses to induce him to instruct his drivers to admit no market baskets on market days, inside of his coaches." Instead, these customers' parcels should be stored up on the roof, she suggested. Why? "[S]he has had more than one elegant and expensive dress smeared over so as to destroy its value, by contact with blood, marrow, and loose hanging fat sticking out beyond the edges of over-filled market baskets resting on the floor of an over-crowded omnibus."[7]

Beef blood and mutton tallow were not the only dangers threatening the delicate and voluminous skirts worn by women in the 1850s. There was also the issue of tobacco spitting, which apparently was particularly bad in Washington. A female omnibus rider wrote to the *National Intelligencer* in 1853 to bemoan the problem:

> *I feel confident that an appeal to the lords will not be in vain; and I am sure, if they will, when they get in an omnibus with their mouths full of the horrid stuff, watch the agonized looks of the ladies, turned from their lips to their dresses, waiting, wondering, in anxious suspense, whose skirts will be the first victim.... I have seen a man get in a crowded omnibus, take his seat opposite to half a dozen expensively dressed ladies, and fill his mouth till you would have thought (knowing he must expectorate presently) that he intended not only to ruin their dresses, but actually to drown them in spit.*[8]

Still, despite these inconveniences, omnibuses were a godsend for many people, so much so that in time omnibus service was seen as an essential public amenity. People who had been used to walking long distances would no longer consider doing so when they could ride to their destination for a small fee. Soon many of the city's inhabitants were dependent on public transportation and felt helpless when it was not available. The *Evening Star* in 1851 ran a letter from a reader who was indignant that the Navy Yard omnibuses had stopped running at night. "I myself was at the stand near the Navy Yard gate one evening, before 7 o'clock, and there was no stage in which to ride to the city. Now I think if the proprietors of the line would be a little more accommodating, that they would be patronized by a large number of citizens.... This is only a hint, and should Mr. Vanderwerken take it, he will not lose thereby."

The People's Carriages

The Mr. Vanderwerken in question—Gilbert Vanderwerken (1810–1894)—would play a key role in the transition from omnibuses to streetcars in Washington. Born in Waterford, New York, Vanderwerken left home at age seventeen to be an apprentice to a stagecoach builder in Newark, New Jersey. This was just as Brower's omnibuses were making their first appearance on the streets of New York. Hoping to cash in on the promising new trend, he opened his own coach-building business in Newark in about 1830. It went bankrupt during the financial depression of 1837, but undeterred, Vanderwerken moved to Mexico and opened a new coach service between Mexico City and Veracruz. After the Mexican-American War disrupted that enterprise, he and his wife finally moved to Washington in the late 1840s. In 1851, he gained control of the Union Line, which by that time was one of two consolidated omnibus companies operating in the city. Then, in 1855, he and his partner, John E. Reeside, bought out the other line, known as the Citizens Line, and merged the two into a single D.C. omnibus monopoly.

Said to be a very distinguished-looking individual, Vanderwerken was famous (or infamous) as Washington's omnibus king, making him the first in a series of entrepreneurs that would dominate development of the city's transit infrastructure. Because of the omnibus business, Vanderwerken was

Design for Gilbert Vanderwerken's omnibuses. *Historical Society of Washington, D.C.*

Early Mass Transit in Washington, D.C.

A late nineteenth-century photograph of Clark Mills's statue of Andrew Jackson. The horse was said to be modeled on one raised by Gilbert Vanderwerken. *Author's collection.*

likely also the city's single largest owner of horses. It has been claimed that sculptor Clark Mills (1810–1883) used one of Vanderwerken's horses as a model for his famous statue of Andrew Jackson mounted on a rearing horse, erected in Lafayette Square in 1853.[9] Vanderwerken's horses were certainly everywhere in Washington, and many were stabled in a vast facility on M Street in Georgetown, where a shopping mall known as the Shops at Georgetown Park is now located. The stables were well known to Georgetown residents for their odor, if for nothing else.

Horses were the unrivaled locomotive engines of their day. If public transport were to be improved in any significant way, it would hinge on leveraging the limited abilities of these beasts of burden. The best solution to this problem was to enhance the horses' carrying capacity by mounting carriages on metal rails, thereby reducing friction and providing a smooth traveling surface. This idea had been around since the late eighteenth century, when the British used it to design a system to haul coal from mines. It wasn't translated to an urban setting until John Mason's New York and Harlem Railroad opened along a stretch of Fourth Avenue in the Bowery in 1832. The new railway featured two streetcars, built by John Stephenson, that were very similar in design to omnibuses but much larger. Each could seat thirty in the passenger compartment, with overflow seating on the roof for more intrepid travelers.

Streetcars offered substantial advantages over omnibuses. An average horse can pull a load of no more than three tons on a good road but as much as ten tons on a railed track. With typical streetcars powered by two horses, this was substantial pulling power. Riders enjoyed a smoother ride and more commodious seating, and the rails allowed cars to be designed with much smaller wheels, which made it easier for passengers to get in and out.

Vanderwerken was likely the first to try to bring streetcars to the District. An ambitious businessman, he began planning for them nearly as soon as he gained control of the city's omnibuses. He first petitioned Congress for a street railway from Georgetown to Capitol Hill in December 1852, but his proposal did not have the political backing to make it through. In early 1854, a rival group of New York street railway men, allied with Washington businessman George W. Yerby, began making the rounds with its own proposal. After city officials had been appropriately wined and dined, the New York group's petition was presented to Congress along with a supporting letter signed by some 1,400 inhabitants living in the vicinity of the proposed line. A letter to the editor published in the *Star* on February 1 gushed with enthusiasm for the proposal: "These neat and beautiful conveyances will emphatically be the people's carriages, decidedly preferable to the noisy, heavy and clumsy omnibuses now in use."[10]

Support for the New Yorkers' project was far from unanimous, however. Many longtime Washington residents couldn't imagine allowing a railroad to run down the middle of Pennsylvania Avenue, both for safety as well as aesthetic reasons. Detractors soon drew up a petition of their own, urging Congress not to grant a charter to the new railway: "The proposed railroad would be a most serious mutilation of the great national thoroughfare of the metropolis, and an interference with the original plans and designs of the founders and engineers of the city."

Further, a functioning street railway "having on it two continuous lines of cars, one each way, constantly passing, would in effect divide the avenue into two streets, and if not suspend, at least greatly interrupt and impede the free and easy communication between the two opposite sides of the street and sidewalks."[11] A veritable disaster in the making!

The *Evening Star* quickly published a letter rebutting the concerns expressed in the counter-petition:

> *One would really suppose, from the phraseology of the document, and the appalling apparitions of deformity and disfiguration which seem to flit across the fancies of these old fogies, that some structure of huge and horrifying proportions was about to be introduced into the limits of our city. And when our citizens are told that this immense structure is to consist of a grooved iron rail, sunk into the earth on an exact level with the surface of the stone pavement—not a hair's breadth above it—and just as is used in New York and other cities of the Union, to the great and acknowledged convenience of the people, they will be amazed and incensed, if not too much amused, at the ridiculous bugaboo which has been conjured up to frighten them from their propriety.*[12]

The bickering would continue throughout the rest of the decade, delaying the introduction of streetcars in Washington for many years. Meanwhile, other cities rapidly built their own systems: Brooklyn in 1853; Boston in 1856; Philadelphia in 1858; and Baltimore, Pittsburgh, Chicago and Cincinnati in 1859. It was a matter of when, not if, they would finally come to Washington. Some city maps from the 1850s even showed a streetcar line already running along Pennsylvania Avenue, although none yet existed.

In December 1861, B.B. French, the D.C. commissioner of public buildings, made an exasperated plea to Congress in his annual report: "A street railroad through Pennsylvania Avenue is a necessity which should no longer be disregarded. The great advantages of this mode of communication upon important city thoroughfares have been so fully demonstrated in all the large cities of the Untied States that no argument upon the subject will be required." He went on to note that repairs on Pennsylvania Avenue would be more expensive than usual that year due to heavy army traffic and suggested that the petitioners to build the street railway would "as a consideration for the privilege, agree to keep the avenue, at least between the Capitol and the President's square, in good repair," thus allowing the government to dodge a significant annual expense.

Capital Streetcars

On May 17, 1862—one year into the Civil War—Congress finally agreed, passing a law incorporating the Washington & Georgetown Railroad. The charter specified three lines: an east–west route along Pennsylvania Avenue from Georgetown to the Navy Yard; a north–south route along Seventh Street from Boundary Street (Florida Avenue Northwest) to the Seventh Street wharves in Southwest; and another north–south route along Fourteenth Street from Boundary Street to the Georgetown–Navy Yard line at Pennsylvania Avenue. To ensure the military utility of the new railway, the company's tracks were to match the width of the Baltimore & Ohio Railroad, and the Pennsylvania Avenue line would connect with the B&O station, located just north of the Capitol.

Curiously, Vanderwerken was not one of the founding incorporators of the new railroad, although he was inextricably linked to it. Perhaps he deliberately stood in the shadows, since he was so closely associated with the fight over the earlier proposals. Whatever the case, the new company soon set to negotiating with Vanderwerken for the purchase of all of his omnibus empire, including cars, horses, stables and all other real property. Although not specified in the law establishing the new company, buying out Vanderwerken's competing omnibus line (and thus eliminating it as a competitor) seems to have been one of the basic requirements for getting the new streetcar operation underway. Vanderwerken offered all of his assets for a flat $65,000 but ended up agreeing instead to sell horses, cars and personal property for $28,500 and leasing his stables and other real estate for $2,500 per year. The railway company would eventually purchase Vanderwerken's strategically located stables in Georgetown, which it converted into a car barn and maintenance facility, as well as his Navy Yard stables.

The war years marked a time of upheaval for Vanderwerken, even more so than for most Washingtonians. In September 1861, he created a scandal when he got into a fight with another very prominent Georgetowner, Major George Hill, over the building on Bridge Street where the two were both living at the time. Apparently, Hill, a prominent paper merchant, leased the ground floor as a storeroom, while Vanderwerken and his family lived on the top floor. The two had a longstanding dispute over the terms of Vanderwerken's lease, and the feud reached a climax one day in September with a pistol fight between Vanderwerken, his son and Hill. Hill fired a few shots but hit no one; in contrast, the elder Vanderwerken fired four times and hit Hill thrice. Vanderwerken was immediately arrested and charged with assault and battery with the intent to kill. His case, which was a sensation in

Georgetown at the time, would be tried twice and drag on for many years, but Vanderwerken would finally be acquitted.

In addition to the Georgetown pied-à-terre he leased, Vanderwerken owned a large estate along the Potomac River in Arlington, Virginia, with a rambling farmhouse called Falls Grove located near the intersection of Glebe and Little Falls Roads. He had bought the property in about 1852 to use as a farm and pasture to raise horses, including both draft horses for pulling omnibuses and fine Thoroughbreds. With the onset of the war, Vanderwerken's property, directly opposite the Chain Bridge, became strategically important. Having few options, Vanderwerken agreed to hand the property over to the army, which turned his farmhouse into a hospital and built two forts (Marcy and Ethan Allen) near the river. The Vanderwerkens spent the war living in Georgetown but returned to their Virginia estate after it was over. Vanderwerken then started up a profitable rock quarry business, cutting Potomac blue stone from his hillside property along the river and selling it in town for use in construction.

Meanwhile, in 1862, the newly chartered Washington & Georgetown streetcar line needed to get rolling quickly. Although Congress had dawdled for ten years on authorizing the railway, it now required the new company to put the first segment of its line between the Capitol and Georgetown into operation within sixty working days of incorporation—an astonishingly short timespan considering that a war was on and no cars, ties, rails or other materiel were on hand. There was certainly no time to lose.

Chapter 2

HORSES IN THE MUD

THE EARLY HORSE-DRAWN STREETCAR ERA, 1862–1888

In 1862, streetcars were finally coming to Washington, and not a minute too soon. The city was in the midst of an urban transformation unlike anything it had ever experienced. Much had changed since the first shots of the Civil War were fired a year earlier at Fort Sumter; public infrastructure and facilities that had been barely adequate in the past were now strained to the breaking point.

Newly conscripted troops from Northern states had swarmed the city. By late 1862, 125,000 Union troops were encamped in the D.C. area, most of them either on the other side of the Potomac or in the rural sections outside Washington City. Suddenly, housing, food, transportation and everything else was in short supply. Officers and their retinues commandeered fine houses in Georgetown. Many larger public buildings, such as churches and boardinghouses, were converted into temporary casualty wards until vast new hospital complexes could be built. Wagons serving as ambulances, blood sometimes dripping from their boards, clattered slowly into the city from the busy southwest waterfront, where the wounded were disgorged from ships and railroad cars. Meanwhile, endless lines of quartermaster wagons filled with army provisions rumbled through the unpaved streets, as did vast hordes of cattle and other livestock. As Commissioner B.B. French lamented, the overwhelming traffic quickly made a thorough mess of Pennsylvania Avenue and other major thoroughfares.

Early Mass Transit in Washington, D.C.

"This Great and Inappreciable Comfort and Convenience"

Amid all of this chaos, the new streetcar tracks were to be installed and the system made operational in a hurry. Several days after President Lincoln signed the law establishing the Washington & Georgetown Railroad, its officers met in room 10 of the National Hotel on Pennsylvania Avenue to get organized. So much had to be done, but luck seemed to be on the side of the fledgling railway. Financing proved easy to obtain, with savvy investors eager to get in on what seemed like a sure thing. In fact, the rooms at the National Hotel where stock in the new company was sold became a madhouse as New York and Philadelphia investors vied with one another for shares in the new venture. As the company's treasurer later recalled, "There was such a rush and clamor of excited men, their hands filled with certificates of deposit, certified checks, and bank bills, pushing, yelling, and surging, each wanting to be the first one waited upon, that the mob overturned the tables across the room which we used as desks, and for a time all was confusion."[13]

Miraculously, construction soon began. Rails were ordered and arrived in time for a crew of forty to begin laying them in early June 1862. Within two weeks, two hundred men were at work digging up cobblestones on Pennsylvania Avenue, laying rails and ties and resetting the stones, progressing at a rate of about a block and a half per day. By early July, the first stretch of track, from the Capitol to the State Department building on Fifteenth Street, was nearly done. "This great and inappreciable comfort and convenience, so long desired and so often defeated, has been...completed with great promptitude," the *National Intelligencer* exulted. "The introduction of passenger railroads into this city of 'magnificent distances' may be regarded as forming an important epoch in the history of the city, second only to construction of the great Potomac aqueduct,[14] and we sincerely congratulate our fellow-citizens, as well as Congress and the Government, on its success."[15]

The first two cars for the new railway arrived from the manufacturer on July 11. They were elegant pieces of craftsmanship intended to entice well-to-do riders who had no previous experience of public transportation. The *Evening Star* described them in detail:

> *The seats on the sides are covered with fine silk velvet, and the windows, which are stained and plain glass combined, are furnished with cherry sash and poplar blinds, beside handsome damask curtains. The top of the car*

Pennsylvania Avenue's first streetcar tracks are seen here, circa 1868, with a car in the distance. *Author's collection.*

is rounded, permitting persons to stand upright without inconvenience, and rods to which loops are attached, are run from end to end.... The car is handsomely painted, both inside and out, the prevailing color being white, while the outside is cream color and white, with a fine painting in the center, and the words "Washington and Georgetown R.R." at the bottom. The wheels are of different colors, contrasting well with the body of the car, and giving it a picturesque appearance. Messrs. Murphy & Allison [of Philadelphia] *are making most of the cars, but others are being built by other makers.... The cars were put on the track last night, and at 11 o'clock run up as far as Willard's* [Hotel], *having on board a number of gentlemen, cheering loudly as they passed up and being greeted with cheers from the few persons on the street at that hour.*[16]

July 29 marked the first day of public operation. The company had ten cars by then, all standard streetcars of the day: pulled by two horses with a driver standing on a platform in front and an enclosed passenger compartment designed to comfortably seat twenty. A conductor, usually stationed on the rear platform, collected fares. On opening day, the cars were packed at times with as many as forty eager passengers. The first car was "crowded almost to suffocation" and screeched to a halt at the curve from Pennsylvania Avenue on to Fifteenth Street "probably owing to the roughness of the rails," according to the *Evening Star*. An extra horse was added, and the car kept rolling. The *Star* wrote admiringly that "[t]he cars in use are handsome and commodious, and the smoothness with which they glide along affords an agreeable change from the rough jolting over the pavements experienced in other modes of vehicular conveyance." The *Star*'s enthusiastic reporter concluded with a wistful, "Farewell, old bus, you're nigh played out," little realizing that one hundred years later it would be the other way around, with buses dancing on the graves of the streetcars.[17]

Construction of the new line had been accomplished in less than two months despite a number of war-related delays. Lumber and iron both were sporadically in short supply, as were able-bodied laborers to lay the tracks. Higher-priority military loads continually interrupted railroad shipments of raw materials. One shipment of iron was delayed for nearly two weeks. Nevertheless, steady progress was made. In August, the new line was extended to Georgetown, where the former Vanderwerken stables were located and where a new frame headquarters building and depot were built alongside the stables. By early October, the complete line from Georgetown to the Navy Yard was in operation. The two north–south lines on Seventh and Fourteenth Streets entered service shortly thereafter, completing the entire system in less than six months.

As the lines were being built, passengers could transfer to the old Vanderwerken omnibuses, which the new company kept running temporarily, to complete their trips on routes still under construction. In October, with all three lines nearly finished, the company's directors donated twenty old omnibuses to the army for use as ambulances. They were much needed and apparently served that purpose well.

Praise for the new streetcars ran high as Washingtonians began shaping their daily routines around them. People from all walks of life took to the new form of transport. "I rode all the way from Georgetown. What a blessing & a comfort," wrote Martha Custis Williams, the great-great-granddaughter of Martha Washington, who lived at Georgetown's stately Tudor Place mansion.[18]

An early horse-drawn streetcar of the Metropolitan Railroad stops outside the east front of the Capitol in the late 1860s. *Author's collection.*

Service in those early days was often praised as efficient and comfortable. In July 1863, the *National Intelligencer* commented on the Seventh Street line, which had opened nine months earlier:

> *We cannot help admiring the regularity with which the cars on this road now run. There is no detention to passengers whatsoever. The energy manifested by the gentlemanly conductors meets the approbation of everyone who rides them. We cannot help speaking of the politeness of Conductor Steptoe T. Tune. His obliging manners and amiability give him the praise of all who chance in his car.*[19]

Early Mass Transit in Washington, D.C.

Once fully operational, the Washington & Georgetown Railroad scheduled cars to arrive at five-minute intervals (known as the "headway") and charged a five-cent fare with a free transfer between routes. The company had a total of seventy cars and 490 horses, the horses wearing bells tied to their harnesses to alert pedestrians that a car was coming.[20] The railway's original routes would remain the core of the city's streetcar network throughout its one-hundred-year history and are still echoed in bus routes that operate today.

"Considerable Hard Feeling Was Expressed"

There would be many more street railway companies founded in the District of Columbia—dozens of them through the rest of the nineteenth century. The second company to get its start was the Metropolitan Railroad, chartered in 1864, just two years after the Washington & Georgetown. It began public service in early 1865, running along F Street downtown, which was soon to become the city's main commercial thoroughfare. While the Washington & Georgetown's line wrapped around the south of the Capitol grounds on its way to the Navy Yard, the Metropolitan line zigzagged across several blocks just to the north and then ran along East Capitol Street, serving the residents of Capitol Hill. On its western end, the line jogged two blocks up Fourteenth Street from F Street to H Street, where it traversed the fashionable residential area north of Lafayette Square on its way to Seventeenth Street. Like the Washington & Georgetown line, the Metropolitan initially featured luxurious cars to appeal to an upscale clientele. Company records show that for a pair of cars costing $1,300 apiece, the company paid an extra $16 per car for "silver-plated handles."[21]

Not everyone was pleased with the city's proliferating streetcar lines and the way they commandeered sections of the roadway for their exclusive use. A major flashpoint for the rivalry between streetcars and private coaches was a stretch of New Jersey Avenue in front of the B&O railroad station near the Capitol, where hacks and private omnibuses would stop to pick up high-paying travelers from out of town. The new streetcar lines threatened to disrupt this loading zone by laying tracks in front of the station's entrance. According to newspaper accounts, the Washington & Georgetown line had originally put down track here but had been compelled to take it up again after strident protests by hack and omnibus drivers.

Two Metropolitan streetcars wait at the end of the line on Seventeenth Street by the old Navy Department building in the early 1870s. *Author's collection.*

The Metropolitan line reopened these wounds in 1864 by laying track in the same spot. As recounted in the *Evening Star*:

> [T]he company laid the track during the night, last night, putting a large force of workmen on the ground, with fires to light them in their operations, and this morning at daylight lo and behold, the track in front of the railroad station was nearly down! Considerable hard feeling was expressed on the part of the hackmen and hotel porters this morning, who think that this is an encroachment upon their rights.[22]

Tempers flared in January 1865 when John Byrne, an omnibus driver from Willard's Hotel, parked his coach over the tracks at the depot. A.C. Richards, superintendent of the metropolitan police, was already on the scene at the time because street railway officials had called him to witness the problems they were having. Richards identified himself as the superintendent of police and directed Byrne to move his omnibus. According to the *Star*,

Early Mass Transit in Washington, D.C.

Byrne "replied, with an oath, that he did not care who he was; that he would go when he was ready." The officer tried to lead the horses on Byrne's team away, but Byrne wheeled them around, keeping them on the tracks. An approaching streetcar then collided with Byrne's coach, and a general mêlée ensued with more swearing, a few punches thrown and the butt end of a whip used as a cudgel. Byrne finally was taken into custody.

An uneasy truce was eventually reached, with precise zones established for hacks and omnibuses on the one hand and streetcars on the other. This time there was no turning back the clock, as streetcars quickly became an established part of the city's infrastructure.

Streetcar routes, each originally chartered as a separate company, were gradually extended along major thoroughfares across the city. Two early companies built extensions of the Metropolitan's lines. The Connecticut Avenue & Park Railway, chartered in 1868, ran up Connecticut Avenue from the end of the Metropolitan line to Boundary Street (now Florida Avenue); it was folded into the Metropolitan in 1874. The Union Railroad

A Metropolitan streetcar turns onto present-day Wisconsin Avenue from O Street, circa 1893. *Library of Congress.*

began at Dupont Circle and ran west along P Street to Fayette Street (Thirty-fifth Street Northwest) in Georgetown, looping back east along O Street. It was absorbed into the Metropolitan line less than a year after starting in 1872.

Another important line that stayed independent of the two big streetcar companies was the Columbia Railway, founded in 1870. Beginning at Fifteenth Street and New York Avenue Northwest, where it met the Washington & Georgetown's main line, the Columbia headed northeast along New York Avenue to Mount Vernon Square, shifted southeast along Massachusetts Avenue to H Street and then ran straight out H Street Northeast to Benning Road. It would remain a profitable independent line for nearly three decades.

The last major early street railway in Washington was the awkwardly named Capitol, North O Street & South Washington Railway, incorporated in 1875. Its route consisted of a loop around the commercial downtown area, starting at the Capitol, traveling north mostly on Fourth Street Northwest to O Street, west along O to Eleventh Street and back downtown on Eleventh Street. From there it made its way across the Mall to Southwest and then circled back to the Capitol via Maryland Avenue Southwest. It was appropriately renamed the Belt Railway in 1893.

"What a Time They Did Have with the Mud"

If you had plenty of time and the car wasn't too crowded, the gentleness of the horsecar ride could be charming. "There was something soothing, rustic, somniferous, and characteristic in the tinkling of bells attached to the harness of the car horses, as they lazily jogged along the quiet streets," one old-timer recalled in 1906.[23] Yet as modern and luxurious as they may have seemed at the time, the city's first streetcars were quite primitive.

Quick construction times sometimes masked poor workmanship in the laying of the rails. Sweltering summer heat could cause improperly laid rails to buckle up from their moorings, as they did in July 1868, when bows in the rails appeared that were several inches high and several feet long. "On the Metropolitan track, near the Patent Office, are a couple of places of this character only a few yards apart, one of which has bulged so high as to admit a man's body between it and the road sills," the *Star* reported.[24] Encountering problems such as this, horsecar drivers might order their passengers to disembark and then try driving their cars off the rails and around the obstacle. Of course, this assumes the adjacent roadway was strong enough to support the load.

It often wasn't. Mud was a severe problem, especially during the winter. The *Evening Star* noted in December 1864 that the new Metropolitan line on F Street was nearing completion "[n]otwithstanding the very disagreeable weather and the great depth of mud."[25] Anna Sherman, a young girl living with her family in a boardinghouse at Fourteenth and K Streets Northwest, later recounted the treacherous impact of the mud. The eldest daughter of a Connecticut man who had moved to Washington to serve as a U.S. Treasury clerk, Sherman witnessed the birth of the city's streetcars:

> *Fourteenth Street was now to have a horse-car road, the first built in Washington. It was not to go very far uptown but was to pass beyond where we were. This was an added entertainment. When the tracks were all down and they finally got the cars on, what a time they did have with the mud. The horses would flounder in it, and the men who were at work would beat them with picks and shovels, and the drivers with the whips, then the cars would get jerked off the track, and it would almost make us cry (I don't know but that we did sometimes) to see the poor beasts. It would seem as if they were expected to do more than horse flesh could do, and finally the men would have to get crow-bars and logs to pry the cars up on to the tracks again. The men would have to do this without the horses' help, and the passengers would all have to get out and find their way to the sidewalk on planks and great pieces of stone, stuck in the mud at long intervals, to wait for the car to get righted. At last the Company paved the road between the tracks and then there was not all this excitement about a short-ride in a horse car.*[26]

The poor horses were always the center of attention. They represented by far the street railway companies' biggest investment, costing as much as $200 apiece, and were, of course, the vital engines that made the whole system work. Yet they were routinely subjected to abuse and were pushed to their limits even when they weren't stuck in the mud. Across the country, horses typically lasted just three years pulling streetcars before they had to be retired.

Horses could pull the cars at a top speed of about four to six miles per hours, just slightly faster than walking. When overloaded (as they frequently were) or facing an uphill grade, they would move much more slowly. If you were in a hurry, the ride could seem interminable. A trip across town, from

Uniformed cadets from Alexandria transfer between a small Belt Line horsecar and a railroad car on Maryland Avenue, circa 1890. *National Capital Trolley Museum.*

Georgetown to Capitol Hill, for example, might take an hour. But unless you could afford a private hackney cab, no faster alternatives were available.

The greatest strain on the horses was in getting the car moving from a stop. Once it was in motion on the rails, it was relatively easy to keep moving. Of course, that offered little relief for the typical streetcar horse, given that the cars were constantly stopping and starting. Early D.C. streetcars would stop anywhere a passenger wanted to get on or off (fixed car stops were not established until 1918).

A typical streetcar was drawn by two horses, although many smaller one-horse cars were also used. Horses would normally run for shifts of about three hours, necessitating the use of several pairs of horses for each car per day. Railway company stables across the city each kept hundreds of horses and were constantly buying new ones and retiring the "worn out" veterans. Streetcar companies originally favored heavy draft horses from Ohio, but eventually consensus was reached that Percherons, a French breed especially valued for their pulling power and stamina, made the best streetcar horses.[27]

Managing a team of horses required skill and experience. First, the two horses had to be appropriately paired; if one pulled harder than the other, it would quickly tire and be overworked. Also, because horses tend to spook

Early Mass Transit in Washington, D.C.

A Metropolitan horsecar and crew pose on Boundary Street (Florida Avenue) near Connecticut Avenue, circa 1892. *National Capital Trolley Museum.*

easily, care had to be taken to keep them calm amid the bustle of street traffic. "Nervous" horses needed special handling. Drivers would often keep them on the right side, away from traffic. A good driver knew just how to keep a firm hand on the reins so that the horses had a sense of being under control and still vary the pressure to give them commands. Too much pulling on the bit and reins could ruin a horse, and reckless use of a whip could cause it to panic. Abrupt stops, especially on slippery cobblestones, could cause horses to slip and fall. The essence of good horsecar driving was smooth, predictable movements.

An important skill was gauging the momentum of the car and knowing how to apply the brakes to assist the horses in stopping the car smoothly without causing them to trip. In the very first public demonstration of horse-drawn streetcars in New York City in 1832, an accident resulted from one driver's inexperience. Two horsecars filled with dignitaries were headed down a section of track, the first driven by an experienced stagecoach driver and the second under the reins of a local hack man. When an official signaled the two cars to stop at the end of the run, the experienced driver gracefully brought his car to a clean stop. The driver behind him, however, tried unsuccessfully to stop his car simply by reining his horses. The car ended up crashing into the rear of the first vehicle. Nobody was hurt, but embarrassed officials quickly learned that they would need to thoroughly train their new drivers.

The biggest challenges for horsecars were the hills, especially in muddy conditions. Generally, horse-drawn streetcar routes were designed to avoid hills. The horses simply did not have the power to carry the cars up them. The hilly areas of the northwest part of the District beyond Boundary Street were out of the question, for example. But a few hills were unavoidable, including two spots on the Washington & Georgetown line—at northbound Fifteenth Street alongside the Treasury Department and on B Street (now Constitution Avenue) by the Capitol. The company maintained dedicated "hill horses" for use at these two spots. The horses were kept at the bottom of the hills and were added to each car's team to help pull the cars up the hill.

Hill horse boys were in charge of this task. "They were hearty, noisy youngsters, the hill horse lads, and there was always a great bustle and stir and shouting and clanking of hooks and chains and so on in front when the hill horse boy tacked his quadruped onto the car," an anonymous observer recalled in later years. Another commentator recalled how passengers could "hear the hill-horse boys' loud greetings to the car drivers as they hitched on their nags to take the long, steep hills; could hear their 'You Jim!' and 'G'long, yuh bum!' addressed to the weary horses as the hard climbs were being made, accompanied by the cracking of the Hankmonkish blacksnake whips." The grueling task was especially difficult in winter months:

> *Very often, during these ascents, especially during the slippery times, one or other of the horses would fall down, and then all of the hill-horse boys, foregathering at the foot of the hill in blustery converse, would rush to the aid of the downed horse, so that the next car to come along to the foot of the hill would have to wait for the return of a hill-horse boy with his nag; and it was music to ears (a music of which there is no echo left now) to hear the hill-horse boy returning down the hill with the clanking of the chains of the horse and his rough repartee exchange with the impatient driver.*[28]

This was exceptionally grueling work, and abuse of the horses occurred regularly. As late as 1893, a certain Joseph Cochran, manager of hill horses for the Belt Railway, was hauled into court for making his animals work nine-hour stretches without being fed. He argued that the horses were fed three times a day and that for nine hours' light work, they would not suffer. "If that's light work," the judge replied, "I don't know what hard work is." He fined Cochran ten dollars.[29]

Going down a hill could be as dangerous as going up—maybe more so. Drivers needed to remember to apply the brakes. One day in 1881, young

Early Mass Transit in Washington, D.C.

Florence L. Clark was riding west on the Washington & Georgetown line at Capitol Hill when "the driver detached the horses and walked them down the hill. The conductor was inside the vehicle [instead of being on the rear platform] and no one left at the brakes. In consequence the car obtained a great and dangerous velocity, and when it reached the abrupt curve at the end of the grade it partly overturned and threw [Clark] violently about, injuring her severely and possibly permanently," according to the *Washington Post*. It was all part of the adventure of riding the city's earliest streetcars.

The Great Epizootic of 1872

Another drawback of horse-drawn cars was disease, horses being subject to a variety of ailments that could affect their ability to pull cars. The most dramatic was the Great Epizootic of 1872 (an epizootic being an epidemic among animals), a type of influenza that affected horses much the way it attacks humans, producing coughing, runny noses, weakness, loss of appetite and so on. As the disease swept down and across the United States from Canada in the fall of 1872, almost every horse in the country was affected.

The disease spread rapidly once it arrived in Washington. It had begun near Toronto in September and progressed south through New York, ravaging New York City horses in October. Beginning on Friday, November 1, dozens of horses in the sprawling stables of Washington streetcar companies started showing symptoms of the disease. Frantic stable hands rubbed affected horses with ammonia, linseed oil and turpentine, and they burned tar, leather and hayseed to "fumigate" the stables—all to little, if any, effect. By Saturday, twice as many horses were affected, and the companies began taking cars out of service. In a number of cases, "horses which started out this morning in apparent health were seized with [the disease] before going half a dozen squares, and had to be withdrawn." Both the Washington & Georgetown and the Metropolitan lines announced that they would suspend all service on Sunday. The Metropolitan reported nearly all of its horses affected to some degree, and half of its cars were already off the road. By Sunday, virtually every horse in the city was sick.

City streets on that Sunday were the quietest they'd been in years, with no streetcars and few other horse-drawn vehicles on the streets. For more than a week, the street railways were completely shut down. The resulting eerie absence of "the musical tinkle of the bells of street car horses" was disorienting to many. The fire department put out a public call for all citizens living near engine houses to help them in bringing firefighting equipment by hand to any fires, although none occurred during the peak of the epizootic.

Finally, on Saturday the ninth, the Washington & Georgetown put a few cars back on the Pennsylvania Avenue line. "To the delight of foot-sore and leg-weary pedestrians, twelve street cars, each drawn by four horses, were put on the avenue line this morning, and of course they were well patronized," the *Evening Star* reported. "The horses were not allowed to run more than one trip, and when taken from the cars did not seem to be any worse for the work."

Streetcars gradually returned to service the following week, although sporadically. Everyone waited anxiously for the plague to abate. "Persons living at the navy yard and in Georgetown, but whose business lies in the central portions of the city, have an enforced walk of several miles every morning and evening, some of them twice a day, and as may be supposed, are considerably disgusted at the tenacious manner in which the 'hoss disease' hangs on," the *Star* observed. By the end of the second week, two-

Exhausted and possibly sick horses attempt to pull a grossly overloaded streetcar in this illustration from *Harper's Magazine*, September 21, 1872.

thirds of the city's streetcars were operating, and the remaining cars returned to service soon thereafter. Although some of the horses succumbed, most survived to go back to their hard jobs of hauling Washingtonians up and down city streets.

Many people pitied the poor streetcar horses and the hard lives they lived. Concern about cruelty to streetcar horses led to the founding of the Society for the Prevention of Cruelty to Animals in 1866 in New York City. Although known today for its work with cats and dogs, the SPCA's initial goal was to protect urban horses. SPCA officials were essentially deputized and took over the role of policing the streets for instances of cruelty and issuing fines or ordering overworked horses to be returned to their stables.

The D.C. chapter of the society, formed in 1870, was poorly organized at first and had little impact. After it was "revived" in 1881, it became more of a force to reckon with. From its offices in the LeDroit Building opposite the Patent Office on F Street, the SPCA sent out its officers to patrol the streets of Washington. As veteran streetcar driver Montgomery Davis later recalled, the SPCA officers could be counted on for surprise inspections:

> *We would be going along when a man in long gray whiskers would appear suddenly at our side, riding a bicycle.... He would order us to stop and would examine the horses. If he found the slightest sore underneath the braces, he would order the horse taken off and we'd have to wait until another horse was sent, pulling the car off the rails to let other cars by. Also, the company would be fined $5 for operating a horse with a sore neck.*[30]

The SPCA gave special attention to the plight of the hill horses, pressuring the Metropolitan Railroad to station more horses at the foot of Capitol Hill, belt them with warm blankets in cold weather and supply storm covers to protect them from rain and snow. Although street railway officials often served on the society's board of directors, raising questions about the objectivity of its oversight, the SPCA unquestionably had a positive impact in the years that horses played such an essential role in Washington society.

The advent of horse-powered streetcars in the nation's capital had been long anticipated and brought the city its first significant mass transit system, easing the lives of many residents and opening the way for the town to grow once the Civil War had ended. But it was a rough-and-ready experience, much limited by the creatures that served stoically as its engines and suffered mightily for the convenience of their masters.

Chapter 3

CLOSE QUARTERS

RIDING THE CARS, 1862–1888

Nearly everyone who could afford the nickel fare rode the city's streetcars in the late nineteenth century. This applied as much to the city's successful and affluent upper-middle classes as to its struggling low-wage earners. Doctors and lawyers, senators and Supreme Court justices—they all rode the cars. "The greatest of the great ride in streetcars here," Frank G. Carpenter, a correspondent for the *Cleveland Leader*, wrote in 1882. "It is not unusual to find yourself wedged in between a Senator whose oratory brings thousands out to hear him, and a General whose deeds will live in history as long as time lasts. Today your companion may be a noted lawyer; tomorrow you may hobnob and chat, if you will, with a member of the President's Cabinet."[31] In effect, streetcars in Washington served as a grand social experiment, a bringing together of the city's diverse strata as rarely happened under other circumstances.

Congressmen and senators—who otherwise might seem oddly interested in a local issue like public transportation—were direct witnesses to the triumphs and trials of the city's only transit system and became engrossed in the details of how it operated. It wasn't uncommon for two members of Congress with oversight of District affairs to get into a passionate debate about the quality of D.C. streetcar service on the floor of the House or Senate—often after both had ridden the cars to the Capitol and been able to formulate their views from direct experience.

Many federal officials sincerely enjoyed riding the cars and participating in their unique conventions. In the 1870s, stern-faced Supreme Court chief

Early Mass Transit in Washington, D.C.

A one-horse car of the Metropolitan Railroad, *at left*, rounds the curve on F Street at Ninth Street in the 1880s. *National Capital Trolley Museum.*

Justice Morrison R. Waite (1816–1888) was a frequent and enthusiastic D.C. streetcar rider. He would invariably be found sitting up front next to the fare box, where he took pleasure in helping pass fares and tickets between fellow passengers and the car's operator (more on that later).

Even President Ulysses S. Grant was known to enjoy riding the streetcar down Pennsylvania Avenue. He would stand in front with the driver, chatting and smoking one of his imposing black cigars. Once he reached the Peace Monument at the foot of Capitol Hill, he would get off and walk back to the White House.[32]

One of the most famous patrons of the city's early cars was poet Walt Whitman (1819–1892), who, according to Whitman researcher Garrett Peck, was a frequent rider when he lived in the city during the Civil War and thoughtfully gave a set of gloves each year to the drivers he knew.[33] Whitman struck up a particularly close relationship with a conductor named Peter Doyle in the war's waning days. As Doyle later described it, Whitman had been dining with his friend John Burroughs on Capitol Hill and hopped on the Pennsylvania Avenue car late one night to head home:

> *The night was very stormy,—he had been over to see Burroughs before he came down to take the car—the storm was awful. Walt had his blanket—*

it was thrown round his shoulders—he seemed like an old sea-captain. He was the only passenger, it was a lonely night, so I thought I would go in and talk to him [instead of remaining on the rear platform of the car, as was customary for conductors].... *We were familiar at once—I put my hand on his knee—we understood. He did not get out at the end of the trip—in fact went all the way back with me. I think the year of this was 1866...*[34]

Born in Ireland, twenty-one-year-old Doyle had moved with his family to Virginia when he was eight years old. He had fought for the Confederacy as an artilleryman and been captured and imprisoned briefly in Washington. Whitman began spending much of his free time with Doyle, riding his streetcar back and forth from Georgetown to the Navy Yard. The sight of Whitman and Doyle together out on the platform became a familiar one on Pennsylvania Avenue.

"Hardly Fit to Carry Hogs In"

While nearly everybody rode them, not everyone considered the cars a godsend. Many old-time Washingtonians disdained the strange new contraptions. Noah Brooks, an early chronicler of life in the city during the war, lampooned these detractors:

> *The fine old aristocrats of the* ancien régime *looked upon these vehicles with great disfavor. They soon discovered that the "c'yar box," as they called the street-car, would not come up to the sidewalk at the wave of a parasol or the beckoning of a hand, as had been the servile habit of the omnibuses, formerly the principal means of public conveyance in Washington streets. And it was a long time before these dignified sticklers for old manners and customs permitted themselves to enter the queer "Yankee contrivance" so lately introduced.*[35]

The corruption scandals of the post–Civil War era set a tone of cynicism about corporate tycoons, and the owners of the streetcar companies inevitably became prime objects of such resentment. Everyone believed that they were making a killing, and resentment only increased as the heavily used cars became worn and dirty and the poorly laid tracks grew rough.

Early Mass Transit in Washington, D.C.

And why couldn't there be more cars? Crowding would remain a perennial problem. During rush hour in the 1870s and 1880s, just as now, people were forced to pack themselves into the cars. Many thought this positively uncivilized, and some complained of the health dangers:

> *How do we know that the man standing so near us that his breath is puffed in our faces may not have a dozen diseases more easily communicated by that means than any other; that the woman clinging to the strap over our heads, and brushing the whole length of her garments against us, may not have been discharged an hour ago from the small-pox hospital. We are the great unwashed who ride in the cars, and we ought to have all the air possible, whereas, under the present system we get none at all...*[36]

By the 1870s, complaints about streetcar companies had already become common. An article apparently written by the owner of a store on Pennsylvania Avenue complained bitterly about the Washington & Georgetown line. "This company was not chartered solely to put money in the pockets of its stockholders," the writer lamented. "As we stated a few days ago, there are not half cars enough to meet the wants of the community, and those in use are hardly fit to carry hogs in.... [P]eople are crammed in the few that are used to the great risk of health and limb.... [W]e have frequently heard ladies say that they would rather pay the expense of a passage to Baltimore to make their purchases than to subject themselves to the discomfort and risk of a ride in the Pennsylvania avenue street cars."

Trunks on Wheels

The larger cars—the ones drawn by two horses—could be crowded with as many as fifty to sixty people at a time, but they were preferred because they were manned by a conductor as well as a driver. After taking their seats or finding a strap to hang on to, customers would pay the conductor as he came through the car calling, "Fares, please!" Conductors would make change, give directions and help people on and off the car, leaving the driver to focus on steering the horses through traffic. It was all very civilized, and it was how the regular railroads operated, so people were used to this arrangement.

But the street railways had thin profit margins and tried to cut expenses wherever they could. One way was to use smaller, one-horse "bobtail" cars,

CAPITAL STREETCARS

Operator and conductor pose with their full-size Belt Line streetcar in this 1890s photo. *National Capital Trolley Museum.*

which earned their nickname because they had no rear platform, just a narrow step under the back door. Riders entered directly into the passenger compartment from the rear and crammed themselves on to benches designed to seat twelve or fourteen. There was no conductor to collect fares or provide any other assistance. Passengers were responsible for depositing their fare with the driver, who sat on the front platform.

Streetcar companies loved the economical bobtail cars. In theory, the companies could provide better and more efficient service using bobtail cars because they could run more of them and thus decrease headway between cars. Also, with fewer passengers, each car would make fewer stops and thus provide more efficient service. In the 1870s and 1880s, streetcar companies put bobtail cars on many of their lines, including Pennsylvania Avenue, where the fare for a bobtail car was discounted to three cents.

When bobtail cars were first added to the Fourteenth Street line in 1867, they were a hit. The new cars "are being liberally patronized and are much commended," the *Evening Star* reported, calling the cars "light and roomy." But the enchantment soon vanished. Even with a discounted fare, bobtail cars became extremely unpopular. The light, poorly suspended cars were cramped, uncomfortable and even dangerous. The driver couldn't see

Early Mass Transit in Washington, D.C.

A small "bobtail" streetcar of the Belt Line makes its way through the snow on Maryland Avenue Southwest. Because of the inclement weather, two horses are pulling this car; in good weather only one would be needed. *Historical Society of Washington, D.C.*

clearly whether passengers were clear of the back door and risked hurting somebody every time he started up. A *Washington Post* reporter described riding a bobtail car into town on the Columbia line in 1888:

> *It was small and dingy, and the oil lamps stuttered and flickered in their boxes at the end of the car, from which the reflectors had been broken. The little bobtail bumped and thumped along over the stones and uneven rails, making a great deal of noise, but little progress, until Massachusetts avenue and a comparatively smooth piece of track was struck. This did not last long, however, and the car was soon jolting over crossings, switches and stones again down New York avenue until it finally stopped at the end of the line, where the reporter got out and wondered why he had not walked down town.*[37]

Worst of all, paying the driver at the front of the car was awkward and difficult. Once people were seated in the car, it was impossible to make one's way to the front. As a result, an informal honor system developed whereby people at the back of the car would pass their tickets or fares up to the front, one hand depositing the coin or ticket in another, until it reached the driver. If a full packet of tickets was being purchased (as it often was—they were cheaper that way), the driver would hand a small yellow envelope of tickets to the rider closest to him. That individual would tear open the envelope, remove one of the tickets, slip it into the fare box and then pass the remainder down the line to the customer making the purchase.

The system relied heavily on the kindness of strangers. Some, like Chief Justice Waite, enjoyed the ritual, but most people were irritated. Aside from the inconvenience, there was the question of whether the money handed to the front would make it all the way and, when change was required, whether it was the right amount and whether it would be returned to the proper recipient. Besides, people felt indignant about being forced to handle transactions for strangers. That was supposed to be the job of the conductor.

In July 1888, the *Washington Post* came out against using bobtail cars on any well-traveled downtown routes:

> *On none of the lines of the Metropolitan Company within the city limit should the bobtail be tolerated any longer. That company is rich. Its franchises are extremely valuable. Its business is great and growing. Its dividends are regular and handsome. It has no excuse for packing its passengers into trunks on wheels and requiring them either to collect their own fares or be annoyed if not maltreated by its drivers.*

The previous year, riders of the Fourteenth Street line had pressured the Washington & Georgetown line to replace at least some of its bobtail cars with two-horse cars. Encouraged by the *Post*, a Northeast citizens committee organized a revolt against the Columbia Railway's bobtail cars in 1888. Participants in the revolt refused to pay their fares unless a conductor collected it personally. The protest cut into company profits but failed to convince management to put two-horse cars on the line. Sympathetic congressmen introduced a bill to ban one-horse cars from the District, and it passed the House but was not taken up by the Senate. The dispute would soon be overtaken by other events, however, as the era of horse-drawn streetcars rapidly drew to a close.

Early Mass Transit in Washington, D.C.

"Worse for Our Country at This Moment than a Defeat in Battle"

A deeper and more fundamental struggle over streetcar service had been fought decades earlier, when the cars made their first appearance on Washington's streets. The struggle was about the right of African Americans to ride the cars as equals with whites. While equal access to public transit became a touchstone for the modern civil rights movement when Rosa Parks (1913–2005) defied an order in 1955 that she give up her seat on a Montgomery, Alabama bus to a white person, Parks was far from the first African American to stand up for her rights on public conveyances. Black citizens in Washington and other eastern cities, including Baltimore and Philadelphia, had been making similar protests since Civil War days.

The introduction of omnibuses in Washington in the 1830s had started the process of bringing different social classes into what many felt was disconcerting proximity. In those days, African Americans had been relegated to riding on the roofs, where baggage was stowed, or the front platforms with the drivers. The arrival of streetcars, carrying larger numbers of people and serving as a more fundamental public service, accelerated the process of social mixing and led to greater friction. White and black citizens frequently found themselves on the same cars, and the streetcar companies at first continued the previous unwritten policies of segregation. Although they paid the same fare as whites, African Americans were required to ride out on the front platforms, separate from the whites who sat inside. This was true in all types of weather—even pouring rain, snowstorms and frigid cold.

As historian Kate Masur has pointed out,[38] streetcars represented a mix of private and public interests that posed unique social challenges. Like hotels and restaurants, the cars were a type of "public accommodation," privately owned but offering essential services to the public. As private entities, streetcar companies could arguably be allowed to set whatever rules they wanted on how their customers would be treated. However, as public utilities providing an essential service, the companies could just as arguably be required to ensure that all customers get the same service.

Common law required the operators of public accommodations to serve the public and not deny service arbitrarily.[39] But there was little consensus on whether this meant that segregation was an unacceptable way for streetcar companies to fulfill that responsibility. A small number of whites wholeheartedly backed unrestricted access for African Americans to all streetcars. Others worried about forcing too much social change too quickly.

Nevertheless, the majority of white Washingtonians opposed giving African Americans the same accommodations as whites. Concerns they expressed about the proper role of the government often masked deeply entrenched racial fears and prejudices. They simply could not imagine having to sit as equals next to African Americans on streetcars—or anywhere else.

The determination of black Washingtonians to resist streetcar segregation grew after the first D.C. regiment of U.S. Colored Troops formed in May 1863. At a June meeting to discuss the recently formed regiment, a white military officer commented that "one of the sins of the District was hatred to the colored men" and pointed to an incident in which "a number of colored men were put off a car" as an example. The audience was incensed. "I'd like to see the driver put me off," answered someone in the crowd. Another speaker, a member of the new regiment, remarked that "he would not ride in the cars until he had his rights and could sit inside." Statements at events like these helped crystallize the importance of the issue in the minds of many black Washingtonians, especially soldiers who wore the uniform of the U.S. Army and sought the same respect that white soldiers received.[40]

In the face of resistance by African American soldiers, the original policy of allowing blacks only on the front platforms of streetcars quickly became untenable. The directors of the Washington & Georgetown Railroad responded in August 1863 with a decision to procure special cars for African Americans. In October, it added six small bobtail cars to the Pennsylvania Avenue line, with signs stating, "Colored people can ride in these cars." This tepid solution did little to resolve the problem. The *Evening Star* noted in November that the bobtail cars were inadequate and that the railway had decided to replace them with ten regular two-horse cars carrying the "Colored" designation. This plan supposedly would result in every third car being a "Colored" car.[41] Whether that many were actually put on the line or how long they were kept in service is unknown, but in the eyes of the railway's managers and many other white Washingtonians, this was ample and fair accommodation.

For African Americans, it was a lingering insult. Even the cars designated for black residents were not always available, as some whites thought their personal preferences could trump African American rights. Noah Brooks recounted that "occasionally a white person of bitter prejudices would stray ignorantly into one of the vehicles conceded to the colored race, and would indignantly demand of the conductor the expulsion of every person but himself, much to his own subsequent discomfiture." Similarly, white passengers as well as drivers and conductors might harass black riders who had the misfortune to

Early Mass Transit in Washington, D.C.

Dr. Alexander T. Augusta. *Oblate Sisters of Providence.*

enter a "Colored" car that was already occupied by whites.[42]

Finally, an incident involving Dr. Alexander T. Augusta (1825–1890), an African American surgeon in the Union army, set in a motion a more lasting change. Born a free man in Norfolk, Virginia, Augusta had learned to read in secret, since it was illegal to teach blacks to read or write. In 1840, he moved to Baltimore to work as a barber while he studied medicine on his own. Frustrated by the refusal of the University of Pennsylvania to admit him, he moved to Toronto in about 1850 to study at the Medical College of the University of Toronto, where he earned a bachelor's degree in 1856. He returned to the United States as the Civil War was beginning and wrote to President Lincoln in 1862, offering his services in support of the war effort. He was appointed surgeon for the U.S. Colored Troops with a rank of major, becoming the highest-ranking African American officer in the Union army. His first post was the newly established Freedmen's Hospital at Camp Barker, just north of present-day Logan Circle.

One rainy day in February 1864, Augusta was on his way to serve as a witness at a trial, and he hailed a car on Fourteenth Street, just one block south of where young Anna Sherman observed the horses struggling in the mud. The conductor allowed him to board the car's platform, but despite the inclement weather and the fact that he wore the uniform of an army officer, Augusta was pushed off when he tried to enter the passenger compartment. He explained what happened in a letter to his commanding officer:

> *I started from my lodgings to go to the hospital I formerly had charge of to get some notes of the case I was to give evidence in, and hailed the car at the corner of Fourteenth and I streets. It was stopped for me and when*

I attempted to enter the conductor pulled me back, and informed me that I must ride on the front with the driver, as it was against the rules for colored persons to ride inside. I told him I would not ride on the front, and he said I should not ride at all. He then ejected me from the platform, and at the same time gave orders to the driver to go on. I have therefore been compelled to walk the distance in the mud and rain, and have also been delayed in my attendance upon the court.

Augusta shrewdly forwarded a copy of his restrained but compelling letter to Senator Charles Sumner (1811–1874), who read it on the floor of the Senate several days later. Sumner was indignant at the affront to Augusta: "Now, sir, I am free to say I think we had better give up railroads in the District of Columbia if we cannot have them without such an outrage upon humanity and upon the good name of our country. An incident like that, sir, is worse for our country at this moment than a defeat in battle." Sumner proposed that Congress consider writing a law banning the exclusion of African Americans from "equal enjoyment of all railroad privileges in the District of Columbia."[43]

Sumner, a leader of the "radical" faction of the Republican Party, was the most strident advocate of equal rights in the Senate. A talented public speaker, Sumner had made an oration against the Kansas-Nebraska Act in 1856 that had enraged South Carolina Representative Preston Brooks, who savagely beat him with a cane on the floor of the Senate. Although severely wounded, Sumner eventually recovered and resumed his Senate duties, leading efforts to enhance the civil rights of African Americans.

Senator Charles Sumner. *Library of Congress.*

Sumner's streetcar proposal was forwarded to the Committee on the District of Columbia, which decided, predictably, that no new legislation was needed. The committee argued that common law required streetcar companies to treat everyone equitably and that if African Americans were having problems, they could sue. But Sumner persisted, and he eventually persuaded his colleagues that the streetcar issue was too important to avoid. Because of his influence, the charter of the new Metropolitan Railroad Company, approved on July 1, 1864, included a provision that "there shall be no regulation excluding any person from any car on account of color." However, the provision applied only to the new railway, not the rival Washington & Georgetown line, which continued to run separate "Colored" cars. The problem had been only partially solved at this point.

Sumner and others in Congress made sure that the issue of African American rights on streetcars was revisited when new streetcar legislation came up. The next opportunity came in February 1865, when a law was proposed allowing streetcar companies to charge higher fares because of wartime inflation. Thaddeus Stevens (1792–1868) of Pennsylvania, a leader of the Radical Republicans in the House of Representatives, raised the issue on the House floor:

> *Mr. Stevens wished to know whether colored persons were not ejected from the cars.*
> *Mr.* [James W.] *Patterson* [of New Hampshire] *said some mean conductors had so acted, but the president of the Washington and Georgetown company had informed him such conductors had been discharged.*
> *Mr.* [Henry L.] *Dawes* [of Massachusetts] *wished to know what was the meaning of the signboard attached to the cars, "Colored persons admitted."*
> *Mr. Patterson replied that that notice was painted in good English, and no man could better understand it than the gentleman from Massachusetts.*[44]

Clearly, tensions were high, but in the end the Radical Republicans prevailed. In March 1865, the law was passed with a provision extending the prohibition against race-based regulations to all street railways of the District of Columbia.

"I Want to Ride!"

The only question at this point was whether the new law would be enforced. African Americans continued to push for their rights and continued to be harassed and physically banned or removed from white-occupied cars. Captain William F. Spurgin, superintendent of refugees, freedmen and abandoned lands for Washington and Georgetown, reported in September 1865 that most Washingtonians didn't respect the rights of African Americans. "Although the law grants them the privilege to ride in the street cars, but few [white people] think the negro should be permitted to do so, and that if he rides at all he should ride on the platform in front."[45] What was needed was a high-profile case that could be used to pressure the streetcar companies into enforcing compliance.

If a symbol of African American dignity and strength were needed, none better could be found than Sojourner Truth (circa 1797–1883), a prominent African American who made a stand for equal access in 1865. Truth was one of the most famous African Americans in the country, having established herself as a proselytizer for civil rights in the 1840s. Born into slavery in upstate New York, Truth's original name was Isabella Baumfree. She led a harrowing young life as a slave before gaining her freedom in 1826 and moving to New York City, where she worked in the households of two Christian evangelists. By 1843, she felt called on to travel the country and preach about the evils of slavery. She changed her name to Sojourner Truth, and with the help of abolitionist William Lloyd Garrison, her memoirs, *The Narrative of Sojourner Truth: A Northern Slave*, were published in 1850. The following year, she gave an extemporaneous speech in Ohio on women's rights, known as the "Ain't I a Woman" speech, for which she became widely celebrated.

In 1864, Truth came to Washington to work for the National Freedman's Relief Association, helping to distribute food, clothing and medicine to former slaves and working to find permanent homes for them outside Washington. However, despite being well known and respected among the reform-minded, on the streets of Washington Truth was just another elderly black woman. In 1865, she found herself facing as much difficulty as any African American in riding the city's streetcars.

Truth's memoirs contain several anecdotes about her run-ins with D.C. streetcar operators.[46] On one occasion, she stood on the street signaling to several cars that refused to stop for her. When the next one came along, she "gave three tremendous yelps, 'I want to ride! I want to ride!! I WANT TO RIDE!!!" Sympathetic onlookers helped her get the car to stop, and she quickly boarded and seated herself. The angry conductor ordered her to "go forward where the horses are, or I will throw you out," but she replied that she knew the law as well as he did. Several soldiers on the car sided with her, and Truth was allowed to keep her seat. "Bless God! I have had a ride," she said when she finally disembarked.

Early Mass Transit in Washington, D.C.

Sojourner Truth, 1864. *Library of Congress.*

On another occasion, she ran after a car in Georgetown that wouldn't stop for her and managed to get aboard when it stopped for other passengers. "It is a shame to make a lady run so," she told the conductor, who threatened to put her off the car. "If you attempt that, it will cost you more than your car and horses are worth," she answered. Again, a man in military uniform intervened on her behalf, and the conductor left her alone.

A third incident proved more harrowing. Truth was out procuring supplies for invalids with a white friend, Laura Smith Haviland (1808–1898), a prominent social activist and former organizer of the Underground Railroad who had been named inspector of hospitals for the Freedmen's Bureau. Truth was harassed by the conductor when she got on a streetcar with Haviland but didn't run into real difficulties until the two of them transferred to a second car. As Truth described it:

> *A man coming out as we were going into the next car, asked the conductor if "niggers were allowed to ride." The conductor grabbed me by the shoulder and jerking me around, ordered me to get out. I told him I would not. Mrs. Haviland took hold of my other arm and said, "Don't put her out." The conductor asked if I belonged to her. "No," replied Mrs. Haviland, "She belongs to humanity." "Then take her and go," said he, and giving me another push slammed me against the door. I told him I would let him know whether he could shove me about like a dog, and said to Mrs. Haviland, "Take the number of this car."*

Truth's shoulder was injured in the incident, and with the help of the Freedmen's Bureau, she pressed charges against the conductor, John C. Weeden, for assault and battery. Haviland testified on her behalf, as did a doctor from the Freedmen's Hospital, who stated that her shoulder had been "much swollen" from being "wrenched."[47] Although the charges against Weeden were eventually dropped, the court proceedings were covered by the local newspapers, and the publicity pressured the streetcar companies to do a better job of enforcing the law.[48]

By 1866, discrimination on D.C. streetcars had decreased noticeably. Without conductors and drivers actively harassing African Americans, intolerant white riders could do little more than silently fume. Washington, though far from stellar in civil rights matters, had become a leader in promoting equal access to public transit.

In February 1866, the popular news magazine *Harper's Weekly* published a cartoon entitled "Holy Horror of Mrs. McCaffraty in a Washington City Street Passenger Car," an image that stands as a strange final commentary on the streetcar crisis in the District. By that time, voting rights were a bigger issue, and a law had just been passed giving black Washingtonians the right to vote. The cartoon mentions that "Mr. McCaffraty voted against Negro suffrage," apparently referring to an earlier non-binding citywide referendum in which D.C. voters overwhelmingly disapproved of black

Early Mass Transit in Washington, D.C.

"Holy Horror of Mrs. McCaffraty in a Washington City Street Passenger Car" from *Harper's Weekly*, February 24, 1866. *Library of Congress.*

voting rights. Congress had ignored the referendum, passing the D.C. voting rights act and even overturning a veto by President Andrew Johnson.

The cartoon expresses support for African Americans, implying that the real problem is with intolerant whites, but it does little to defuse racial hostility and prejudice. Instead, it redirects animosity toward Irish Catholics. The African American woman is well dressed and appears dignified and refined—implicitly the type of person who should be welcomed on city streetcars. Mrs. McCaffraty, on the other hand, is crude and animal-like, leering menacingly at the serene black woman. Perhaps this Irish termagant is the one who should be thrown off the car! She carries an overflowing market basket with fish dangling from the end, undoubtedly creating a stench throughout the car. Her uncouthness is further emphasized by the liquor bottles sticking out of her basket, emblems of the stereotypical Irish propensity for drink.

The conflicted message of this cartoon seems to sum up the state of civil rights in Washington and the country at large in 1866. Society still had a long way to go to achieve racial tolerance, and the right of African Americans to ride in peace on D.C. streetcars had not been settled and would be threatened repeatedly in the future.

Chapter 4

ᎻARD ᏟHOICES

MODERNIZING THE STREETCAR SYSTEM, 1888–1897

*The shades of night were falling fast
In one box car were fifty massed,
While thirty more were packed outside,
The tenor-voiced conductor cried,
   "Move forward, please!"*

*At every corner more piled on,
Till every inch of space was gone,
No nickel-bearer was denied,
And still the meek conductor cried,
   "Move forward, please!"*

*The shivering shop girls stand in groups,
Who fain would ride within those coops,
To board the cars they vainly tried,*

*And yet the slim conductor cried,
   "Move forward, please!"*

*To realize th' ideal jam
'Twould need a big hydraulic ram
To crowd the passengers inside
Who heard not when the fellow cried
   "Move forward, please!"*

*One day a man of fearful might
Packed all the people in so tight
They stuck together in a lump,
As solid as a hickory stump—
   "Move forward, please!"*[49]

B y the late 1880s, Washington's streetcars were perennially overcrowded and out of date. Although they were essential to the smooth functioning of the city—thousands of early commuters rode them every day—they were hopelessly outmoded. The fundamental problem was the continued reliance on horses. Why should D.C. streetcars still be horse-drawn when other American cities were rapidly converting to cable and electric?

Horses had never been an ideal solution. They were expensive, could only work a few hours a day, pulled cars slowly, needed lots of care and made a mess of city streets. Their limitations as locomotive engines had become painfully obvious as American cities grew in the 1880s. The population of the District of Columbia had more than doubled from 75,080 in 1860 to 177,624 in 1880, and it would continue climbing to 230,392 in 1890. More than ever, these people lived in widely dispersed communities. Some form of "rapid transit," as it was being called, was desperately needed.

Congress was key to making any improvements; it retained the power to charter streetcar companies and set requirements on how they operated. Congressional debates about the D.C. streetcar "problem" had been going on for years. In 1888, Senator George Graham Vest (1830–1904) of Missouri, one of the city's severest critics, railed against the horse-powered D.C. network, calling it "the most infamous system of street railroads ever inflicted upon any people." According to the *Evening Star*, he "condemned the entire system of streetcar service here, and declared that it ought to be abolished; that horse cars are obsolete, and it is time the national capital had a modern service."[50] Public sentiment was clearly in his favor. The following January, when he called the Washington system "the worst in the United States," it led to a rare instance of bipartisan agreement on Capitol Hill. "There was a unanimity of Senatorial sentiment in this regard, which was surprising. Each Senator present was ready to say something on the subject and quietly awaited his turn to express himself," the *Washington Post* reported.[51] The time for modernizing the city's streetcars had come. The only remaining issue—and it was a thorny one—was choosing which propulsion technology to use.

The Evil of Overhead Wires

Controversy had erupted with the inauguration in 1888 of the Eckington & Soldiers Home Railway, a streetcar line that connected the new Northeast community of Eckington with downtown (the following chapter includes details of its development). The Eckington line was not only the first mechanized streetcar line in Washington, but it was also the city's first electric trolley line—the word *trolley* referring to a streetcar that gathers electric power from overhead lines through a pole on the roof of the car. The way the pole reaches up to the overhead wires reminded people of a fisherman's pole trolling in a stream, and thus the term was coined. For many Washingtonians, the revolutionary new Eckington trolley was a marvel to behold. But for other observers, notably Crosby S. Noyes (1825–1908), editor of the *Evening Star*, it was the incarnation of evil.

Under the editorial leadership of Noyes, the *Star* had already been waging an aggressive campaign against the use of overhead wires for the distribution of electricity to downtown buildings. The *Star*'s primary arguments were that the wires were unsightly, posed a danger of electrocution, would interfere with the operations of the fire department and would be impossible to eradicate at a later date if ever allowed to gain a foothold in the city. The worry about overhead wires in Washington was in keeping with rising concerns among civic leaders around the country about crowded, dirty, unsafe conditions in urban centers. These concerns were one of the chief drivers of the City Beautiful movement, which would gain prominence at the Columbian Exposition of 1893, just five years later. Eventually, the McMillan Commission would produce a grand plan to beautify Washington's monumental core. But in the meantime, the proliferation of hundreds of tall wooden poles strung with colossal nests of wires was a particular evil that, in the view of Noyes and others, had to be stopped. Electric streetcar systems, adding even more wires strung out over the centers of major roads, would make matters that much worse.

When plans for the Eckington project were first made public in August 1888, the *Star* responded with a fierce editorial. "The reform of abolishing overhead wires in the District seems to be progressing backward," it warned. "[N]ow the Commissioners add a new species of overhead wire to the existing network by permitting the Eckington railway to construct an overhead electric system." They should instead be working to "secure to the city the benefits of rapid transit without aggravating the evil of overhead wires," the *Star* insisted.[52] To support its position, the newspaper cited a consultant's report, prepared expressly for the D.C. commissioners, on how rapid transit should be introduced in the District. The report recommended that overhead trolley wires be banned within the city (i.e., south of Boundary Street) and allowed only in suburban areas of the District.[53]

The *Star*'s cause was quickly taken up in the Senate by George F. Edmunds (1828–1919) of Vermont. Edmunds had a reputation for being a biting inquisitor as well as a staunch champion of the status quo, always suspicious of new developments. The new electric trolley was a classic subject for his wrath. In a hearing just days after the Eckington announcement, he accused the D.C. commissioners of violating the law and defying the will of

An 1880s view of the Treasury Department building and Fifteenth Street. Horse-drawn streetcars still ply this route, and overhead power and telecommunications wires have been installed. They would soon be banned. *Author's collection.*

Congress in allowing the project to move forward. "Not for many a day have the District Commissioners had such a severe raking over as was given them in the Senate yesterday," the *Washington Post* observed.[54]

The Eckington line's defenders, including the *Post*, countered that the railway was essentially suburban in nature, and thus overhead wires were consistent with the recommendations of the city's consultant. Further, the company had already made purchases and other contract commitments, and it would be wrong to force it to change after the fact. The irate senators backed down, and the Eckington line was allowed to proceed with its plans, but it would be only a temporary victory.

Spurred to action, Congress soon required D.C. streetcar lines to convert. In March 1889, it passed an act authorizing D.C. streetcar companies to "substitute for horses electric power by storage or independent electrical batteries or underground wire, or underground cables moved by steam power." A year later, another law decreed that if downtown streetcar companies didn't convert within two years, they would forfeit their corporate franchises.[55] While deadline extensions and special accommodations were subsequently granted to various companies, the edict to move away from horsecars had been established. What to replace them with was not at all obvious. The law included an explicit prohibition against trolley systems using overhead wires after July 1893.

The city's streetcar companies had their marching orders. They were required to mechanize their cars, but they were also prohibited from using overhead electric wires—the cheapest and most widely used propulsion technology of the day. Complying with the Congressional mandate would be a tremendous challenge, both financially and technologically, for every company operating in the District.

THE MOTOR OF THE FUTURE

The Washington & Georgetown Railroad Company—first, largest and most successful of the city's streetcar lines—was a sound, conservatively run operation in the late 1880s. Knowing that it would sooner or later be forced to abandon horse-drawn cars, the company decided to take action. In 1887, the company's board of directors commissioned board member Charles C. Glover (1846–1936) and company president Henry Hurt (1844–1916) to make a thorough study of advanced propulsion technologies and come back to the board with a recommendation on how to proceed.

Glover and Hurt were great friends. Glover was one of the city's most prominent and influential business leaders. Born to a family who had been in Washington since its founding, Glover had joined the banking firm of Riggs & Company when he was nineteen years old and had risen to become one of its partners. He had been on the board of the W&G since 1875. Hurt, a Virginia native, had served in the Confederate army during the Civil War. Shortly thereafter, he started his career as a streetcar driver and gradually worked his way up through the ranks of the company. At six feet tall and weighing nearly two hundred pounds, Hurt was a commanding and assertive figure. He was confident that he knew the streetcar business inside out and understood which direction it was heading.

The two made a grand five-week tour across the country to observe streetcar systems in Cincinnati, St. Louis, Kansas City, Los Angeles and San Francisco. When they returned to Washington in May 1887, Hurt announced that the W&G would convert to cable. "We are firmly convinced," he told the *Washington Post*, "that the cable is the motor of the future, and we will adopt it, even if it necessitates the discarding of all our cars, our tracks, our buildings—in fact, even if we have to begin over again with an entire

An undated portrait of Charles C. Glover. *Library of Congress.*

new plant."[56] Hurt envisioned a thoroughly modern and luxurious new cable system in the District, including cars as elegant as those he saw in San Francisco. "They are beautifully finished in hard wood and brass and it is our intention to duplicate them for Washington when our cable road is started."

At the time, it was hard to argue with Hurt's conclusion. Cable was a tested and stable technology. In contrast, electric systems were still experimental and had a reputation for being unreliable. Andrew S. Hallidie (1836–1900), a wire-rope manufacturer, invented the first cable-drawn streetcar system in the early 1870s, demonstrating it successfully in San Francisco in 1873. For most of the 1880s, cable was the best available alternative to horse-drawn streetcars; electric wouldn't become widely available until the end of the decade.

Cable systems are conceptually simple. Engines in a central steam-powered plant propel a looped steel-rope continuously through an underground conduit that extends the length of a cable car route. The cars are equipped with "grips," powerful metal rods that reach down through a narrow slot in the street and clamp on to the moving steel cable, which then pulls the cars along the track.

The straighter the route, the better a cable system will work. The vast majority of the energy involved in running the system is actually spent in circulating the cable beneath the roadway, so the extra burden of the cars grabbing hold of it adds only a marginal load. Thus cable systems are especially efficient for hauling cars up steep hills, such as in San Francisco. Multiple cars can be carried at the same time without losing speed. And the cost of operating cable cars in the late nineteenth century was only about half that of horsecars—a fact that caught the attention of many streetcar company executives.

Early Mass Transit in Washington, D.C.

The biggest drawback was the huge initial investment required. Trenches had to be dug under the streets and fitted out with iron yokes to form conduits for the cable loop. An elaborate steam power plant had to be built with massive engines to circulate the cable, and the enormous cable itself had to be installed, maintained and frequently replaced.

When Chicago opened its first cable line in 1882—still several years before electric systems were perfected—it seemed to prove to many street railway men that the technology was reliable enough to operate in harsh summer and winter climates and could handle the load of many cars running simultaneously in a concentrated urban environment. It was soon the darling of the streetcar industry.

Having made its decision, all that the Washington & Georgetown line needed was Congressional approval, which came in March 1889. Work began immediately afterward on converting the Seventh Street route, an almost perfectly straight line that was the easiest of the company's three routes to convert. In September, a crew of some four hundred men began digging the massive trench that would form the cable conduit and fitting it with cast-iron yokes made in Dayton, Ohio. New grooved rails from the Cambria Iron Works in Johnstown, Pennsylvania, were laid on the surface. Work on the conduit was finished by the end of the year, and in January 1890, an enormous iron-and-wood spindle, twelve feet in diameter, arrived at the Baltimore & Potomac Railroad's freight yard. Weighing ninety-seven thousand pounds, it contained the thirty-four-thousand-foot cable that would span the length of the Seventh Street line, from the wharves on the Southwest waterfront up to Boundary Street, where a popular new baseball park, eventually to be called Griffith Stadium, was to open the following year.

The line finally went into service on April 12, 1890. Veteran cable car "gripman" Lawrence Ody of San Francisco skillfully operated the first car, which was packed with dignitaries. Crowds lined the streets cheering the speedy new cars and jostling to get aboard wherever they could. Many people rode all the way down to the Seventh Street wharves to see the new powerhouse at the end of the line and watch its great engine wheels turning the cable. Just four trains (consisting of a grip car pulling two unpowered "trailer" cars) ran the first day because only four trained gripmen were on hand. More trains were added in subsequent days as additional operators were trained.

Even before the Seventh Street line opened, the W&G began to convert its other two lines, on Fourteenth Street and Pennsylvania Avenue, and those lines opened in August 1892. The Pennsylvania Avenue line in particular represented a much more complex engineering task, having a total of

In addition to the W&G, the Columbia Railway converted to cable power for a brief period in the late 1890s. Here a class of schoolchildren takes an excursion on a Columbia cable car in 1899. *Library of Congress via Maryland Rail Heritage Library.*

thirty-four curves, but the technology had advanced by then, and relatively few problems were encountered. After the cable went into operation, a trip from Georgetown to the Navy Yard, which previously took an hour, lasted just forty minutes, and a ride up Fourteenth Street to Columbia Heights ran twenty minutes. According to the *Evening Star*, the railroad spent $3 million to build the entire cable system, including its two powerhouses—the equivalent of at least $460 million in today's money.[57]

The crown jewel of the new system was the imposing new powerhouse on Pennsylvania Avenue, between Thirteenth and Fourteenth Streets, that powered both the Fourteenth Street and Pennsylvania Avenue lines. The real estate alone for this massive edifice had cost $500,000. Designed by Kansas City architect Walter C. Root (1859–1925), who specialized in railroad-related architecture, the grand six-story Romanesque Revival structure was perhaps the largest privately owned building in the city at the time and filled an entire block. A carved stone arch resting on marble piers framed its ceremonial main entrance. Inside, eight massive iron boilers were arrayed on the ground floor, which was structurally separate from the rest of the building so that vibrations would not be felt on the upper floors. Corporate

Early Mass Transit in Washington, D.C.

An 1897 drawing of the Capital Traction cable powerhouse on Pennsylvania Avenue. *Washington Times*, September 30, 1897.

offices and rented space filled the stories above them. A soaring 150-foot smokestack stood at the rear of the site.

The system had its biggest test less than a month after it began operation, when the Grand Army of the Republic—a huge fraternal organization of Union veterans of the Civil War—held an encampment in Washington. On one day during the convention, cable cars shuttled 170,000 passengers, almost four times their usual load, and encountered few problems. Washington's mass transportation system had entered a new age.

"Follies Little, If Any, Short of Criminal"

The Washington & Georgetown's cable cars were the earliest rapid transit cars to run on busy downtown Washington streets. The Seventh Street cars traveled at nine miles per hour, twice as fast as the average pace of horse-drawn cars. For safety reasons, the railroad set a rule that the cars could not be hailed mid-block, as had been customary with horsecars, and would only stop at the far side of intersections. Patrons were cautioned not to attempt to board or alight when the cars were moving—another common practice with horsecars. Unfortunately, Washingtonians had no experience with the kind of power and speed the new streetcars represented, and they were slow to recognize their unique dangers. An editorial in the *Washington Post* in 1893 expressed exasperation at the lack of common sense displayed by cable car patrons:

> [W]*e persist in jumping on and off while the trains are in motion, in alighting on the side on which we may be struck by passing cars, and, generally, in committing follies little, if any, short of criminal. One cannot take even the shortest ride upon the cable car without having his heart in his throat a dozen times. The way in which men and women tempt Providence is beyond belief. They act as though they expected all the physical laws to be suspended for their benefit, and nature itself to wait upon their caprice.*[58]

The newspapers regularly reported on cable car accidents, fueling the technology's dangerous reputation. Several fatalities occurred when pedestrians walked casually in the path of oncoming cars, expecting them to be able to stop as quickly as horsecars could. Others suffered injuries when, as standing passengers, they were knocked down by the sudden acceleration of the car gripping the cable, another unfamiliar experience.

Especially dangerous was alighting on the street side of the cars, as passengers would land directly in the path of streetcars coming in the opposite direction. George H. Rhodes, of 111 Third Street Northeast, was one such victim who jumped off a moving car and was struck by another car coming the other way. His injuries proved fatal. Mrs. John P. Anderson was struck by a southbound car as she tried to board on the street side of a northbound car on the Seventh Street line. She was pushed "some distance" along the rails by the cable car's fender but was lucky to survive her ordeal. Eventually, streetcars would be designed to allow entry and exit only from the curbside.

All the while that riders were creating unnecessary hazards for themselves, the newly hired gripmen were busy trying to keep their cars moving. Controlling how the car's grip grabbed and let go of the cable was not an easy task. A gripman had to be of a strong physique to handle the long, heavy lever that controlled the grip, and it took great skill for him to do so without jerking the car forward or damaging the grip or the cable. The biggest potential safety horror was the specter of the grip becoming so entangled in a frayed cable that it couldn't let go. If that were to happen, the car would continue zinging along the roadway at nine miles per hour with no way to stop until it crashed or the power plant stopped the cable. How often this may have actually happened in D.C. is not known.

Another challenge occurred when two cable routes crossed, as they did at Seventh Street and Pennsylvania Avenue Northwest. The gripman whose cable passed underneath (in this case, the Pennsylvania Avenue line) had to let it go before the intersection, coast through and then grab the cable again on the other side. Such intersections were dangerous for pedestrians, horses and other vehicles because the cable cars were largely out of control as they coasted through. In April 1896, the *Washington Times* warned that "death will reign" at the intersection of Fourteenth Street and New York Avenue Northwest because three rapid transit lines—the Washington & Georgetown's Fourteenth Street cable car line as well as the Eckington and one other electric line—all crossed at the same intersection. "Flagmen, be they ever so attentive, cannot prevent the unwary citizen or rural visitor from getting bewildered, and a whole squad of police would not give adequate protection," the newspaper feared. While collisions did occur, the predicted mayhem at Fourteenth and New York never materialized. Beginning in 1898, D.C. street railway companies were required to pay the salaries of traffic policemen at such intersections to protect public safety.

A Model City

Meanwhile, the city's other streetcar lines had to make their own decisions on how to convert. Even as the W&G's cable lines went into service, the *Evening* Star kept up its drumbeat against overhead-wire trolleys, which were fast becoming the preferred choice of streetcar companies across America.

In February 1888, less than a year after Henry Hurt and Charles Glover decided to convert the W&G to cable, the first large-scale urban electric trolley system entered service in Richmond, Virginia, proving the economic and technical viability of overhead electric systems. Connecticut-born inventor Frank J. Sprague (1857–1934), who had spent several years working for Thomas Edison, had been wrestling with the problem of how to distribute electricity efficiently to streetcars for many years. He had formed his own electric railway company in 1884 and worked for years on small demonstration projects, as did other inventors. These small-scale demonstrations failed to prove decisively that the technology would work in major urban settings, where dozens of cars would be operating simultaneously on the same line. It was hard to believe that the electric current sent out over those thin little overhead wires would be strong enough to power all those cars.

The trolley system that Sprague built in Richmond dispelled those concerns. While there were glitches when it first came on line, Sprague was a master at resolving them. He had also solved key technical problems, such as how to mount trolley poles on car tops so they would link reliably with the overhead wires. In the months following the opening of the Richmond system, executives from street railways across the country came to observe the new Sprague trolleys, and they were universally impressed. Sprague famously orchestrated a demonstration one evening in which he lined up twenty-two cars and had them all start up briskly one after another without straining the electrical power system. Soon orders for electric overhead trolley systems based on Sprague's patented methods were coming in from all over America.

But the proliferation of trolleys only steeled the determination of the *Washington Star* to prevent such systems from taking root in the capital. In October 1892, the newspaper ran a lengthy feature written by Theodore W. Noyes (1858–1946), son of Crosby Noyes, after he returned from an extensive European tour of modern streetcar systems. Noyes chided American (and particularly Washington) streetcar companies for their lack of inventiveness:

> *Our national boast is that nothing is impossible to American inventiveness, that what other people have failed or neglected to achieve we accomplish speedily and thoroughly. A notable exception to this national self-confidence is found apparently in the great electric companies and many street railway magnates, who declare with one accord in a concert of self-deprecation that no form of electric railway motor but the trolley can be made commercially practicable in America, and that the only substitute for the antiquated car horse that American ingenuity can devise, even for our large cities, is the aggravation of the overhead pole and the wire evil.*[59]

Surely, Noyes argued, there were other viable alternatives. He was particularly intrigued by the system operating in Budapest, Austria-Hungary, an electrical system that used underground conduits to feed power to the cars. He described the system in great detail, noting that it functioned perfectly well in inclement weather, contrary to worries by American streetcar company officials that rain or snow would short out underground electrical conduits and cause them to fail. Drawing many comparisons between Budapest and

Washington, Noyes concluded that Washington streetcar systems could readily convert to battery-powered, cable or underground conduit electrical systems. By doing so, Washington would become "a model city, not only of America, but of the world, to which students from all parts of the globe will resort for suggestions concerning the latest and best forms of street railway motor."

"This Superb Improvement in Electric Propulsion"

For the Metropolitan Railroad, chief competitor to the Washington & Georgetown line and the city's second-largest streetcar company, the pressure was on. The Metropolitan had struggled with the conversion issue and had delayed making a final decision as long as it could. Company executives ruled out cable technology because they felt that their lines had too many bends and turns to make cable feasible. With overhead wires also out of the question, where else could they turn? In 1889, they decided to adopt a battery-based electric system. The Metropolitan would become the first large streetcar system in the country to adopt battery-powered cars.

"Storage batteries," as they were called at the time, had the advantage of being less expensive than cable because no underground conduits were needed and no expensive cable had to be installed and maintained. However, battery power had few other advantages. The batteries of the day couldn't retain a charge for very long, took a long time to recharge, were very heavy and had to be replaced often. Most significantly, battery-powered cars tended to be sluggish, especially around curves, and thus were unpopular with riders. The Metropolitan tried to phase them in, running a mix of battery and horsecars on its lines; however, taking the less expensive path proved to be a bad idea. Batteries were abandoned after three years, in October 1893.

At this point, the Metropolitan was in dire straits. The Congressional deadline of July 1893 to convert away from horsepower had passed, and the Justice Department accordingly began proceedings to revoke the company's charter. Meanwhile, the archrival Washington & Georgetown line had fully converted to cable and was happily providing fast, efficient service to its satisfied customers. The Metropolitan needed something—anything—to replace its antique horsecars and get back in the game.

The *Star* began worrying that the Metropolitan would insist that it had no choice but to convert to an overhead wire–based system. The newspaper claimed that most Washingtonians didn't believe the company had really run out of choices. "[T]here is a wide opposition to the conclusion…that Congress will have no alternative but to grant permission to the road to introduce the trolley," it warned. "There is a very large contingent who do not swallow the statements that, in the first place, the road could not be equipped with the cable system, and, second that the underground trolley is not a practical success."[60] The day of reckoning seemed to be close. If the Metropolitan were allowed to adopt overhead wires, there was little doubt that the city would soon be virtually cocooned with them.

Fortunately, the Metropolitan backed down from the fight, opting to spend the money to build an underground electrical conduit system. With the company's support, Congress passed a new law in 1894 giving the Metropolitan time and authorization to convert to such a system. The company's engineers reached out to the operators of the Budapest, Austria-Hungary system, who assured them that an underground system would work in Washington.

Construction began in late 1894, with the Ninth Street line being first to go into operation on July 29, 1895. During a trial run, the *Star* noted approvingly that the Metropolitan's new electric streetcars ran much more smoothly than the cable cars of the Washington & Georgetown line:

A typical 1890s electric streetcar of the Metropolitan Railroad. *Robert A. Truax Collection, courtesy of Jerry A. McCoy.*

> *In spite of the fact that the track was very dirty—made so by excavating and other work done beneath and on each side of it—the running was remarkably smooth, and especially was this noticed at the curves, where there is commonly much extremely discomforting motion of a decidedly jerky sort. The stops and starts were without jar, and, in fact, there was no opportunity for even the most critical passenger to speak of either the cars or the underground system by which they are operated in any other than terms of hearty commendation.*[61]

Distinguished banker John Joy Edson (1846–1935), one of the dignitaries who rode on the line's first official trip, credited the *Star* for the success of the new system:

> *The building of this road is due as much to The Star as anything else—I might say more than to any other cause.... Its brave and insistent fight against the trolley made it impossible for that kind of rapid transit to gain foothold in Washington, and so this superb improvement in electric propulsion was made imperative.*[62]

The Metropolitan soon began to convert its other lines to underground electric conduit, completing the changeover of its entire system by early 1897. As the turn of the new century drew near, the Metropolitan, which had procrastinated for so long and agonized over its choices, was suddenly the city's technology leader. It had leapfrogged the smug and conservative W&G, whose jerky cable system now seemed obsolete. In fact, the Metropolitan's underground conduit system would become the de facto standard for all Washington streetcar lines in coming years, but not before more agonizing decisions were made and much more drama was played out.

Chapter 5

GRID-IRONING THE CITY

THE RISE OF STREETCAR SUBURBS, 1868–1899

The Washington & Georgetown and the Metropolitan remained the city's two largest street railways, but many other lines were chartered in the late nineteenth century. Building new streetcar lines, especially ones extending out of the core of the city into newly developing neighborhoods, was seen as the key to progress in the Gilded Age. In fact, investors at times were downright frantic to build new lines. Like the gold and silver deposits that were luring miners in the West, streetcar systems in Washington and other cities were seen as sure bets for outsized profits. Even if their day-to-day operations didn't make any money, it was believed that the new lines would still enrich their owners by transforming worthless fields and forests into pricey suburban real estate.

In 1892, a reporter for the *Star* marked down on a map of Washington the routes of all the street railways and extensions that were being proposed to Congress. "When he had finished the task, which is not a slight one, he found that nearly every street in the city would be supplied with a street railroad if all the bills became laws," the newspaper reported. "A number of streets would have more than one railroad along some sections, so that altogether the city would be pretty well gridironed."[63]

Views were decidedly mixed as to whether this headlong development was a good thing. An 1890 Senate debate on the proliferation of streetcar lines captured the pros and cons as they were commonly perceived. Senator John James Ingalls (1833–1900) of Kansas, a champion of labor rights, saw streetcars as benefiting the common man:

Early Mass Transit in Washington, D.C.

I have no doubt that they are built for profit; but the street railways of this and every other city are built for the poor. They are built for the laboring people.... I know of no reason why street railroads should not be constructed.... They relieve the congestion of the city. They increase the public health. They are great sanitizing agencies that enable people of small means to escape from the heat and from the crowd and from the inconvenience, the unsanitary condition of the city, into the country...

Aside from health concerns, cities like Washington desperately needed to expand to better accommodate their burgeoning populations, and streetcar systems clearly facilitated that growth. But not everyone agreed that it was for the best. Senator Eugene Hale (1836–1918) of Maine objected to Senator Ingalls's views:

These roads are not built at the demand of the people. There has not been...any great rush and tide of public sentiment and petitions from the poor for these roads. Everybody knows why they are asked for.

A syndicate...buys a large tract of land out in the country. It seeks to better its fortunes, to double and treble its money.... There is no movement on the part of the laborers or of the poor of the city to build the road, but this syndicate comes forward with its plans and ruthlessly takes possession of every avenue that the people of the District ought to have.... The truth is [the streetcar developers] *are the lords of the manor here.... They are the men who have their way and we do not scrutinize them enough. Nobody does.*[64]

Against the backdrop of these conflicting attitudes, the city's most prominent developers, many of them northerners aspiring to transform the sleepy southern capital, set out to build the District's new streetcar suburbs. Their quests were often filled with frustration and disappointment.

"The Citizens of Uniontown and East Washington Are Delighted"

The story of the rise of Anacostia is one example. Anacostia began when several developers purchased a truck farm on the far shore of the Eastern Branch of the Potomac in 1854. The old farm was located directly across from the Navy Yard and was accessible via a bridge that crossed the river at that point. It was this same bridge that John Wilkes Booth would gallop across eleven years later, fleeing the scene of his assassination of Abraham Lincoln. Here developers laid out streets and house lots in a community they dubbed Uniontown, which slowly attracted settlers through the 1850s and 1860s.

As early as 1868, local businessmen led by prominent wood and coal merchant Leon William Guinand (1825–1880) petitioned the Metropolitan Railroad to extend its line across the Navy Yard Bridge to Uniontown. Guinand, a native of Switzerland who owned a wharf on the city side of the Eastern Branch, hoped to spur faster growth in the sluggishly developing Uniontown outpost. But with fewer than seventy families living there at the time, the Metropolitan was unwilling to invest in the proposed line. Undaunted, Guinand succeeded in 1872 in convincing Congress to charter an independent Anacostia & Potomac River Railway Company.

One of the Anacostia & Potomac line's biggest promoters, and one of the most successful developers of the Anacostia community in general, was not Guinand but a northerner who came to town in 1874. Henry Adams Griswold (1847–1909), born to a prominent family in Wethersfield, Connecticut, had worked as a lawyer with his brothers in Chicago after the Civil War. When he moved to Washington, it was initially to help handle the business affairs of his recently widowed sister. He settled in Anacostia, purchasing one of its oldest houses, situated on a generous tract of land overlooking the city. According to a posthumous tribute, Griswold was "reserved in his nature, but warm-hearted and deeply attached to those to whom he was allied by ties of kinship." At the same time, he had a "delicate physical organization and an extremely sensitive spirit."[65] Although he would be credited with helping build Anacostia into a thriving and prosperous suburb, Griswold also engaged in bitter struggles over the development of the streetcar line.

When Griswold came to Anacostia, no work had yet been done on the proposed streetcar line because little money had been raised to pay for it. Griswold helped inject new energy into the project, both by investing in the project himself and by bringing in other investors, allowing construction to finally begin in October 1875. The railroad began operations in July 1876 with Guinand as its first president. When Guinand died in September 1880, Griswold took charge.

It took time to build the company's operations. Initially, the A&P's two small cars made a short run from what is now V Street and Martin Luther King Jr. Avenue Southeast, in the heart of Anacostia, across the Navy Yard Bridge to Seventh and M Streets Southeast, near the main gate of

Early Mass Transit in Washington, D.C.

A horsecar of the Anacostia & Potomac Railway is seen at the foot of Asylum Hill in this 1890 photo. *Historical Society of Washington, D.C.*

the Navy Yard. The line was certainly popular with Anacostians, who were thrilled to no longer have to walk the length of the bridge to get into the city. "The citizens of Uniontown and East Washington are delighted and patronize the road so well as to exceed the expectations of the company," the *Evening Star* claimed at the time.[66] Several more cars were soon added, and within a year, the line had been extended west along M Street to the Southwest waterfront, where passengers could connect with the north–south Washington & Georgetown line.

With the streetcars bringing more people to Anacostia, Griswold in 1879 subdivided his large real estate holdings and began selling house lots in what was called Griswold's Addition, adjacent to the original Uniontown development. When he took over the presidency of the A&P the following year, he was also its principal owner. He pushed for extensions of the line into downtown Washington, including extending the waterfront end of the line north into the heart of downtown. After years of wrangling with Congress, the proposed extensions were approved, and in January 1891, Griswold took the reins of the first car to travel from Anacostia to the Center Market on Pennsylvania Avenue, passing the Baltimore & Potomac train station on the Mall along the way. An additional branch on Capitol Hill that led east to Congressional Cemetery and the

Capital Streetcars

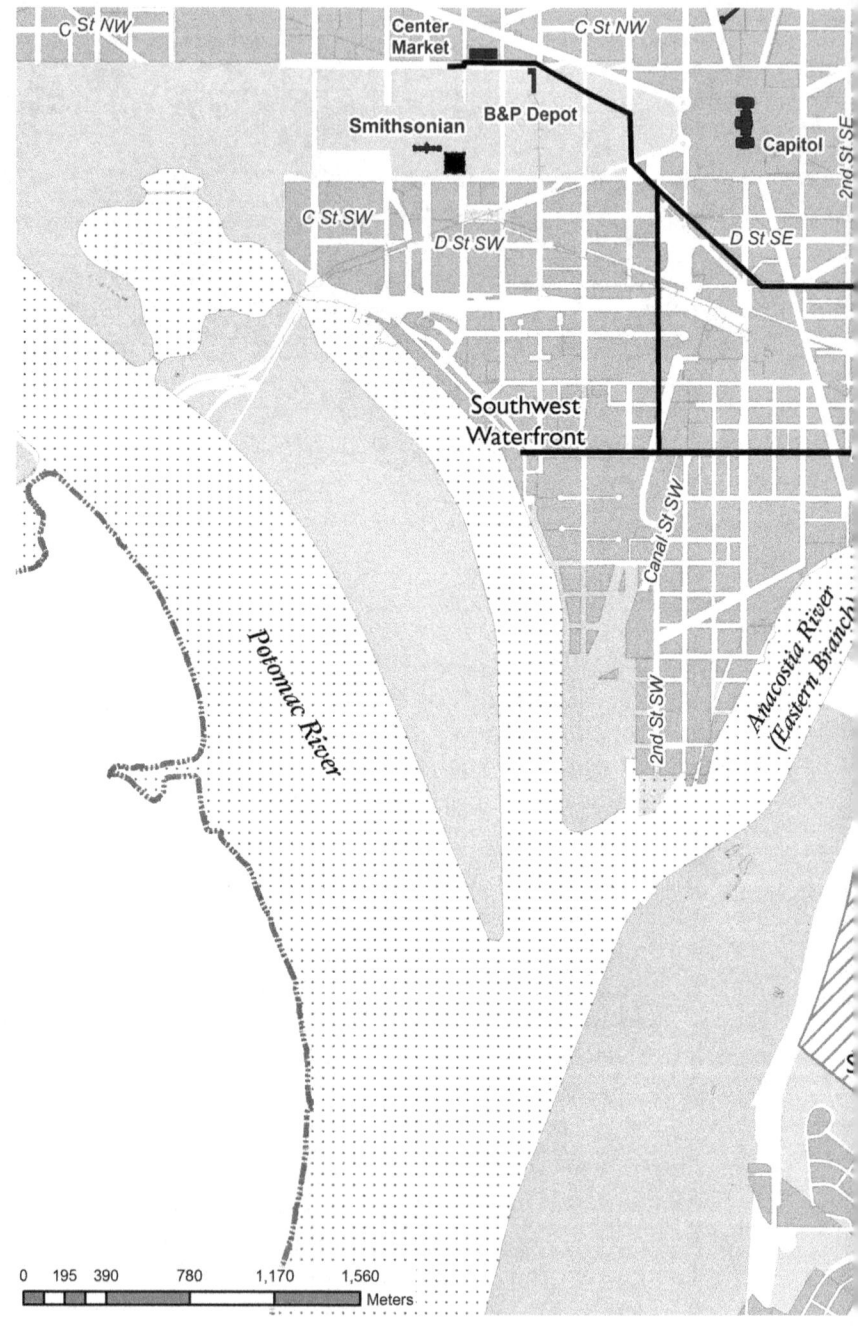

A map of the route of the Anacostia & Potomac Railway. *Matthew B. Gilmore.*

Early Mass Transit in Washington, D.C.

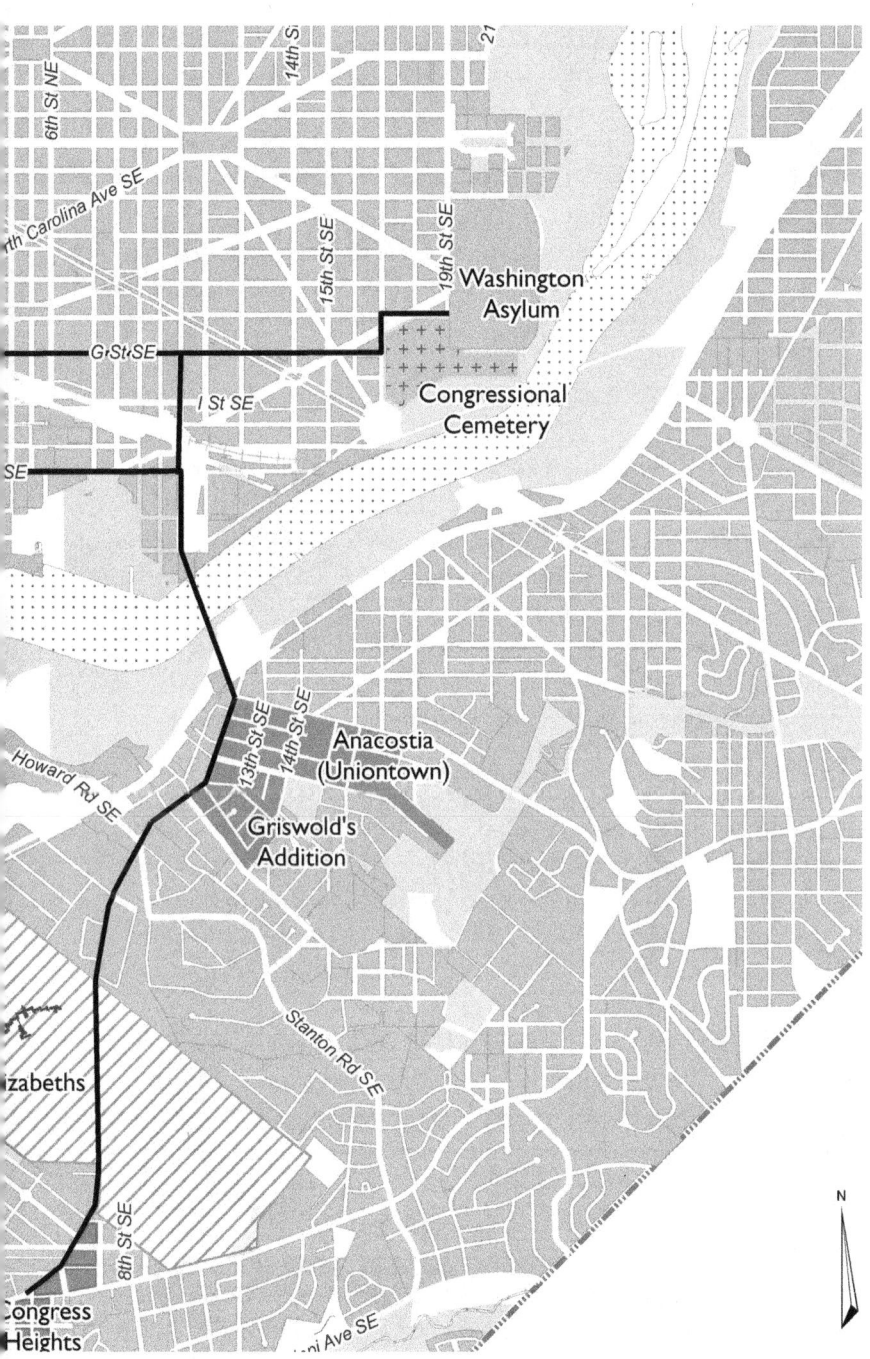

Washington Asylum was also added in 1891.[67] By 1893, the railway had fifty-two cars, 230 horses and eight and a half miles of track carrying hundreds of thousands of passengers annually.[68]

By the 1880s, Griswold had become a successful attorney and real estate developer in addition to heading the growing A&P railroad. He even served as Anacostia's postmaster for a time. Residents came to refer to him as the town's "mayor." But much of his success turned out to be more fragile than it appeared. The A&P's expansion had been hinged on the assumption that patronage would grow substantially, allowing development loans to be repaid and profits to be earned. That did not happen, at least not as rapidly as Griswold had planned. As Anacostia continued to grow at a measured pace, ridership rose slowly.

The A&P's Congressional Cemetery branch, known as the "ghost line," turned out not to be profitable at all. Griswold curtailed service, and in return complaints piled up about the small, dirty cars and the limited remaining service. "The ghost line, which runs from 11th and G streets to the work house, is a disgrace. And there is not a person who has ever used it that will not agree with me," one disgruntled passenger wrote to the *Evening Star* in 1892. "These cars run at any time—I mean this car, for the company is operating at present but one car—and visitors to the Washington Asylum and the Congressional cemetery have to wait in all sorts of weather for this one poorly equipped car to make the long round trip, which usually takes from half to three-quarters of an hour and sometimes more."[69] Superstitious people claimed that empty cars operated at night without passengers or drivers.[70] By 1896, service had stopped altogether on the ghost line, and the tracks were soon overgrown with weeds and filled with dirt.[71]

While Griswold shrugged off the complaints, service declined throughout his system. The spacious two-horse cars with drivers and conductors that originally plied the A&P were replaced with smaller bobtail cars, even after such cars were banned within Washington city. Anacostians felt that they were being treated as second-class citizens. Griswold, like other suburban streetcar company executives, insisted that he couldn't make money if he had to pay the wages of both drivers and conductors.

By 1895, the remaining poorly paid drivers and conductors had had enough. They went on strike in July, insisting that their wages be increased from $1.25 per day to $1.50. Service on the A&P was shut down as the strike dragged on. Anacostia residents had to walk into town or ride hastily arranged coach service. Merchants worried that their businesses would be ruined. Then, after insisting for almost three weeks that he couldn't afford the higher wages, Griswold suddenly changed his mind and agreed to the workers' demands. When his decision was announced at a large union meeting, "there was a wild explosion of enthusiasm, and the audience cheered till the gas lamps winked responsively."[72]

But the workers' problems weren't over. After only a few more months, Griswold announced that he could not afford to pay the higher wages after all. He presented an ultimatum to the union: either the wages would have to be reduced or service would be cut back. When the workers balked, Griswold locked them out of their jobs. He hired scab drivers to operate the A&P's cars at the lower wages. Some of the angry locked-out workers resorted to jumping on the backs of the A&P's cars as they came across the Navy Yard Bridge and forcing them to derail, terrifying the passengers. Many Anacostia residents sympathized with the workers and joined in a boycott of Griswold's streetcars. Patronage plummeted, and the A&P's financial woes worsened.

Of course, as a horse-powered line, the A&P was woefully outmoded in 1895 anyway. Many observers assumed that Griswold was pocketing profits from the railway and refusing to modernize it merely to avoid making the necessary capital investment. The likely truth is that the company simply had no reserves to fund a conversion. Meanwhile, competitors saw an opportunity. In 1896, Arthur E. Randle (1859–1929), a real estate developer who had purchased a large old farm on a hill overlooking Anacostia, succeeded in winning a Congressional charter for a new streetcar company, called the Capital Electric Railway, to offer electric trolley service over the same Anacostia route that the A&P traveled. In 1897, the new electrified route was extended up the hill to Randle's development, called Congress Heights, a trek that would have been impossible for the A&P's horsecars.

By the following year, the A&P was bankrupt and in receivership. Griswold resigned as president, and soon the company was sold to a large syndicate that was buying up many of the District's formerly independent streetcar companies. Ironically, the Capitol Railway within a few years would default on the bonds used to fund its construction, and the railway would be sold in 1900 to the syndicate-controlled A&P. Like the other lines swallowed up by the syndicate, the parts of the A&P and the Capitol Railway that stayed in service were eventually unified and converted to underground electrical conduit power.[73]

The quiet, sensitive Griswold went into retirement at his Mount View estate in Anacostia. He suffered from "nervousness and insomnia," according to the *Evening Star*, and it finally caught up to him in March 1909. One day, while his wife was out shopping, he retired to an attic that had not been used in years and shot himself in the chest with a shotgun. He died instantly.

Griswold left his wife and sons an estate worth about $20,000. The newspapers wrote piously of his great success in promoting and expanding Anacostia, but it's unclear how burdened Griswold may have been by the ultimate failure of the Anacostia & Potomac Railway to turn a clear profit. It had been the centerpiece of his efforts to build up Anacostia, but it had never been a financial success.

Obnoxious Obstructions

The history of Eckington, a community located along the east side of North Capitol Street above Florida Avenue, makes for an interesting comparison. Eckington was perhaps the first "true" streetcar suburb in the District in the sense that it was designed from the start as a streetcar destination. It originally had been one of a scattering of nineteenth-century country estates that dotted the hills overlooking Washington City. On a tract of 112 acres, Joseph Gales Jr. (1786–1860), publisher of the *National Intelligencer* newspaper and one of the city's early mayors, built in 1815 a country house, which he named Eckington after his birthplace in England. For most of the nineteenth century, the only development to mar the rolling, forested hills surrounding the Gales mansion was the laying of the Baltimore & Ohio's Metropolitan Branch railroad line, which cut through the eastern portion of the tract in 1873.

Real estate investor Colonel George Truesdell (1842–1921) bought the Eckington tract in 1887 with the idea of building a modern bedroom suburb on it. Originally from Fairmount, New York, Truesdell had fought with the Twelfth New York Volunteers during the Civil War and was badly wounded at the Battle of Gaines Mill, Virginia. He was confined as a prisoner for a time in the infamous Libby Prison in Richmond, Virginia, but was released and later became paymaster of the army, rising to the brevet rank of lieutenant colonel. Imbued with military discipline and ambition, Truesdell always used his military title. He moved to Washington in 1872 to buy and sell real estate and spent fifteen years building up his practice before making his move in Eckington.

Truesdell laid out his new subdivision as an idyllic suburban community with large house lots, stunning views of the city and desirable modern amenities—including paved streets, stone sidewalks and electric streetlights—that more established District neighborhoods still didn't have. In 1890, the *Washington Post* called Eckington "Washington's prettiest suburban addition" and marveled how in just three years it had grown out of "a virgin forest." "It is almost like a glimpse of fairyland to witness the illumination of Eckington by electricity every evening, the brilliant spectacle being heightened by the

An undated photograph of George Truesdell. *Library of Congress*.

CAPITAL STREETCARS

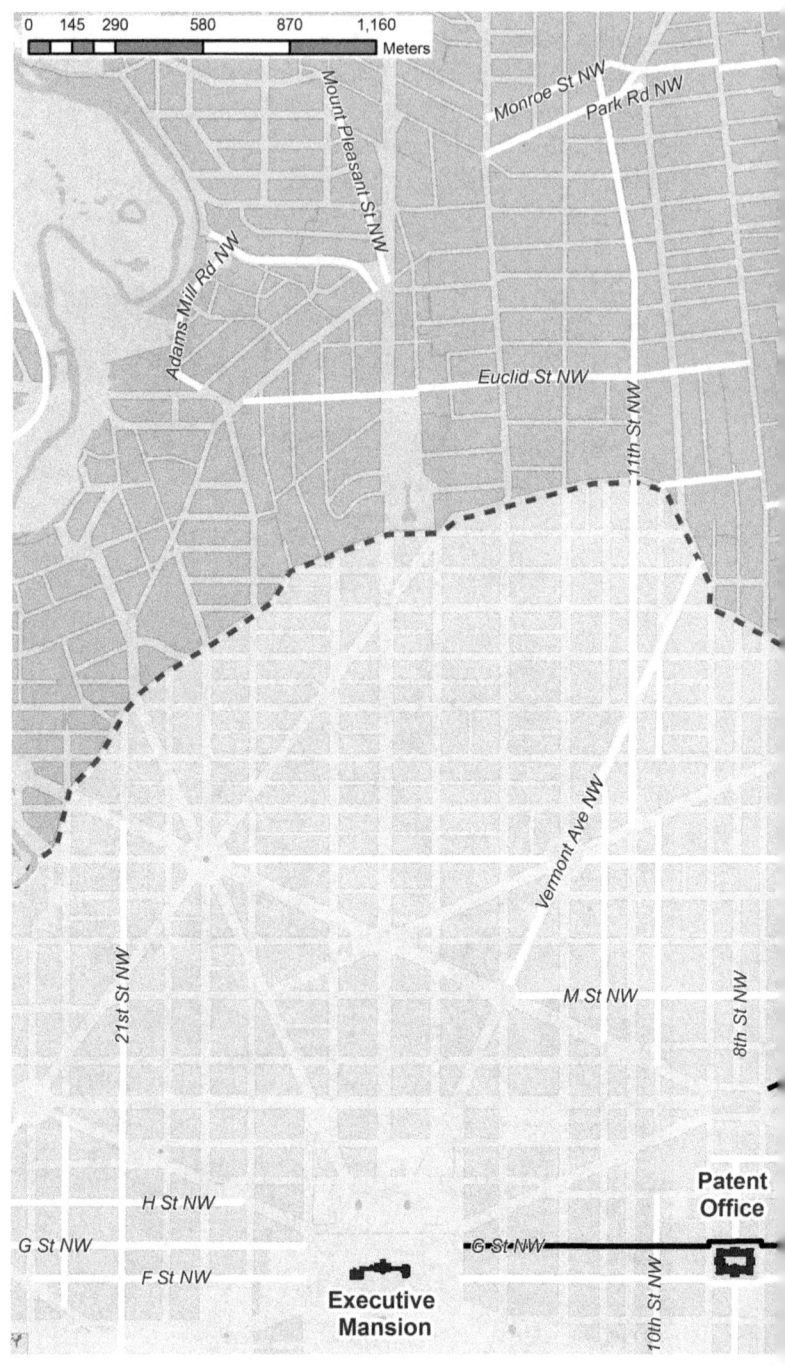

A map of the route of the Eckington & Soldiers Home Railway. *Matthew B. Gilmore*

EARLY MASS TRANSIT IN WASHINGTON, D.C.

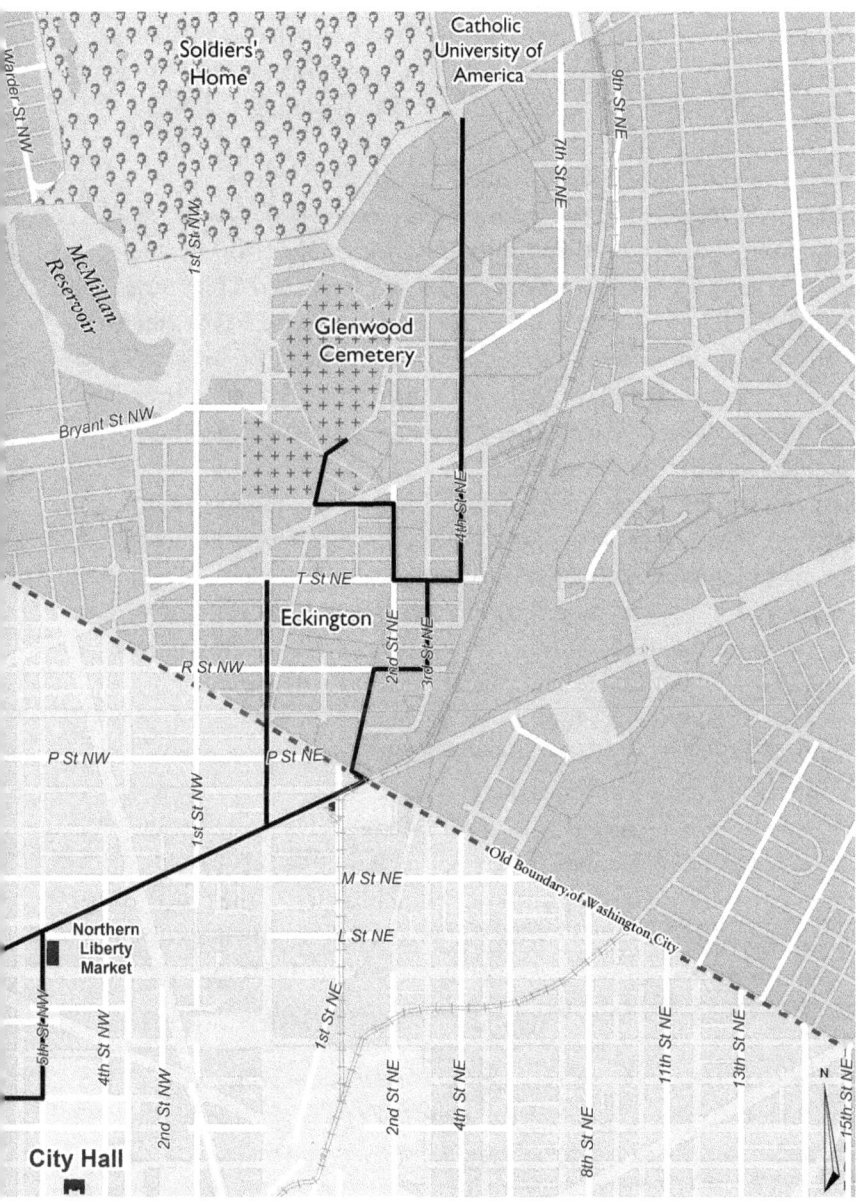

appearance of the streets and approaches, a transformation indeed having been accomplished."[74]

In 1888, Truesdell obtained a Congressional charter for the Eckington & Soldiers' Home Railway, planned specifically to serve his pretty new suburb. The line would include an electric station to power the railway as well as the brilliant streetlights that made Eckington so attractive at night. It was an ideal arrangement.

The railway's original route started downtown at Mount Vernon Square, at the intersection of Seventh Street (the main commercial corridor of the day) and New York Avenue. It ran northeast from there along New York Avenue, quickly leaving the commercial downtown behind, until it reached Third Street Northeast, where the B&O railroad had a small one-room station. From there it turned north along Third Street, passing through the heart of Truesdell's new Eckington development, and continued into the countryside along Fourth Street until it finally ended at the southern entrance to the Soldiers' Home grounds, a popular spot for Sunday outings.

As the first electric streetcar line in the District, the Eckington railway stirred a firestorm of controversy by using overhead wires to deliver electric power. The controversy undoubtedly was frustrating for Truesdell. After the successful inauguration of Richmond's trolley system early in 1888, it was universally understood that trolleys were the cheapest and most efficient way to power mass transit systems. Trolley systems were already being planned and built in cities all over the country. From a technical perspective, it was difficult to fault Truesdell for insisting that the Eckington line use this latest and most economical form of propulsion.

The new railway, constructed by the Thomson-Houston Electric Company, a predecessor of General Electric, opened in October 1888. It began with just three electric trolley cars. Poles were installed in the center of the roadway to carry the overhead wires. An engineer from the Thomson-Houston Company reassured a *Washington Post* reporter that the system's high-voltage electricity posed no safety hazards:

> *There is no possible danger to any one, unless he was tall enough to take the place of the car. In other words, if a man would touch the overhead wire with his feet on the rail he would receive a slight shock. It would not, under any circumstances, be fatal or even dangerous.*[75]

Such a claim could hardly have been true, and it's unclear how many people believed it, but the new trolley cars were nevertheless a great

Early Mass Transit in Washington, D.C.

A scene from opening day of the Eckington & Soldiers' Home Railway, 1888. *Historical Society of Washington, D.C.*

sensation. For several days, crowds formed along New York Avenue, not only to see the streetcars zipping along without horses but also to see the street lit up at night by the electric lights mounted on the iron poles in the center of the roadway.

Like Griswold in Anacostia, Truesdell soon set about expanding his new railway to serve a wider clientele. Extensions were first built on the northern ends of the lines, one heading north along North Capitol Street and the other extending from the Soldiers' Home to the Catholic University of America, which had just been established in 1887, and the adjoining new village of Brookland, where developers Benjamin F. Leighton and Richard E. Pairo were busy laying out house lots. With luck, the new destinations would soon fill with streetcar riders.

However, like Griswold, Truesdell eventually became frustrated with his railroad venture, both because of restrictions on how he could expand and disappointing patronage. He had always wanted to extend the line on its southern end farther into the downtown area, but that meant coming up with an alternate power source because of the ban on overhead trolleys inside the city. Truesdell was determined to find a propulsion technology

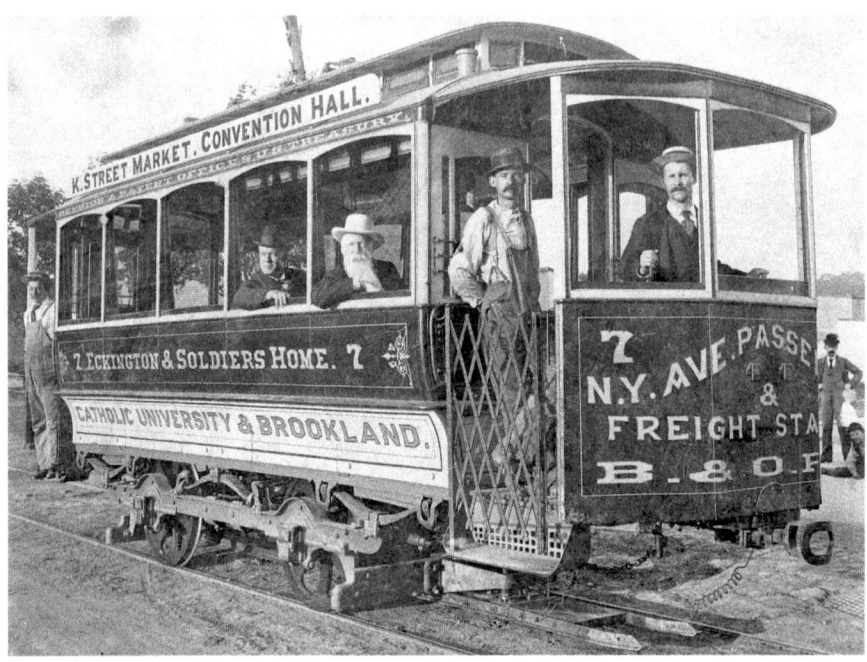

A circa 1890 photo of an experimental surface-contact electric streetcar on the Eckington & Soldiers Home line. *Library of Congress*.

that wouldn't break the bank. He, like other railway directors, was convinced that underground electrical conduits were not economical.

One alternative was to set electrical contacts right in the pavement between the tracks on the roadway, which was certainly a much less expensive approach than digging conduits. Each streetcar would get power momentarily from one of these contact plates as the car passed over, propelling it on to the next plate. The company experimented with such a system in late 1890 on a stretch of test track along North Capital Street north of Boundary Street. However, the "surface contact" system they tried was a bust. The contact plates in the street were supposed to be electrified only when a streetcar was directly over them, but there was no practical way to ensure that they did not stay charged when they were in the open. It was soon obvious that the railroad couldn't deploy a system that might randomly electrocute people or horses stepping on the plates, and the experiment had to be abandoned.[76]

When in late 1890 the company finally began building its downtown extension, it tried using battery-powered cars like the Metropolitan. The extension ran south from New York Avenue along Fifth Street Northwest and then turned east on G Street and ran all the way to the Treasury

Early Mass Transit in Washington, D.C.

Department at Fifteenth Street, bringing the Eckington line into the heart of the downtown commercial district. With this southern extension in place, the company could offer a twenty-five-minute ride all the way from Brookland down to the Treasury Department, although it required a transfer at New York Avenue from a trolley-powered to a battery-powered car. For the new Southern extension, the company bought the latest Robinson electric cars, elegant carriages finished in mahogany with gold trim that had three sets of wheels intended to facilitate going around curves. "Keeping abreast of the time is a characteristic of Mr. George Truesdell, to whose untiring energy and enterprise so much of the success of the Eckington Railway is due," the *Washington Post* raved.[77]

Reality was considerably harsher. Pretty as they may have been, the Robinson cars still encountered the same problems that the Metropolitan line experienced. They were too pokey, and recharging the batteries was slow and expensive. In 1893, after just two years, the company gave up on storage batteries.

Technical problems were not the only issues the Eckington & Soldiers' Home Railway faced. Like the Anacostia & Potomac's ghost line to Congressional Cemetery, the Eckington extension to Brookland was expensive to operate and didn't attract many passengers. The company began reducing service, angering Brookland residents. Truesdell argued that he couldn't run cars more frequently than every twenty minutes without losing money. The Brooklanders didn't believe him. In a February 1892 letter to the *Post*, the secretary of the Brookland Citizens Association insisted, "We have endeavored for the past year to secure proper facilities from this company, all to no purpose. Cars have been run upon the hit-or-miss principle. No effort has been made to afford accommodations to the patrons of the line. The road is doing a good business, but fails in the very important respect of affording quick transit from city to suburbs."[78] The following year, Truesdell stepped down from the presidency of the railroad, perhaps disillusioned by the difficulties he had encountered.

The railway soldiered on, its fight for overhead wires soon degenerating into a game of chicken with the *Star* and the D.C. commissioners. Exasperated that an overhead trolley system could not be installed to replace the failed battery cars, the railway converted its downtown extension to horsecars, ignoring the fact that horsecars were supposed to have been phased out by that time. More horsecar lines were added in 1894, all while that original overhead trolley line along New York Avenue and to the north continued to operate. The company's directors figured that people would be so fed up with these outmoded cars that Congress would give in and allow them to install an overhead trolley system.

The *Evening Star* editors were doubly upset about this turn of events. Not only were horsecars back, but the Eckington company had also missed a July 1, 1895 deadline for taking down the poles and overhead wires on New York Avenue, which the newspaper referred to as "obnoxious obstructions." After the *Star* redoubled its public complaints, the company tried a new tack. The overhead wire system on New York Avenue was removed, and that portion of the Eckington line began running…yes, more horsecars! As the *Washington Post* commented, the switch to horses

> *will mean a considerable increase in the expense to the company, which already has its stables full of horses that are not in condition for use, and it will give the residents on the line a poorer service. But the company is taking a rather grim satisfaction in the matter, as they are already losing money on their horse service, and they think that the additional loss will be a sort of investment as an object lesson to the public on the benefit of rapid transit, trolley or otherwise.*[79]

As it turned out, the public was the one giving the lesson. "Eckington is at present a very much disgusted community," the *Post* reported.[80] Customers stayed away from the balky, outmoded horsecar service, which they found insulting. Ridership plummeted as rapidly as expenses soared.[81] A year later, the overextended company was bankrupt, and the courts soon appointed former vice-president William Kesley Schoepf (1864–1927), an experienced streetcar engineer, as its receiver.

Schoepf oversaw a last desperate effort to make the Eckington line viable, short of installing an underground conduit system. In early 1896, the company hosted the demonstration of a streetcar powered by compressed air, which it gambled would be both publicly acceptable and economically viable. The compressed air system used the pressure of air from canisters stored underneath the passenger seats to push pistons that turned the car's wheels. The compressed air was heated with steam to increase its force as it moved out of the canisters.

With no money for an initial investment in the new system, Schoepf managed to convince the Hoadley-Knight Company to send a car at no charge to Washington for trial runs on the Eckington line. Joseph H. Hoadley, president of the company, was on hand for the first run in March 1897 and was very effusive about his new contraption: "We are perfectly satisfied with all our tests, and are amazed at the possibilities they have opened up. As surely as electricity is taking the place of horses and men, the air motor will take the place of electricity in all but lighting—may be it will do that."[82]

Hoadley's enthusiasm was misplaced. The public did not care for the compressed air cars, finding them smoky, dusty and smelly. The cars also tended to be slow on uphill grades. The compressed air experiment, on which the hopes of the company had been pinned, was soon abandoned.

At this point, the bankrupt line had already been purchased by the same syndicate of investors that took over the Anacostia & Potomac Railway, a group led by financier Oscar T. Crosby (1861–1947). In 1898, the Crosby syndicate also gained control of most of the other street railway lines in the District with the exception of the Capital Traction Company and was operating them under one holding company, called the Washington Traction and Electric Company. In compliance with the Congressional edict, the new conglomerate began installing underground electrical conduit systems on the portions of the former Eckington line that were within the downtown area. The struggle to find an alternative propulsion system had failed.

Born in Ponchatoula, Louisiana, Oscar T. Crosby was another key figure in the long line of moguls that shaped public transportation in the nation's capital. Crosby had graduated from West Point to join the Army Corps of Engineers in the early 1880s, at a time when electrical power was on the cusp of widespread adoption. Learning the ins and outs of electrical power while in the corps, he resigned in 1887 to join in building the nascent industry. He served for a time as general manager of the Sprague Electric Railway and Motor Company, which had built the first practical trolley system in Richmond. With the financial backing of New York investors, Crosby in 1896 became the first president of the local Potomac Electric Power Company (PEPCo), which built a large power plant on the Virginia side of the Potomac River at Chain Bridge. Once the source of electric power for the D.C. area was under their control, Crosby and his partners set their sights on acquiring their most important potential customers, the street railway companies, and converting them all to electric power.

CAPITAL STREETCARS

WHIZZING ACROSS THE DISTRICT

Since the late 1880s, streetcar lines had been radiating out along all the major roads connecting downtown Washington with the rest of the District and suburban Maryland. In 1888, the same year the Eckington line was established, the Brightwood Railway was chartered as an extension of the Metropolitan's Seventh Street line, carrying it out Seventh Street Extended (now Georgia Avenue) to the historic Brightwood community on the D.C. border, which had seen the only fighting of the Civil War to reach the District when Confederates tried unsuccessfully to attack Fort Stevens in 1864. After experimenting with an exotic patented pneumatic propulsion system, the Brightwood Railway converted to overhead electric trolleys. It eventually was absorbed into Oscar Crosby's conglomerate.

Also in 1888, the Georgetown & Tenallytown Railway was formed to build a streetcar line along what is now Wisconsin Avenue from Georgetown to the small suburban village of Tenallytown (the name was changed to Tenleytown in 1922). Georgetown had never been considered part of

A Brightwood Railway car on Georgia Avenue near Florida Avenue, early 1890s. *National Capital Trolley Museum.*

Early Mass Transit in Washington, D.C.

Washington City, and thus the new line could safely adopt an overhead trolley system without having to face the ire of the *Evening Star*. When the line opened in April 1890, a ceremonial first run carrying company officials was met with much celebration. "It was just a little past 3 o'clock when the excursionists entered the beautifully painted coaches at M and Thirty-second streets and were sent whizzing over the new line," the *Washington Post* reported. "Hundreds of men, women, and children gathered along the street to witness the inauguration, and from the windows ladies waved their handkerchiefs as the electric cars went speeding along."

The Georgetown & Tenallytown line, which connected two previously well-established communities, was one suburban project that paid handsome rewards to its owners. The line's first president, retired brigadier general Richard C. Drum (1825–1909), was among a group of investors whose real estate holdings in upper Northwest appreciated nicely. "President Drum has a farm near Tennallytown for which he paid $187," the *Post* observed. "Since then he has refused forty times that amount."[83]

Founded in 1892, the Washington and Great Falls Electric Railway was one of the District's best-loved lines. The route ran from Prospect Street in

A trolley on High Street (Wisconsin Avenue) in Georgetown, headed for Tenallytown, circa 1900. *Historical Society of Washington, D.C.*

Georgetown along the heights of the Potomac to Glen Echo and Cabin John in Maryland and was built specifically to bring visitors to those two resorts. It took several years to lay out the railway's exact route through the riverside hills and to settle disputes with angry farmers whose land it crossed, but in the end it made for one of the most scenic lines in the region. The railway opened late in 1895, offering riders spectacular views as they crossed trestles spanning deep ravines on their way to what was then the Chautauqua camp at Glen Echo or to Cabin John's resort hotel farther north.

Two brothers from Philadelphia, Edmund and Edwin Baltzley, had planned Glen Echo to be an exclusive haven for Washingtonians wealthy enough to afford summer cottages there. Disappointed with the results, the Baltzley brothers sold their property in about 1903 to the streetcar company, which redeveloped the site into an amusement park that became a great success and remained popular until the 1960s.

The Rock Creek Railway

One of the longest and perhaps most ambitious of the many streetcar extensions that were built in the 1880s and 1890s was the Rock Creek Railway, a line that ran for seven and a half miles from Eighteenth and U Streets Northwest up a newly extended Connecticut Avenue to the fledgling community of Chevy Chase, just past the border with Maryland. The new community, the streetcar line and the extended road were all elements of Francis G. Newlands's grand vision for turning a vast wooded wilderness into an elite suburban residential enclave.

Born in Mississippi, Newlands (1848–1917) moved to Washington with his family during the Civil War, when his stepfather began working as a clerk for the Treasury Department. Young Newlands studied law and was admitted to the bar in the District but decided to seek greater opportunities in San Francisco, where he moved in 1870. As a successful lawyer there, he met and became closely associated with William Sharon and William Ralston, two wealthy tycoons who had made a fortune from Nevada silver mining. Newlands married Sharon's daughter in 1874 and gained control of much of her inheritance when Sharon died in 1885. Visiting Washington in 1887 to handle the affairs of the Sharon estate, the future U.S. senator from Nevada met D.C. real estate speculator Colonel George Augustus Armes (1844–1919), who gave him the idea to

Early Mass Transit in Washington, D.C.

Francis G. Newlands, circa 1910. *Library of Congress*.

acquire and develop a vast stretch of land in the upper Northwest section of the city.

Newlands was never one to think small. Beginning in 1887, he had his agents discreetly buy up real estate all along the streetcar route that he was secretly planning. With deep pockets from the Sharon estate, Newlands spent more than $1 million to buy 1,712 acres of property. The following year, a charter for the Rock Creek Railway was approved by Congress, and in 1890, Newlands gained control of the company. That same year, he founded the Chevy Chase Land Company to own all of the land he had purchased and to develop the Chevy Chase community at the end of the line, conveniently located in Maryland, where its well-to-do residents would be able to vote.

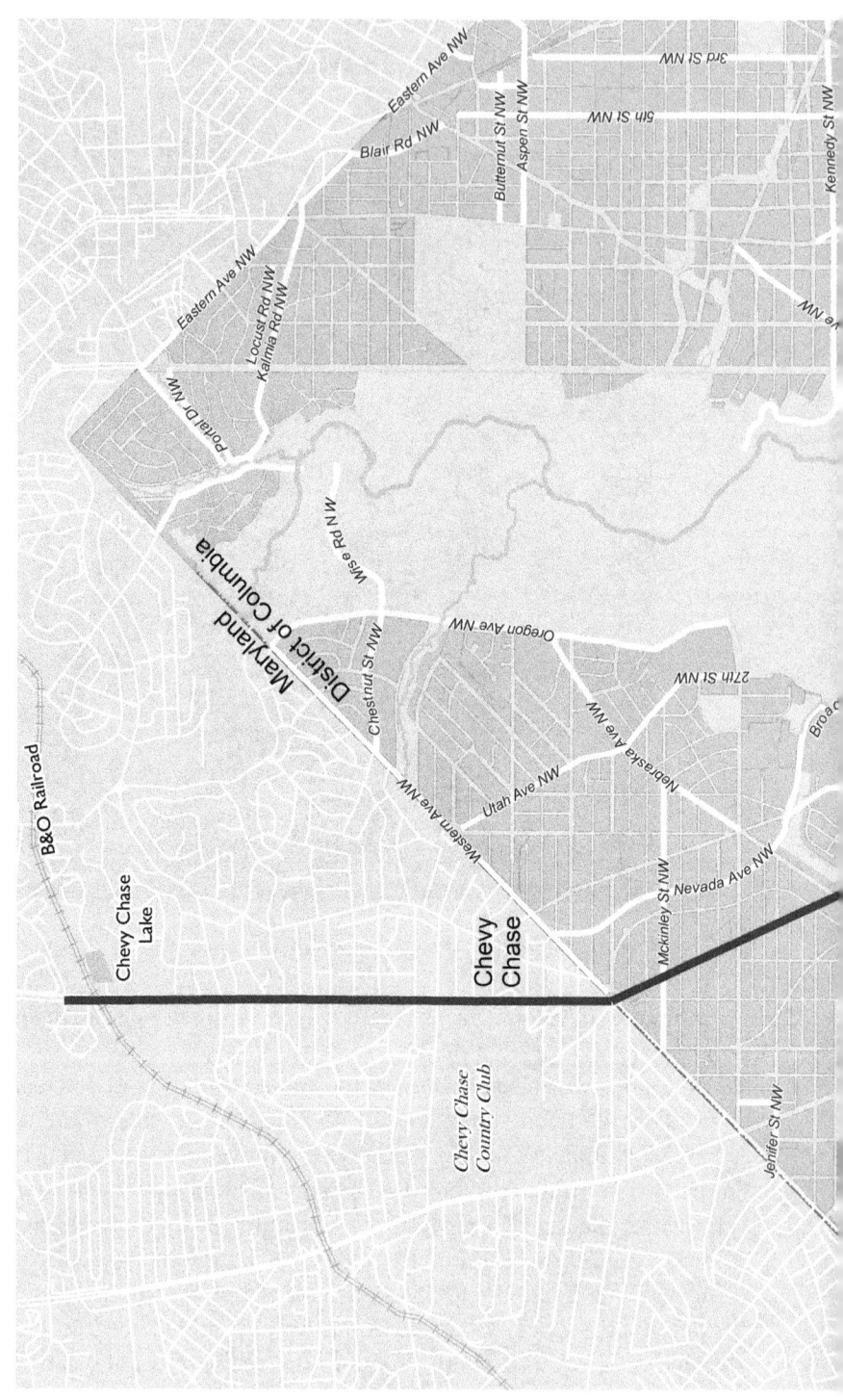

Early Mass Transit in Washington, D.C.

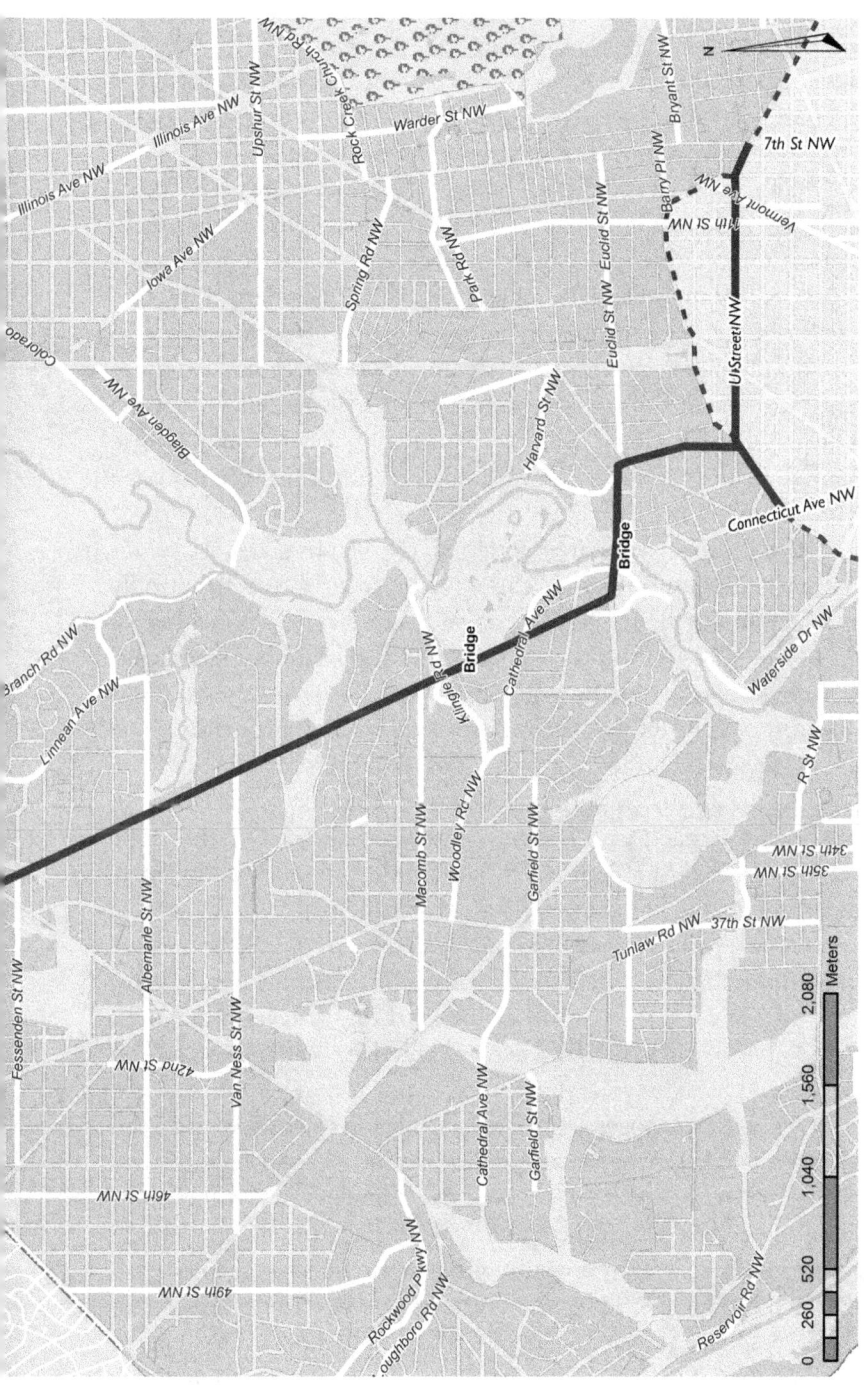

A map of the route of the Rock Creek Railway. *Matthew B. Gilmore.*

Newlands's close ally, Senator William M. Stewart (1827–1909) of Nevada, invested $300,000 in the Chevy Chase venture and helped shepherd a favorable charter for the Rock Creek Railway through Congress, despite grumbling and resentment from members who weren't in on the deal. When the bill came up for consideration in the House of Representatives, David B. Henderson (1840–1906), an inveterate supporter of the common man, led a two-hour debate on it, at one point sarcastically suggesting that it be called "a bill to boom real estate in the District of Columbia." Henderson worried that the new line would cater primarily to the wealthy: "He didn't want to see the poor and the needy discriminated against, and especially he did not want to have the colored brother discriminated against. He knew that the Woodley Lane and Rock Creek district was a region where nabobs were going to flourish in the future, and he for one did not want to encourage their growth by legislation."[84]

Henderson's objections were well founded. Newlands's vision for his development was emphatically as an elite enclave, which meant that only whites were likely to live there. Newlands was infamous for advocating an amendment to the U.S. Constitution to disenfranchise African Americans. But most Washingtonians at the time supported his efforts because his plans contributed substantially to the city's development and prosperity. The Rock Creek Railway accordingly received its Congressional charter on very favorable terms. Other important investors joined the project as well, including George Truesdell, who was appointed to its board of directors, and Samuel W. Woodward (1848–1917), co-founder of the Woodward & Lothrop department store company.

Construction of the new road and streetcar line required a massive investment. At more than $1.5 million, the cost of grading, bridges, interest and taxes was higher than the cost of all the land that had been acquired along its route.[85] The planned road ran across rugged forested hills, requiring many deep cuts into hillsides and voluminous fills of the valleys in between. Two large and expensive bridges were needed, one over the wide and deep valley of the Rock Creek, which had previously cut off upper Northwest from the rest of the city, and the other over the Klingle Valley, which runs just south of present-day Cleveland Park. The steel girder bridges, which eventually were replaced with more substantial stone structures, were each more than five hundred feet long and more than one hundred feet tall. Newlands hired engineer William Schoepf—who would move on to manage the failing Eckington & Soldiers' Home line—to oversee construction. Work was largely completed in 1892.

Early Mass Transit in Washington, D.C.

When it opened in September, the Rock Creek was the city's second electric trolley system. Traversing the natural beauty of the wooded countryside, it promised a healthful respite from the crowded city. The *Washington Post* reported:

> *From the first hill a fine view of Washington and the surrounding country is had. Through woody glens and deep cuts the road gradually climbs till Chevy Chase, the highest elevation in the District is reached. This suburb, which is destined in a short while to rival all competitors, stands at an elevation of 500 feet above the Potomac. When the heat in the city is intense and citizens are sweating, the temperature on the heights along the Rock Creek road is cooled by brisk breezes from the hills of Virginia. Chevy Chase is to be the most attractive village along the route.*[86]

An article in the trade journal *The Electrical World* raved about the potential of the elegant new suburb and its convenient streetcar connection:

> *It is safe to predict a handsome return for money invested in property in Chevy Chase, as it will, in all probability, be a popular place. The city terminus of the Rock Creek Railway will, without doubt, be in close proximity to the Capitol within one year, and this will afford Congressmen an opportunity to step aboard of an electric car, and in 40 minutes, possibly less, be taken right to the door of their suburban homes, without change of cars. It is not unreasonable to suppose that the time will come when this line will run special palace cars, heated and lighted with electricity, from the Capitol to Chevy Chase without stop, simply for the accommodation of Senators and Representatives.*[87]

Creating this elite railway (that had so rankled Congressman Henderson) required building extensions to connect it seamlessly to the city's already established streetcar lines. In particular, the company wanted an eastward extension at the southern end of its line, along U Street, to Seventh Street Northwest, where it could connect with the Metropolitan's Seventh Street line. However, the pesky ban on overhead trolley wires within the city meant that another form of propulsion was needed.

In May 1893—two years before the Metropolitan completed its first segment of underground electric conduit—the Rock Creek Railway installed the first such system in the District along its U Street extension. Cars continued to use the overhead wires along Connecticut Avenue and

Two electric streetcars of the Rock Creek Railway on Connecticut Avenue, circa 1900. *National Capital Trolley Museum.*

then switched to underground power at Eighteenth and U Streets. There the cars would stop over a "plow pit" and, in less than a minute, would be converted from one power source to the other. The overhead trolley pole would either be extended up to the wires or folded down and stowed on the roof of the car. Down in the pit, a special forked pole with electrical contacts known as a "plow" would be attached to (or removed from) the underside of the car.

The Rock Creek's prototype underground conduit was of a kind known as the Love Conduit system, designed by Philadelphia engineer John E. Love. The U Street segment was the only D.C. streetcar line that ever used this technology. Underground conduits on other lines, beginning with the Metropolitan in 1895, standardized on a different design, based on the system used in Budapest, Austria-Hungary.

Newlands seems not to have gotten much involved in these technical details. In fact, he had little interest in running his streetcar line; his focus was on the exclusive new Chevy Chase community. The streetcar was merely a means to get owners to and from their suburban properties. To further enhance access to Chevy Chase, Newlands soon began casting about for a partnership with another streetcar firm. After several potential schemes fizzled out, in 1895 he set his sights on the Washington & Georgetown, the city's most successful streetcar company.

Early Mass Transit in Washington, D.C.

One of the unique provisos of the Rock Creek's charter, as it had been revised in 1891, was that it could acquire other streetcar firms, something none of the city's other streetcar companies could do. With this unique power in hand, Newlands approached banker Charles C. Glover, who was not only a highly influential member of the board of the W&G but also the owner of extensive real estate holding in upper Northwest. Newlands proposed selling his company outright to the Washington & Georgetown company. Formally speaking, the Rock Creek Railway would "buy" the W&G—because it had the legal authority to do so—but in reality the W&G would take over the smaller line.

Glover was ecstatic about the idea, and in September, the deal was consummated. The merged companies were renamed the Capital Traction Company, and Newlands was given a seat on the new company's board, which otherwise was made up of former W&G board members. As a result of the merger, passengers were able to transfer at no cost among all of the company's combined lines. "Think of what we are doing right now—a 15-cent ride for 5 cents!" Glover exclaimed to the *Washington Post*. "A man may board one of our cars on the Potomac River front and enjoy one continuous ride to the northern limits of the District of Columbia for the small sum of 5 cents, or if he buys [a book of] tickets, for even less. [The newly acquired Rock Creek line] passes through a magnificent strip of country, which is bound to develop in population, and forms the nucleus of a line which may some day involve extensions… And when you consider the price we paid for it it is a right down bargain."[88]

"A Volcano in a State of Wrath"

As cheering executives shook hands and workmen began painting "Capital Traction Company" on the sides of all of the company's cars, the new conglomerate went into operation with three different propulsion technologies: overhead trolley wires along upper Connecticut Avenue, a short underground electric conduit along U Street and an extensive cable system on all the rest of its lines. Then, just two years later, the cable system came to a sudden and cataclysmic end when its enormous power station on Pennsylvania Avenue burned to the ground in a spectacular nighttime blaze.

At about 11:00 p.m. on the night of September 29, 1897, the fire started in the third-floor print shop of William Gettinger, one of the building's tenants.

CAPITAL STREETCARS

The ruins of the Capital Traction powerhouse, October 1897. *D.C. Public Library, Washingtoniana Division.*

It was shortly after his employees had all left for the evening, so no one was around to put it out. Within minutes, the five-year-old building was engulfed in flames, its pine floors and large bins of coal serving as so much tinder for the extraordinary bonfire. According to the *Washington Times*, it was "the fiercest and most brilliant fire in a single structure that has ever occurred in Washington." The *Washington Post* reported that a "huge tongue of flame" shot up in the sky as if from "the crater of a volcano in a state of wrath," lighting up the night sky so intensely that thousands of awestruck bystanders were drawn to the spectacle. The *Post*'s offices were just across Pennsylvania Avenue, and a *Post* reporter was one of the first on the scene when the blaze broke out. He went inside with a fireman and witnessed the building's self-destruction from the third floor of a large stair tower:

> [T]he scene of the big machinery room below was spread in full view. Not a man was to be seen, but the engines were running and the big wheels turning, turning with the same monotonous rumble while from the burning floor above huge blazing pieces of woodwork, furniture, glass, and iron crashed down, to be churned into tiny fragments.
>
> All this time, too, the cars were running, but at 11:20 a big piece of iron crashed into the midst of the revolving wheels and brought all to a

Early Mass Transit in Washington, D.C.

sudden stop. A moment afterward the engine machinery room was filled with flames.[89]

All of the streetcars powered by the station that were in service across the city were instantly frozen in their tracks as the cables stopped moving. The great powerhouse and its equipment were a total loss. All that remained were fragments of the heavy brick and stone outer walls and the great central smokestack, said to be the tallest structure in the District after the Washington Monument. While the rest of the site was soon cleared of rubble, the smokestack would remain until 1902, when it was finally taken down brick by brick to make way for the new white marble headquarters of the District government.

The young Capital Traction Company displayed astonishing efficiency and resolve in responding to this unparalleled disaster. Even as firemen battled the fierce blaze, Capital Traction employees began working to locate horses that could be used on an emergency basis to pull the cable cars, just as they had done in days past. According to streetcar historian G.F. Cunningham, "Horses and harness were begged and borrowed during the wee hours of the morning. Practically every Washington business concern which used a large number of horses turned over its stock to the Capital Traction Company."[90] By the morning rush hour, horse-drawn cars were operating on all of the affected Capital Traction lines, pulling the trailers that had been attached to the company's powered cable cars. Former gripmen found it relatively easy to take up the reins of their teams, and given the catastrophe that had just occurred, there were few immediate complaints about the slower, old-fashioned service.

Capital Traction's cable cars had been running for just five years. Although they wouldn't admit it publicly, company executives knew immediately that they would never rebuild the cable system. As soon as the board of directors had a chance to meet, it quickly ratified the decision to convert to electricity.

Cable technology had turned out to be a dead end. The elaborate mechanical engineering required to install and maintain the system was a nightmare. How much simpler and more elegant, in contrast, were electrical systems that delivered power so efficiently through wires or rails. Once practical electric trolley systems became available, streetcar companies around the country were as anxious to get rid of their cable cars as they had been a few years earlier to acquire them. In that sense, the destruction of the Capital Traction power plant fire must have seemed like a blessing in disguise; it cleared the way for a swift change in direction.

CAPITAL STREETCARS

After the great fire in 1897, horses temporarily pulled cars that were previously used as trailers in cable car trains, as seen in this view of a horse-drawn cable car turning onto Pennsylvania Avenue from Fifteenth Street near the Treasury Department. *National Capital Trolley Museum.*

By July 3, 1898, just nine months after the fire, Capital Traction's lines had all been converted to electric power, the old cable having been removed from the underground conduits and replaced with electrical conductor rails. The company adopted the same system that the Metropolitan had installed, confirming it as the permanent de facto standard for D.C. streetcars. Remarkably, the conversion of the entire cable system was accomplished without any interruption of service. Even the Seventh Street line, which had its own power station, kept its old cable cars running through the conversion process while electric lines were being installed in the live cable conduit. When the former Rock Creek Railway Love Conduit system on U Street was converted and integrated with the larger system in 1899, the system-wide conversion was complete.

And what of Francis G. Newlands and his cabal of wealthy investors, poised to make a killing on the Chevy Chase project? The venture was considered a success, but for years it paid meager returns. The timing had not been good. A financial panic in 1893 had kept business sluggish, and sales of home sites were practically nonexistent in 1898, the year of the Spanish-American War. In fact, stockholders in the Chevy Chase Land Company received no dividends at all for many years. According to Newlands biographer Albert W. Atwood, from 1890 through 1917 disbursements exceeded receipts by $172,000. It was only after World War I that development of upper Northwest really took off and the company started to make substantial profits.[91]

Newlands was independently wealthy and could easily afford to be patient with his Chevy Chase venture. He had much larger investments out west, in Nevada and California, that made far greater contributions to his wealth. He had moved to Nevada in 1888, becoming a congressman from that state in 1893 and a senator in 1903. Senator Newlands championed irrigation projects in the West and was an expert on the nation's railroads. As chairman of the joint committee on transportation, he was at his desk in the Senate office building on Christmas Eve 1917, working on issues of how to put the railroads on a wartime footing, when he suffered a sudden heart attack and died later that evening at his posh Massachusetts Avenue mansion on Sheridan Circle. His contributions to the development of Washington were widely praised. "He was not merely able to foresee, but was able to plan and construct," the *Washington Post* observed.[92]

Chapter 6
BIGGER CROWDS AND BIGGER CARS

THE NEW CENTURY'S CHALLENGES, 1900–1918

I sing the song of the open car,
And the man at the end of the seat,
Who never is willing to move along,
Or even retract his feet.

He sticks to his seat, the selfish churl,
As if he were stuck with glue,
And his whole manner says,
as plain as words,
"I don't care a hang for you."

Oh, he is a selfish, selfish man,
I call him the end-seat hog;
He's the kind of man who
would kick a cat
Or torture a faithful dog.

The world will be better when he is dead
And laid on a tomb's dark shelf;
I hate and despise him with all my heart,
For I want that seat myself.[93]

By the turn of the century, the boom era of streetcar expansion was at an end. Henceforth, aside from adjustments and extensions to existing lines, no major new routes would be added to the city's network. The Gilded Age drive to build streetcar lines out into the wilderness had vanished. In its place were less glamorous issues—how to make the cars run profitably, how to accommodate more and more passengers and how to do it all without jeopardizing comfort and safety.

Nothing epitomized the turn-of-the-century streetcar experience like riding in the "open" cars that ran in the warm-weather months. Open cars had been around since the horse-drawn era, but in the late 1890s, after all the city's lines had been mechanized, they were more common, often serving as trailers in two- or three-car trains. These cars were completely open on both sides, with benches like church pews stretching across the width of the car. Each bench was meant to accommodate up to five people. Passengers boarded and took their seats directly from the platform (right) side of the car, while a wooden bar kept them from attempting to get on or off the other side, in the middle of traffic. Most people were very fond of riding in these cars in good weather.

Fun as they might be, they posed their own unique hazards for the riding public, some more significant than others. Just as the new open-car season was starting in April 1907, the *Evening Star* published a tongue-in-cheek essay on "Open Car Etiquette," facetiously applauding, among other things, the women who sat in the back row and bitterly complained about men who smoked there, even though those seats were meant for smokers. "Why should any particular section of a car be reserved for men, when no particular section is correspondingly reserved for women?" these progressive females wanted to know. Likewise earning mock praise from the *Star* were the "woman who spatters Somebody's German Cologne all over herself before leaving home and the man who gets his hair soused in some rancid sort of bay rum at the barber shop," both of whom inevitably sat at the front of the open cars, where the breeze would waft the objectionable scent over everybody sitting behind them. "The effluvia thus shed upon all of the passengers in the

An open car of the Metropolitan Railroad on East Capitol Street near Ninth Street, circa 1890. *National Capital Trolley Museum.*

other seats fills them with visions of the islands of lotus and crime," the *Star* proclaimed.[94]

Far more notorious than these minor discomforts were the "End-Seat Hogs," people who would board and sit immediately at the end of the bench, where it was easiest to alight, forcing other patrons to climb over them to find their own seats. The peculiar design of the open cars made this problem inevitable. Anyone who voluntarily slid to the inside of the bench risked being trapped by other passengers packing in after them. Naturally, nearly everyone tried to get the end seat if they could, and they complained about the end-seat hogs when they couldn't. Complaints filled the newspapers in the 1890s and 1900s, both in Washington and other cities around the country. "Men are the offenders; and their bad habits are not easily changed," wrote one *Star* subscriber, who had observed "[a]t Glen Echo, at the close of the theatrical performance, when the [cars heading back into town] approach the entrance, there is a mad rush of young men for the seats. They spring upon the running board while the car is in motion, at the risk of their limbs, and occupy all the end seats before the car stops."[95] The *Washington Post* likewise declared the end-seat hog a universal and despicable presence. "The party entering [the car] may be old or feeble or embarrassed by bundles and packages…It makes no difference. The holder of the end place, no matter of which sex, refuses to make the smallest concession. Young or old, weak or strong, sound or crippled, active or unwieldy, the outsider has to struggle past the obstruction of rowdyism or lose the ride…It is a disgrace to the community—a wonder and a sorrow to the looker-on. It is an exhibition of vulgarity which one would hardly expect to witness in any city claiming to be civilized."[96]

The streetcar companies paid little attention to such day-to-day nuisances, focusing instead on improving the efficiency of their routes. The Capital Traction Company, which had fully electrified in 1898, began simplifying its routes in the early 1900s and improving complicated street crossings, such as the one where New York Avenue, Pennsylvania Avenue and Fifteenth Street met near the White House.

Capital Traction's competitor, the Oscar T. Crosby syndicate, had acquired almost all of the city's other streetcar lines between 1895 and 1899 and likewise concentrated on improving its routes. The myriad early streetcar companies, all operating in competition with one another and sometimes offering overlapping service, had been very inefficient. Travel around the city could be complicated and expensive, with no free transfers between lines. The entrepreneurial Colonel George Truesdell, founder

Clifford Berryman penned this cartoon of "The Man on the End," for the June 21, 1907 edition of the *Evening Star*. *National Archives*.

of the Eckington line, was named the Crosby syndicate's president in 1899, and he oversaw streamlining and consolidation of these complex lines, even though the former companies nominally retained their separate identities. In addition to abandoning excess and unprofitable routes, the syndicate also completed installation of underground electric conduits throughout the city, all powered by PEPCo, the electric company it controlled.

That meant bringing electrification to the remaining lines that were still horse-powered and even one that was cable-driven. The Columbia Railway,

The busy intersection of Fifteenth Street and Pennsylvania Avenue in the 1910s. *Library of Congress.*

operating on New York Avenue and H Street Northeast to Benning Road, was the only D.C. streetcar company other than the Washington & Georgetown to adopt cable. After experimenting briefly with compressed air technology in 1892, the company decided in 1894 to replace its horsecars with a cable system, even though the superiority of electric propulsion had been well established by that time. Construction began in October 1895, making the Columbia the very last streetcar system in the country to convert to cable. When the Crosby syndicate took over just four years later, the company's brief cable adventure ended, and its tracks were quickly converted to underground electric.

Forward thinking as the Crosby syndicate was, it still managed to bite off more than it could chew. Many of the lines Crosby acquired—like the Anacostia & Potomac and the Eckington & Soldiers' Home—were unprofitable and saddled with debt, and they dragged Crosby's holding company down. In 1901, the company, called the Washington Traction and Electric Company, defaulted on its debt and was sold in foreclosure. The following year, a new company was formed with a slightly different

Early Mass Transit in Washington, D.C.

Horse-drawn carriages and wagons compete with streetcars powered by underground electric conduits in this scene on Pennsylvania Avenue at Seventh Street, taken in February 1901. *Library of Congress.*

name: the Washington Railway and Electric Company (WRECo). It took over and formally merged all its nominally separate subsidiary lines. This finally left D.C. with just two major streetcar companies—Capital Traction and WRECo—that would run independent, competing services for the next thirty years.

Once out of the D.C. streetcar picture, Oscar T. Crosby turned to other interests. An amateur anthropologist, he went on a grand expedition to Tibet and central Asia in 1904, publishing a book on his travels the following year. He continued traveling to exotic locales the rest of his life and increasingly became involved in international affairs, serving as the director of a relief commission in Belgium during World War I and, later, as an assistant secretary of the Treasury Department. He died in Warrenton, Virginia, in 1947.

The irrepressible George Truesdell put much of his energy into real estate investment, although he reportedly faced financial difficulties in his later years. In the 1880s, he had purchased a large tract of land in the Kalorama neighborhood northwest of Dupont Circle, which would become one of the city's poshest residential suburbs. Here he built an immense "summer home" there called Managasset, akin to the mansions of the wealthy along the Hudson River in New York. In the early twentieth century, Truesdell gradually sold off much of his Kalorama property, and in 1911, he razed Managasset and replaced it with a luxury apartment house called the Altamont. He died in his apartment at the Altamont in 1921.

"The Present Conditions Are a Menace"

Meanwhile, with consolidation issues out of the way and electric power firmly established, Capital Traction and WRECo became the entrenched mass transit providers for the sprawling city, their service intertwined with Washington's daily life. Several Capital Traction lines began operating mobile post offices in converted streetcars that were attached as trailers to passenger-carrying cars. Patrons could deposit their letters in slots built into the sides of the cars, which transferred the mail among various locations around the city. For outlying suburbs, an even more comprehensive service was sometimes provided. The Cabin John streetcar delivered a crate of bread and cakes each dawn from a downtown bakery to the small food store at Glen Echo. "People would stop your car, hand you a basket, a list and a $10 bill," Isaac B. Goad, a former conductor, recalled many years later. "I'd drop the basket off at the grocery and pick it up on the next trip, and take it back. We'd do banking for these folks, or pick up a prescription."[97]

In the early 1900s, the two companies also began modernizing their rolling stock. Manufacturers had been producing faster and significantly larger cars, allowing for greater loads and more efficient use of drivers and conductors. For example, cars purchased by the Capital Traction Company in 1898—just after the great cable power station fire—seated only twenty-six passengers, whereas cars purchased between 1909 and 1919 seated between forty-four and forty-eight.[98] Strap-hangers could virtually double that number.

Although they may have made good design sense, the larger cars could be loud and menacing and tended to alienate the public. In 1900, a group of Eleventh Street citizens signed a petition complaining about the noise the new cars made: "[T]he health of the residents near and along this line will be endangered and their comfort greatly disturbed as it is almost impossible to converse while the cars are passing, and the noise at nightfall greatly disturbs our rest." The residents went on to "call your attention to the rapid and unlawful rate of speed at which these cars are being run, altogether resulting in great damage to the value of our property and the loss of tenants," a remarkable concern given that just ten or twenty years earlier they had enthusiastically welcomed the streetcars, celebrating increased property values they brought.[99] In 1905, similar complaints were raised by merchants on F Street downtown, who found WRECo's big cars annoyingly loud and dangerous.

The new streetcars could indeed be hazardous. None was equipped with speedometers, and thus motormen had no idea whether they were exceeding the speed limit. Even if they realized when they were speeding, they were still motivated to travel as quickly as possible because they would be severely penalized for failing to adhere to their strict schedules.

Perhaps motorman James Reilly was worried about keeping on schedule when he headed down the Second Street hill in Eckington during the morning rush hour on August 1, 1919. At the bottom of the hill, the tracks turned sharply to the right on to R Street, and Reilly's streetcar probably was going too fast when it took that curve. The car overturned, and the ninety-five passengers crowded onboard were thrown in a heap amid a shower of flying glass. "For a few moments after the crash pandemonium reigned. Women screamed as they were thrown to the left side of the car. The passengers fell in bunches, with fragments of the car and pieces of glass flying around them."[100]

Thirty-five passengers were injured, six seriously, including Miss Ruby Edmunds, whose skull was fractured. All eventually recovered. A number of the injuries likely resulted when passengers stepped on one another as they frantically tried to escape the overturned car. Reilly told police that the car had not been going more than ten or twelve miles per hour, but a professional army driver who had been onboard estimated that the speed was likely twice that. WRECo investigators concluded that the accident was a result of Reilly applying the car's air brakes too suddenly as it sped around the curve.

Only two months later, another serious accident occurred on the Georgia Avenue (Brightwood) line just outside Walter Reed Army Hospital. Witnesses told police that a WRECo streetcar was speeding down Georgia Avenue when an army truck emerged from the entrance to Walter Reed. The streetcar slammed into the side of the truck, pushing it more than one hundred feet down the street. Edward Sothern, one of the four soldiers on the truck, was killed instantly, and three passengers on the streetcar died in following days at Walter Reed. The streetcar's motorman, Carroll Nash, miraculously survived, although his post at the front of the car had been turned into a mass of twisted steel. Seventeen others were injured in the wreck. Two months earlier, after the Eckington accident occurred,

A crowd gathers at the scene of the overturned streetcar in Eckington, August 1, 1919. Note the ambulance from Casualty Hospital on the right. *Library of Congress.*

officials at Walter Reed had complained to WRECO about the speed of streetcars on Georgia Avenue. Apparently nothing had been done to slow down the cars.

The early 1900s marked the rise of the women's suffrage movement, culminating in the first Woman Suffragists parade on Pennsylvania Avenue in 1913. With the push for the right to vote came also a broader assertiveness about issues that affected women's lives, including the inconvenience of traveling on streetcars designed by and for men. Women were leading increasingly independent lives, traveling more extensively outside their homes for work, entertainment or shopping, and they needed streetcars they could ride in comfort.

The biggest problem was the height of the steps into the passenger compartment. Many streetcars had a gap of fourteen inches or more from the ground to their first step; climbing aboard was a struggle for many people. Women in particular faced challenges because of their clothing. When Capital Traction began running a new series of cars with high steps on its Fourteenth Street route in 1908, the women living along the line fought back. Mrs. Frederick L. Ransom of 1455 Belmont Street organized a

Early Mass Transit in Washington, D.C.

A wrecked WRECo streetcar outside Walter Reed Hospital, October 13, 1919. *Library of Congress.*

protest movement after witnessing other women struggling to get on and off the cars. She would ask them if they wished to support the cause, and "[t]hey always gladly assented—as soon as they caught their breath."[101]

Matters were only made worse with the advent in 1910 of the fashion craze for hobble skirts, which severely constricted a woman's gait even when she was walking on level ground. The streetcar company executives patronizingly offered their sympathy but little else. One commented that women wouldn't have such problems if they would just avoid wearing hobble skirts, infuriating Ransom and her supporters, who argued that the high steps were dangerous regardless of what style skirt a woman might wear. By 1912, a committee of representatives from several D.C. women's clubs had been formed to meet with Capital Traction and WRECo executives and convince them to modify their cars. "We respectfully ask that a well-graded, lower step be added to the cars, or else a new type of car introduced," the committee wrote. "The continuance of the present conditions are a menace to the health and lives of all women of Washington."[102]

A woman tries to climb aboard an open streetcar of the type commonly used during the summer. Although the scene is from New York, Washington had the same type of cars, with the same challenges for women. *Library of Congress.*

In March 1912, stepless "hobble skirt" streetcars were introduced in New York, adding more pressure on D.C. companies to take action. WRECo followed suit in April by introducing new cars with doors in the middle and lower steps. The women pronounced satisfaction, and the flap over hobble skirts (which were already going out of fashion) quickly subsided. Along with traditional cars, WRECo's fleet of sixty elegant center-door cars would remain a component of the streetcar system for several decades.

Despite the higher capacity of the newer cars, complaints still poured in about overcrowding, especially during rush hour, just as had they had for as long as streetcars had been running. "The limit of caution seems to have been passed too often of late," the *Evening Star* protested in 1900. "The practice of allowing or compelling passengers to crowd in between filled seats is dangerous and highly objectionable."[103]

Replying to a complaint in 1902 about crowding during rush hour on the Columbia (H Street) line, a WRECo spokesman vaguely replied that the company's manager "tries to do what he can for the good of the citizens as well as the company."[104] Conventional wisdom within the industry held that crowding riders was the only way to make streetcars profitable. When

Early Mass Transit in Washington, D.C.

A center-door streetcar stops at Union Station. *Historical Society of Washington, D.C.*

Charles Tyson Yerkes (1837–1905), the well-known Chicago street railway tycoon, was once asked why he didn't put more cars out to better handle the passenger load, he replied, "It is the straphangers that pay the dividends."[105] With such attitudes, real improvements were unlikely.

Riders chafed at the companies' indifference, and sometimes nerves were frayed to the breaking point. One day in February 1911, a certain Alexander C. Black, clerk at the War Department, was sitting on a car that grew very crowded. An elderly woman boarded, and Black decided that he should give her his seat but vowed to do it only if he were compensated for the inconvenience. He "extricated himself from the several inches of seat on which he was wedged and gallantly gave his place to the woman passenger. He then wormed his way to where the conductor was standing and demanded either a seat or his ticket back." When the conductor wouldn't meet his demands, Black scuffled with both him and the driver and then jumped off to sit in the middle of the tracks in front of the car, refusing to move until his fare was returned. Black's act of defiance was reported admiringly in the newspapers but had no lasting impact. The police carted him off to jail and charged him with disorderly conduct.[106]

Capital Streetcars

The newspapers relished stories of people, young and old, achieving small personal victories against the mighty streetcar companies. A simple delight in causing trouble seems to have motivated eight-year-old Draper F. Horton, who decided one day in June 1901 to stick an iron awning rod down into the conduit slot at Eleventh and G Streets Northwest. As expected, the rod promptly entangled itself in the plow of the next streetcar that rumbled by. "Besides tying up the cars, the boy caused serious damage to the system, and the current had to be shut off for quite awhile to make repairs," the *Washington Post* reported. "The boy was arrested by Officer Harry Warren, of the First precinct, charged with malicious mischief."[107]

Increasing concern about safety, as well as dissatisfaction with the way streetcar companies dealt with complaints, led to reforms in how they were regulated. Since 1862, Congress had directly legislated major aspects of streetcar operations in the District, leaving the District's commissioners a very limited role. In 1909, Congress granted authority to regulate D.C. streetcar systems to the Interstate Commerce Commission (ICC), a federal agency mostly concerned with matters unrelated to the District.

One of the biggest impacts the ICC had was in instituting a rule in 1910 that led to the end of two-streetcar trains. In the early days of cable and electric power, two-car trains—composed of a powered motorcar pulling an unpowered trailer car—were common on D.C. streets. They were an efficient way to serve a large number of passengers with just two operators: a motorman and a conductor. However, with larger cars and heavier traffic, these mini trains could become dangerous for passengers, particularly if conductors were not on board the trailers to signal the motorman when it was safe for the train to move. The commission became concerned for the safety of both passengers and conductors. It ruled in 1910 that two-car trains must have two conductors on board, one each for the motorcar and the trailer. The rationale was that it wasn't safe for a single conductor to handle both cars because it was dangerous to step across the space between the cars while the train was operating.

The streetcar companies insisted that they couldn't afford to pay for two conductors on each train. Rather than doing so, they opted to discontinue using two-car trains altogether. Eventually, even having one conductor on a streetcar would be considered prohibitively expensive, but it would take several more decades before conductor-less streetcars (like the old-fashioned bobtail cars, which had been banned in the 1890s) would be allowed again on D.C. streets.

Early Mass Transit in Washington, D.C.

The ICC's streetcar reign proved to be short. In 1913, a new D.C. Public Utilities Commission (PUC) was established, modeled on similar commissions that had been created in New York City and elsewhere, and it took over the role of regulating streetcars and other public utilities in Washington. The three District commissioners were designated as the PUC's commissioners, making the PUC a direct extension of the D.C. government. From this point forward, regulation of streetcar operations in the District would be the province of local officials.

The commission's first act was to require air brakes on all of the larger streetcars, which were too big for the handbrakes used on older cars. The move improved safety and helped to reduce the noise problem.[108] As it gradually became better established, the PUC would go on to arbitrate changes in routes, the number and types of cars in service, how track was maintained, what fares could be charged and many other aspects of operating city streetcars.

How fares were collected was the subject of much tinkering. Street railways before the early twentieth century had collected fares the same way that regular railroads did, using conductors who would collect fares individually from passengers after they had boarded and taken their seats. This system posed problems for larger cars, which might carry upward of one hundred passengers during rush hour. Conductors simply could not monitor all the passengers, and the streetcar companies feared that they were losing significant revenue. The solution was to require passengers to pay their fares immediately upon entering the cars. In 1909, D.C. streetcar companies began introducing patented "Pay as You Enter" cars, which had been designed specifically for this purpose and were first used in Montreal, Canada. The cars had separate entrances and exits, with fare boxes manned by conductors at the entrances. A variation of this theme—called "Pay Within" because the conductor and fare box were stationed farther inside the car—was soon developed by rival manufacturers to compete with the patented Pay as You Enter concept.

Even a small change like this inevitably rankled some patrons, who objected to being shaken down for their fare immediately upon entering a car. It seemed disrespectful. In particular, the direct gaze of the conductor could discomfit women as they attempted to retrieve their fares. But daintiness had never been a strong suit of the streetcar business, and such concerns were swept aside. Payment upon entry quickly became a standard practice. The adoption of fare boxes would ultimately lead to the introduction of metal tokens shortly after World War I. Tokens were much

A conductor follows passengers onto a crowded car on the former Columbia Street Railway line on H Street Northeast in the 1910s. *Library of Congress.*

easier to process than paper tickets and would become a standard way to pay mass transit fares for the rest of the twentieth century.

Washington's Oddest Occupation

Motormen and conductors worked long, grueling hours—often twelve to fifteen hours a day, seven days a week—and many of them faced considerable dangers on a daily basis. In horsecar days, operators had been required to stand on the open platform at the front of the car, exposed to the elements in all kinds of weather. With the advent of faster-moving electric streetcars, the motormen faced worse exposure on these open platforms. Many suffered from hypothermia. In some cities, streetcar unions pushed to eliminate open platforms, but company officials resisted, arguing that the glass front of a closed compartment would become fogged or soiled and prevent operators from clearly seeing where they were going. The struggle for closed vestibules came to the attention of the Woman's Christian Temperance Union, which in 1903 collected signatures on a petition to Congress to ban open platform cars in the District. The drive was successful, and a law requiring closed vestibules on D.C. streetcars passed that same year.

Conductors braved hazards that are unthinkable today. One of the most harrowing was having to work the open cars that were so popular and crowded in the warmer months. Because there was no center aisle, they were obliged to balance themselves on the narrow running board that ran along the side of the car to reach each passenger and collect his or her fare. "Thus the conductor was constantly swinging along this narrow footboard all day, with a fare box in one hand, a punch and bunch of transfers in the other, trying to keep his balance, like a goat on a narrow precipice," an early streetcar union executive recalled.[109]

One day in September 1903, twenty-two-year-old William Smallwood, who lived on Benning Road, was working as a conductor on a crowded open car near the far eastern end of the Benning Road line at Chesapeake Junction on the Maryland border. Of course, the streetcars on these suburban stretches used overhead trolley lines, which were mounted on poles that stood between the two sets of incoming and outgoing tracks. Smallwood had just started to make his rounds collecting fares from the many commuters who were headed

Passengers, including military servicemen, crowd on to a WRECo open car in July 1918. Note the conductor on the running board at the rear of the car. *Maryland Rail Heritage Library.*

into the city when he leaned far over the side to get around two men who were standing on the running board. Unfortunately, the fast-moving car passed a trolley pole at that exact moment, and Smallwood was struck in the head and thrown off the car into a ditch. The passengers "gave the alarm, and as quickly as possible the car was stopped and backed to the scene of the accident. Smallwood was unconscious. He was placed on one of the seats and carried to the Casualty Hospital," where doctors said he "had only the very smallest chance for recovery, as the right side of his skull was crushed."[110] Despite their dangers, the popular cars continued in service for many more years; the last one was not removed from service in Washington until the 1930s.

Perhaps the most dangerous streetcar job was the one the *Washington Times* called "Washington's Oddest Occupation," that of the "pitman," who spent his days attaching and removing electrical plows to the undersides of streetcars. Pitmen were stationed in "plow pits," small enclosures just beneath the street surface that were located at a handful of sites around the city where underground conduits ended and overhead trolley lines began. Prominent plow pits were located on Fourth Street in Eckington, at Fifteenth and H Streets Northeast, at the Calvert Street bridge over Rock Creek, at the Navy Yard bridge in Anacostia and on Prospect Street in Georgetown, where the Glen Echo line connected with downtown routes. When a streetcar arrived and rolled to a stop over one of these plow pits, it was the job of the pitman to either attach or detach the plow on the underside of the car as another worker connected or disconnected the trolley pole on top of the car. Once the pitman had completed his task, he would ring a bell to signal the driver to continue on his way.

It was a fairly simple job, carried out hundreds of times a day, but it was fraught with danger. The pitmen worked in proximity to the electrified third rail, as well as numerous other live wires: "Thousands of volts of electricity are chained in those wires which crawl about on every side of the cave [plow pit]. Let a single loose installation occur or a wire be snapped in a storm, and the pit would be instantly charged with a voltage equal to that of the death chair in Sing Sing," the *Washington Times* ominously noted.[111]

In August 1900, the first recorded plow pit fatality occurred when John C. Page, a native of Austin, Texas, who had served in the Spanish-American War, was found electrocuted in his plow pit at Fifteenth and H Street Northeast. The motorman of a streetcar waiting over the pit to have its plow attached became impatient when he heard no bell signaling him to move on. He found Page senseless in the pit. Authorities later determined that Page's left arm had come in contact with the electric conduit rail. The pitmen

Early Mass Transit in Washington, D.C.

A pitman rests with his legs dangling in the plow pit at the Columbia Railway Car Barn at Fifteenth Street and Benning Road Northeast. The barn was built in 1895 and demolished in 1971. *National Capital Trolley Museum.*

were supposed to flip switches to turn the current off when they attached or detached the plow, and electrocutions might occur if the switches weren't set properly. Similar incidents occurred in 1901, when WRECo employee James Looney was electrocuted in his Prospect Street plow pit in Georgetown, and in 1911, when an Italian immigrant named Tony Scoffetti was electrocuted as his pit flooded with rainwater.

But electrocution wasn't the only hazard. A more gruesome end came to those pitmen who happened to poke their heads up out of the pit at the wrong moment. Such was the case with Edward Cosack, who was working the Anacostia pit one day in January 1902. He had just attached a plow to a southbound car headed over the Navy Yard bridge into the city when he moved over to the adjacent pit on the northbound side of the tracks and looked up to see what was going on, thinking that side was clear. A northbound car was arriving at that very instant. "The car struck him, crushing his skull and lacerating his face and scalp in a frightful manner," the *Washington Post* reported. He was killed instantly.

Pitmen might attach and detach the plows hundreds of times in a shift. For this they earned about two dollars per day. The job was hard and lonely, but pitmen made the most of their isolated outposts in the middle of the streets. The plow pit at Eckington was fitted out with a potbellied stove for heat in the winter, as well as a bench, books, magazines, a checkerboard and pictures taped to the walls. When traffic was busy, pitmen might stay down in their pits for most or all of their shifts. On lighter routes, they would come out and wait by the side of the road between cars. Passengers on arriving cars were often fascinated to watch the pitmen scurry out into the middle of the street and disappear in the hole just before the car rode over them. An odd occupation indeed!

Will You Drive That Front Car?

Streetcar workers had struggled to organize themselves and be treated fairly for as long as street railways had been in the District. Little more than a year after the first horse-drawn cars went into service during the Civil War, operators suffering from steep wartime inflation went on strike for increased wages. Additional strikes occurred throughout the late nineteenth century. As often as not, drivers and conductors would simply stop their cars in the middle of the street, usually somewhere downtown in the middle of rush hour, as they did at Fourteenth and F Streets Northwest in December 1894 after wages had been cut from $2.00 per day to $1.67. "The drivers slapped on their brakes, tied the reins about the brake handles and stepped off the platforms, followed by the conductors," the *Washington Post* reported. "[A]nd then one after another the cars lined up until they extended for several squares in both directions." President Samuel Phillips of the Metropolitan Railroad was summoned to this chaotic scene to try to resolve the problem. "Will you drive that front car?" he asked an aged driver. "I will not" was the prompt and emphatic reply, according to the *Post*, which noted that "it was evident that [Phillips] was at a loss as to the next step to take."[112] Despite the high drama, this strike, like most, was soon settled. Without experienced negotiators to aide them, the drivers and conductors squeezed out only a small concession, settling for $1.75 per day, which was still a twenty-five-cent pay cut but was not quite as bad as the original proposal. President Phillips continued to insist that he was losing money and would go bankrupt if he didn't cut wages.

On the heels of the Metropolitan strike, the first concerted efforts were made to create a union of District streetcar workers. Called the Protective

Street Railway Union, it represented streetcar workers for several years, but when the Metropolitan and other lines were consolidated under the Crosby syndicate, the union seems to have been sidelined. It's unclear when it was formally dissolved.

The next big push for unionization came in 1916, when Rezin Orr (1854–1917), secretary-treasurer of the Amalgamated Association of Street, Electric Railway & Motor Coach Employees of America and a veteran of efforts to organize workers in other cities, came to Washington to help create local union chapter 689. In March, Orr sent a committee of newly minted union representatives to Capital Traction and WRECo with a proposed labor agreement that included more pay, shorter hours (i.e., nine or ten hours per day instead of twelve to fifteen) and recognition of the union. The two companies rejected the proposal and began summarily firing union leaders and members from their rolls. The union responded by calling a massive strike to shut down all streetcar service in the District.

The strike generated sensational headlines in the newspapers, and Washingtonians braced themselves for a crippling shutdown of their public transit system. Many feared that violence would erupt among strikers and company representatives, but little trouble ensued. The strike, which began on Sunday, March 5, lasted only until late the following day. The District's commissioners intervened with a deal to arbitrate differences between the union and the two streetcar companies, and both sides agreed. Workers returned to their jobs as an agreement was hammered out. The companies agreed to modest fixed wage increases, and workers agreed not to strike for one year.

From this point, the city's two streetcar companies took opposite tacks. Labor relations went remarkably well at the Capital Traction Company, which recognized the union and thenceforward maintained an excellent relationship with it. In fact, no further strikes occurred against Capital Traction for another thirty years. WRECo, on the other hand, under the leadership of president Clarence P. King, stubbornly refused to negotiate with the union or even accept its existence as legitimate.

In March 1917, as the required one-year waiting period ended and just a month before the United States entered World War I, the union struck against WRECo. This time, a protracted struggle ensued. The seven-hundred-man metropolitan police force was mobilized for disturbances, but strikers again remained generally well behaved. On the first day, conductor Harry Hargrove was one of the few arrested. He was charged with "applying language prohibited by law to a strikebreaking conductor," a rather odd offense. Hargrove was soon released from custody.

This cartoon from the February 8, 1918 edition of the *Evening Star* reflects the popular animosity toward street railway executives, who seemed out of touch with patrons and employees alike.

At some spots downtown, strikers would swarm around WRECo cars, immobilizing them in their tracks. Service was disrupted across the city, but strikers were never able to entirely stop WRECo from running. King had offered individual contracts to all WRECo employees, and some had signed and agreed to stay on through the strike. King also temporarily hired operators from New York and other cities to run the cars as strikebreakers. He issued a statement "that the company is determined to stand firm and not recede an inch from its position and that this is being done to wipe out the union, and thus forestall further strike possibilities." The union, at least at first, was not intimidated by his threats.

Washingtonians had always been suspicious of the industrialists who ran the city's street railways, and most people strongly sympathized with the strikers. The strikebreakers from out of town were seen as unruly

Left: A train of two open streetcars turns onto Pennsylvania Avenue headed toward the Capitol in this summertime postcard scene from the early 1900s. Note the many pedestrians crossing the street wherever they please. *Author's collection.*

Below: Postcard view of streetcar traffic on Pennsylvania Avenue in the early 1900s. *Author's collection.*

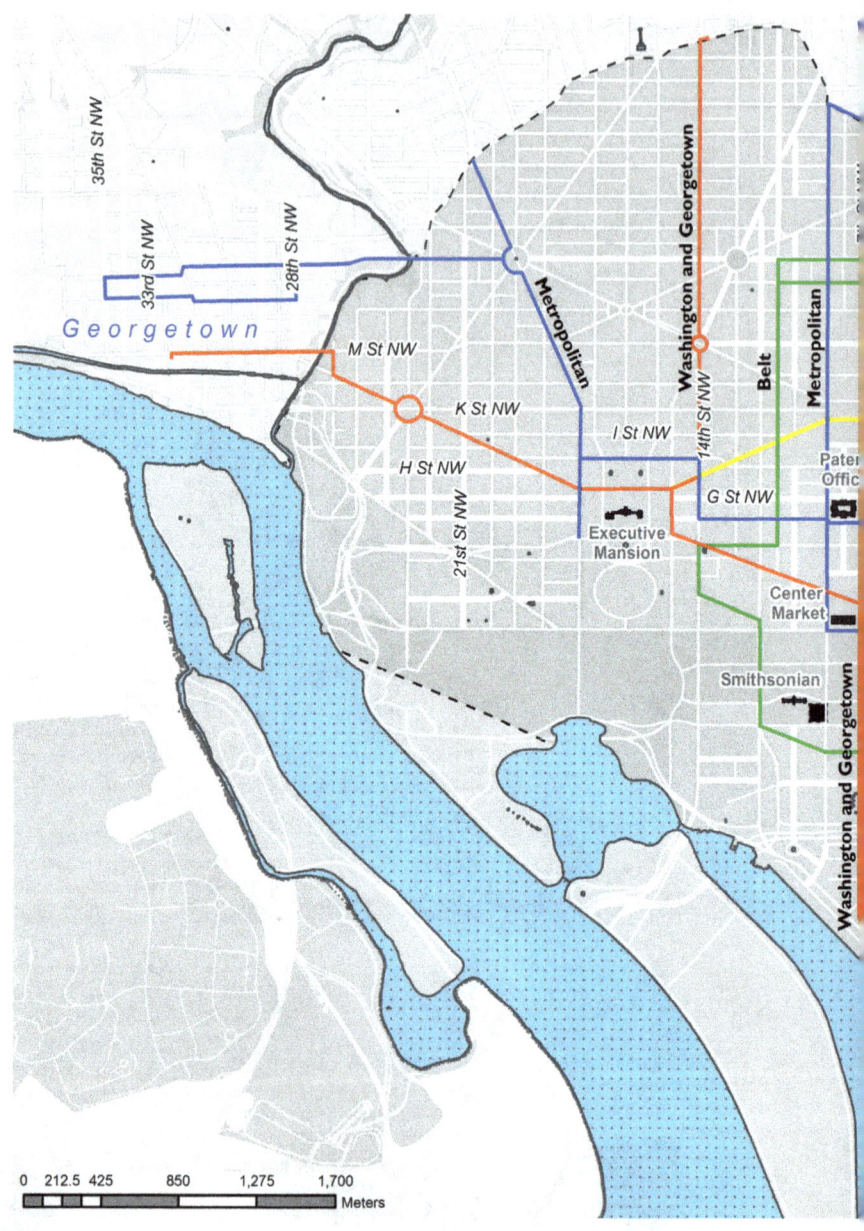

Map of streetcar lines in Washington, D.C., in the 1880s and early 1890s. The routes are overlaid on a contemporary map. *Matthew Gilmore*.

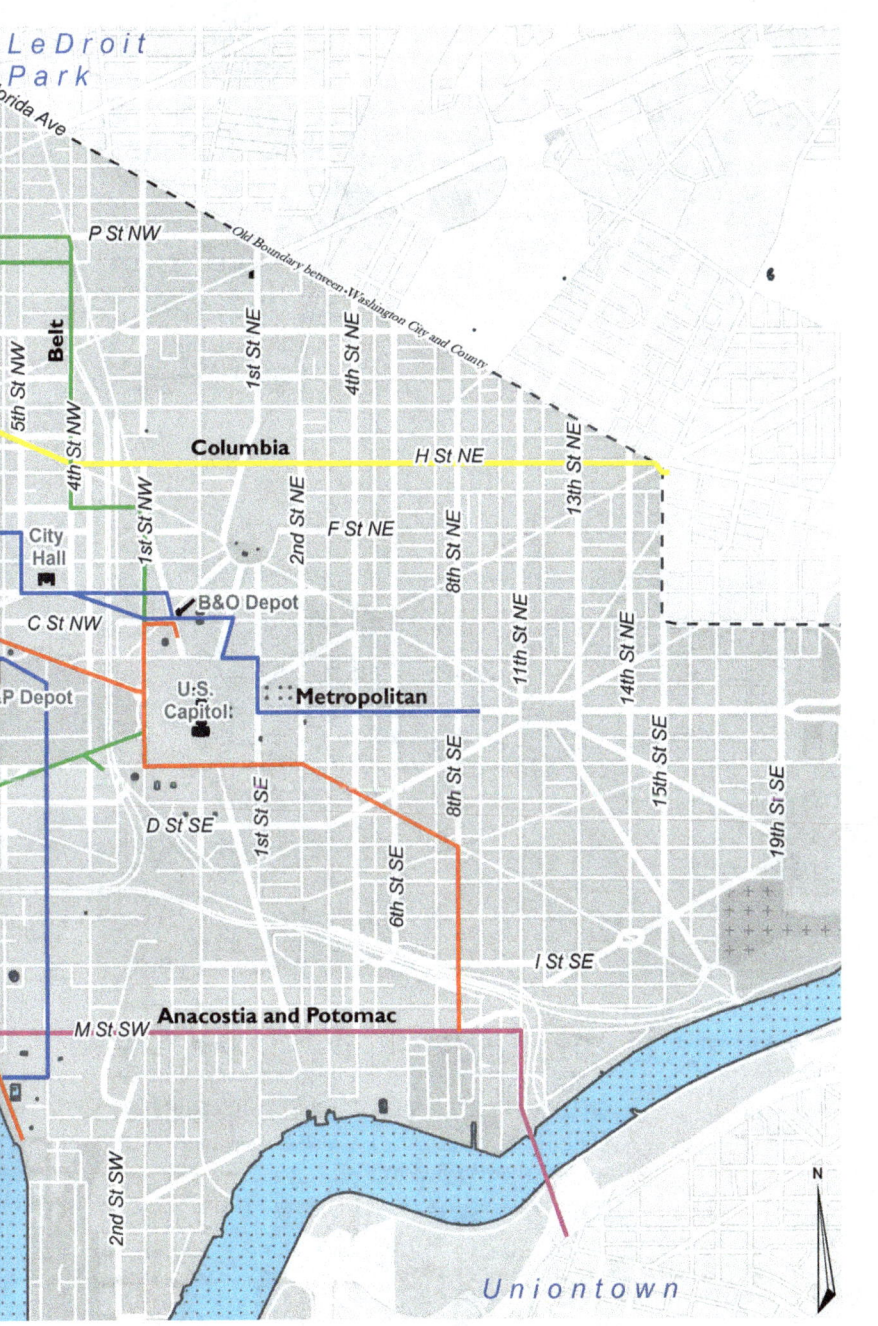

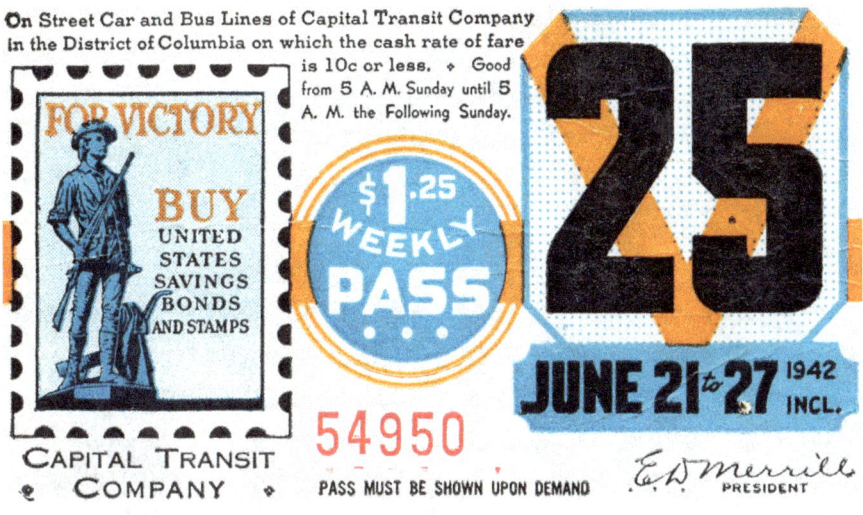

A wartime weekly pass encourages the purchase of savings bonds. More than half of Capital Transit's riders used weekly passes in the 1930s and 1940s. *Author's collection.*

This Capital Transit car was specially painted to encourage women to join the wartime Women's Auxiliary Transit Service. *National Capital Trolley Museum, Leonard Rice Collection.*

Opposite, top: Postcard view of an eastbound WRECo streetcar on F Street negotiating a bend in the tracks as it crosses Ninth Street. *Author's collection.*

Opposite, middle: A streetcar train on the Fourteenth Street line heads around Thomas Circle shortly after the turn of the century in this postcard view. *Author's collection.*

Opposite, bottom: A colorful Capital Transit weekly pass from 1934, the year such passes were introduced, celebrates the Glen Echo amusement park. *Author's collection.*

This circa 1960 photo shows a D.C. Transit streetcar stopping for passengers at Thirteenth and D Streets Northeast. *National Capital Trolley Museum.*

Fire is potential threat wherever electrical connections may be interrupted, as happened at this switch on Florida Avenue in the late 1950s. *Historical Society of Washington, D.C., Joseph Jessel Collection.*

A Route 30 streetcar waits for passengers transferring from a bus at the Friendship Heights terminal on Wisconsin Avenue in 1959. *Author's collection.*

Two D.C. Transit streetcars wait at the turnaround that marks the terminus of the Route 40/42 line on Mount Pleasant Street in 1961. *Author's collection.*

A D.C. Transit streetcar stops at Glen Echo Amusement Park, circa 1960. *Historical Society of Washington, D.C., Joseph Jessel Collection.*

A D.C. Transit streetcar stops to pick up passengers from the platform on Connecticut Avenue just north of the Dupont Circle underpass, circa 1960. *Author's collection.*

A Route 54 streetcar pauses next to the Peace Monument (out of view to the left) on its way to the Navy Yard car barn in the late 1950s. *Author's collection.*

Not all routes followed urban streets. This photo shows D.C. Transit's vintage 1918 streetcar on the Cabin John line in Maryland in September 1959. *Author's collection.*

A restored 1890s Capital Traction streetcar takes fans on a ride along G Street downtown in 1958. *Photo by Clark Frazier.*

Another photo of the restored 1890s car, this time seen on Fourth Street Northeast turning on to T Street. The Eckington car barn is just out of view on the right. *Photo by Clark Frazier*.

D.C. Transit's vintage 1918 streetcar passes in front of the Howard Theater at Florida Avenue and T Street Northwest on the last day of streetcars in January 1962. *Historical Society of Washington, D.C., Joseph Jessel Collection.*

Contemporary photo of preserved streetcar tracks on O Street in Georgetown. *Photo by the author.*

The Capital Traction Car Barn on M Street in Georgetown. *Photographs in the Carol M. Highsmith Archive, Library of Congress.*

Detail of the stone carving on the front of the Georgetown car barn. *Photo by the author.*

Contemporary photo of the Navy Yard car barn. *Photo by the author.*

The former car barn on East Capitol Street Northeast was once WRECo headquarters. It is now the Car Barn condominium. *Photo by the author.*

Historic PCC car no. 1101 stops at the passenger platform of the National Capital Trolley Museum in 2014. *Photo by Ken Rucker, National Capital Trolley Museum.*

An 1890s streetcar, similar to the one now on display at the Smithsonian's National Museum of American History, undergoes restoration at the National Capital Trolley Museum. *Photo by Ken Rucker, National Capital Trolley Museum.*

The City of San Francisco operates restored streetcars on its Market Street line, including this PCC car that has been painted in the livery of the D.C. Transit System. *Photo by the author.*

One of the new streetcars made in the Czech Republic arrives in Baltimore in December 2009. *District Department of Transportation.*

A Czech-made streetcar undergoes testing in Greenbelt, Maryland. *District Department of Transportation.*

and disruptive; patrons who still rode WRECo's cars claimed that the strikebreakers pocketed the fares they collected. After several days, many of them wearied of their jobs and began leaving town. Fourteen workers deserted seven cars on Eleventh Street one day, complaining that WRECo was making them sleep in its car barns. The impoverished men reportedly paid their fares home to New York and Philadelphia in nickels and dimes.[113] King responded by hiring yet more strikebreakers from other cities.

King's unapologetic attempt to crush the union made him a pariah, as Washingtonians rallied around the struggling strikers. Special emergency funds were established to provide sustenance to the workers and their families, keeping them going through much of March. On the twenty-seventh, legendary workers' rights activist Mary "Mother" Jones (1837–1930) addressed a packed meeting at the National Rifles Armory, joining other community leaders in advocating a government takeover of the city's street railways. Jones was adamant that King and his fellow executives were the culprits. She told the strikers that they would be "measly miserable cowards to make any settlement with the robbers" and urged them to "get some fighting blood in them."[114]

It was no use. WRECo continued to hire strikebreakers to cross picket lines. The scabs managed to keep many of the company's lines running, although service was never at pre-strike levels. By April, WRECo began unilaterally announcing that the strike was over, even though union officials insisted that it wasn't. A resolution mediated by the Public Utilities Commission finally brought most of the original WRECo workers back to their jobs but didn't include recognition of the union. King continued to reiterate his steadfast opposition to the union when Congressional hearings were held in May and June but won little sympathy on Capitol Hill. The special Senate committee holding the hearings excoriated him in its final report, singling out his opposition to the union as the root cause of the strike:

> *In our opinion, if Mr. King had not been obdurate; if he had understood present-day social economics; if he had been willing to meet at all—not half way, but measurably—the men, some of whom had worked for him more than a quarter of a century, there would have been no strike in the city of Washington in last March, the public would not have suffered the grossest inconveniences, the capital of the nation would not have presented a sorry spectacle to the world, and what is more important, there would not have occurred the misery and heart-breaking of men admittedly of good character and of their wives and their children.*[115]

The strongly worded report did little to directly aid workers, however. While there was talk of a possible government takeover or stronger oversight by the Public Utilities Commission, nothing concrete was done to rein the company in. The ultimate impact of the strike and King's ruthless response was to further sour the public about streetcar companies in general, leaving fewer supporters to defend the system in future years when it would be imperiled by competition from automobiles and buses. Meanwhile, WRECo tamped down opposition by quietly approving three wage increases between May and November 1917, satisfying its employees at least temporarily.

Taming Crush Hour

America's entry into World War I in April 1917 accelerated problems of overcrowding and inefficient service that had been festering on both Capital Traction and WRECo car lines throughout the 1910s. The population of the city had grown more than 20 percent, from 331,069 in 1910 to 395,947 in late 1917, and it would soar to 526,000 at the peak of the war effort in April 1918. Thousands of new wartime government workers crowded into apartment houses, hotels and temporary quarters that had sprung up around the city. Most of the new arrivals took streetcars to their jobs, many of which were located in temporary office buildings near the Mall in East Potomac Park. Streetcar line extensions were planned to service those locations, although the war ended before they were finished. Capital Traction had cars running to Potomac Park in June 1918, while WRECo's line was completed in April 1919.

The biggest problem, as usual, was overcrowding. Not only did congestion slow the cars down, but it was also harder and harder just to keep them on the streets because conductors and motormen were leaving to join the military. In December 1917, the Public Utilities Commission hired New York transit consultant John A. Beeler (1867–1945) to study streetcar congestion in D.C. Beeler deployed an army of observers on downtown D.C. streets to record precise details of how fast the cars moved and how frequently they were spaced. In his report, Beeler noted that delays due to traffic congestion were "most exasperating to the public" and were the worst during rush hour, which he considered a misnomer for D.C because "the cars do anything but rush. A better name would be the 'crush hour.'"[116]

The worst congestion was around Fifteenth Street and New York Avenue Northwest, which Beeler called the "throat" of the Capital Traction network.

Early Mass Transit in Washington, D.C.

Streetcar patrons crowd a platform on F Street in 1918. *Library of Congress.*

A total of 211 cars was scheduled on an average workday to pass through the intersection between 4:30 p.m. and 5:30 p.m. In January 1918, the packed cars crawled through at an average speed of about four miles per hour. By 6:00 p.m., that had dropped to just under three miles per hour, not much faster than a brisk walk. No wonder that anybody who could walk to work preferred it to being wedged into these slow-moving cars.

Beeler made many recommendations, not only for the Capital Traction "throat" but for the rest of the city's car lines as well. The cars made too many stops—sometimes several within a single block. Beeler recommended eliminating many stops to keep the cars moving. He also advocated better-designed streetcar platforms to improve passenger loading and unloading, changes in traffic patterns and better fare collection methods, including the use of fare boxes. Automobiles were a big problem; Beeler said that parking should be much more severely restricted and that on some routes automobiles should be banned altogether to prevent obstructions to streetcars. Numerous other recommendations were made as well.

Not all of Beeler's recommendations were implemented—particularly the limits on automobiles—but many were. After the war, service improved, but streetcars had cemented their reputation as slow, crowded and unpleasant.

A view of pedestrians and streetcars on Fifteenth Street just south of New York Avenue in 1918. *Library of Congress.*

However vital Beeler's improvements may have been to achieving respectable service levels, they were never enough to reverse this increasing disenchantment. And for some passengers—notably African Americans—a streetcar ride could at times be a downright harrowing experience.

Chapter 7

A VAST AMOUNT OF HARM

THE STRUGGLE TO MAINTAIN EQUAL ACCESS, 1900–1920

Twenty-two-year-old Joseph Smith was fortunate to start the twentieth century with a new job—night laborer with the Washington Traction and Electric Company. Smith, an African American, lived on Champlain Street near Meridian Hill in what surely was a humble abode. His new job was to serve in a group of workers that went out on the lonely streets of Washington late at night to clean the streetcar conduits after the cars had stopped running.

At two o'clock in the morning on June 27, 1900, Smith was hard at work on a conduit at Eleventh and G Streets Northwest when he received a devastating shock. The electric power, which had been cut off for the cleaning work, unexpectedly came back on momentarily and electrocuted Smith. As he lay in the street "turning and writhing with pain," a beat policeman arrived at the scene and immediately "sent a hurry message to the Emergency Hospital, stating that the young negro was probably dying."

Identifying him as an African American was a bad call. The responding hospital physician apparently was highly displeased at having to rescue a black man. It took twenty-five minutes for him to get to the scene in his horse-drawn ambulance, despite the very short distance (about five blocks) from the hospital. Smith's white supervisor, who was on the scene, "thought it was an outrage to delay so long."[117] When the doctor finally arrived, he apparently started cursing at Smith. According to the *Evening Star*, the physician later refused to admit his irresponsible behavior: "The doctor denies having used the language ascribed to him, and says there was no unnecessary delay in responding to the call."[118] Fortunately, Smith seems to have survived the ordeal.

The incident was emblematic of whites' growing hostility toward African Americans at the turn of the century. The legal framework that had protected African American rights had been crumbling since the end of Reconstruction in 1876. A turning point had come in 1896, when the Supreme Court infamously ruled that "separate but equal" public facilities were acceptable under the Constitution, paving the way for states to begin enacting Jim Crow segregation laws, often limiting access to streetcars. By 1900, neighboring local jurisdictions, including Alexandria, Virginia, had segregated both their streetcar and railroad systems. Virginia passed a statewide Jim Crow streetcar law in 1906. Conductors on railroad cars entering Virginia from the District often scrupulously followed the rules, going through the cars at the border and ordering passengers to separate themselves into white and "Colored" cars. Whites and blacks alike had to follow the humiliating rules. In one case, Robert E. Lee's daughter Mary Custis Lee was arrested for refusing to move out of a car designated for African Americans as the train left Washington for Alexandria.[119]

Astonishingly, D.C.'s streetcars remained officially integrated throughout this difficult period. The 1864 law establishing equal access to D.C. streetcars was never overturned, and African Americans made good use of their streetcar rights. "Colored people are very fond of car riding, and constitute a large percentage of our patrons," one anonymous conductor told the *Evening Star* in 1900. Many white Washingtonians supported integrated streetcars, as evidenced by the opinions of the local press. In a 1902 editorial, the *Washington Post*—not particularly known as a liberal newspaper at the time— commented on the failure of New Orleans's Jim Crow streetcar law: "Upon the whole, we think that the Jim Crow street car is both nonsensical and mischievous. It does no good. It may do a vast amount of harm."[120]

African American community leaders, including prominent church ministers, began organizing in the early years of the twentieth century to express their opposition to Jim Crow laws that were taking hold elsewhere in the country, as well as the threat of Jim Crow hanging over Washington. As they feared, D.C.'s integrated streetcars increasingly came under attack, mostly from southern congressmen. The first major case involved James Thomas "Cotton Tom" Heflin (1869–1951), a white supremacist from Alabama who was elected to the House of Representatives in 1904. In 1906, he first introduced a bill to amend the D.C streetcar law, and in February 1908, it was debated fiercely on the floor of the House before being soundly defeated by a vote of 140 to

58 that closely followed party lines. Heflin's controversial argument was that it was better for both races to be separate because trouble inevitably ensued when the two races mixed. After the acrimonious debate over his bill was well publicized in the press, Heflin decided to obtain a permit to carry a concealed handgun in public, ostensibly for self-protection.

Just a month later, on March 27, 1908, Heflin ended up playing out his own imagined fears. As he rode a streetcar that night on Pennsylvania Avenue, two African Americans boarded who had been drinking and were carrying a bottle of whiskey. There was also a white woman aboard, and Heflin, who was on his way to deliver a lecture on the merits of temperance, apparently told the men not to drink in the presence of the lady. An argument ensued, voices were raised and when the streetcar stopped in front of the St. James Hotel at Sixth Street, Heflin pushed the two men off the car. He then proceeded to shoot at them through an open window. One shot hit one of the men, Lewis Lundy, in the neck, critically injuring him. Another ricocheted off the pavement and struck a bystander, Thomas McCreary, in the leg.

The brazen attack made headlines around the country. While some readers were outraged, many others supported Heflin's violent aggression. The police, to their credit, arrested him immediately after the incident and

HEFLIN OF ALABAMA.
Cries Heflin, "No fame do I crave;
The country my colleagues may save;
I'm just standing pat,
For my face is so fat
I can't cut myself when I shave."

A caricature of "Cotton Tom" Heflin appeared in the *Washington Post* on February 6, 1908.

charged him with assault. However, as he was brought to a nearby police station, more than a dozen of his fellow representatives, mostly from southern states, gathered at the station in a show of support. In the coming days, Heflin openly boasted of his feat, suggesting that his irresponsible act had actually helped preserve the social order. "He Shot a Bad Negro," read the headline in the *Baltimore Sun*, capsulizing a widely held sentiment. After the mysterious white woman he was supposedly protecting failed to materialize as a witness, prosecutors dropped charges against him. Lundy, who was an ex-con, recovered from his wound but was soon in jail because of a separate incident, fueling the smug conclusion that he deserved what he'd gotten from Heflin. The bystander, Thomas McCreary, also eventually recovered from his wound.

Tempers flared again after another streetcar altercation on Pennsylvania Avenue three years later. This time it involved Seaborn A. Roddenbery (1870–1913) of Georgia, who had been elected to the House of Representatives in 1910. Roddenbery, like Heflin, was a strident white supremacist. In his short tenure in Washington, Roddenbery was best known for proposing a Constitutional amendment outlawing interracial marriage. One day in 1911, Roddenbery and three other congressmen, including Speaker of the House Champ Clark (1850–1921), were riding on a Pennsylvania Avenue streetcar when an African American couple boarded at Tenth Street. The couple tried to sit down in the space available next to Roddenbery, but it was a tight fit. The man squeezed in next to Roddenbery, allegedly elbowing him. This enraged the high-strung southerner, who immediately started slugging the black man in the face. As other frightened passengers screamed to be let off the car, Roddenbery's colleagues intervened to stop the fight. Although the unnamed African American man was injured, no charges were filed against Roddenbery due to the brief mêlée. Neither of the two newspapers that reported the incident, the *Washington Post* and the *Washington Herald*, challenged Roddenbery for resorting to violence. Instead, both celebrated his pugilistic skills, noting that he was much smaller than the African American man.

While incidents like these were certainly not a daily occurrence, they contributed to increasing anxiety among African Americans, who never knew when sudden violence might be directed their way as they rode on city streetcars. The cars remained a mixing bowl for the races, just as they had been during the Civil War, and uncomfortable whites repeatedly attempted to segregate them. In December 1911, just six months after the Roddenbery incident, Representative Frank Clark of Florida introduced another District streetcar segregation bill in Congress. Once again, it failed to pass.

Early Mass Transit in Washington, D.C.

An out-of-town newspaper, the *Chicago Defender*, smugly asserted that Washington's African Americans had nothing to worry about. Ignoring the fact that Congress was the chief regulator of public life in the nation's capital, the newspaper claimed that there were three reasons why D.C.'s streetcars would never be segregated:

> *First, the traction companies do not want to be bothered with the expense or embarrassments that such a separation would entail upon them; second, the rich white people, who ride in their own automobiles, carriages, etc., are not concerned about the present mixing of the races; third, nobody is worked up over the matter except a few out-of-the-way neighborhood associations, representing, in most part, a bunch of non-voting poor white folks, and their narrow-minded protests are not likely to weigh very heavily against the two influences just mentioned. So the Negro needs to lose little sleep over the prospect of having "jim-crow" street cars in the District of Columbia.*[121]

Neighborhood associations did weigh in on the issue, but for every one that favored segregation, such as the Citizens Northwest Suburban Association, which represented Tenallytown, there was another that openly opposed it, like the Randle Heights Citizens Association. Resolutions by such organizations had little impact on D.C. streetcar laws and regulations.

Meanwhile, southern congressmen made many more attempts to push segregation. Senator James K. Vardaman of Mississippi announced a streetcar segregation bill in 1913, as did Representative Byron P. Harrison, also of Mississippi. In 1915, Frank Clark of Florida reintroduced his version. African American ministers protested each time. Reverend Simon P.W. Drew, president of the Colored Baptist Evangelic Alliance of America, called for forty days of fasting and prayer against Clark's bill, which he called "unwise and unchristianlike in motive and an insult to every colored citizen and a disgrace to our country."[122] None of the bills passed.

"Beaten Unmercifully from Head to Foot"

These scuffles must have seemed minor in comparison to the extraordinary outbreak of racial violence that occurred on the streets of Washington from Saturday, July 19, through Tuesday, July 22, 1919. The riots that took place in D.C. were the first to gain national attention that year, but many other cities saw racial violence as well, including Chicago, Knoxville, Omaha and many smaller towns, mostly in the South. It was as if the decades of increasing white hostility to African Americans in cities around the country had finally reached a boiling point, touched off by the end of World War I. The D.C. rioting, which was centered downtown but spread across the city, claimed seven lives and injured hundreds more. Unlike the riots of 1968, the focus in 1919 was not on looting or destruction of property; it aimed to attack individuals.

Commentators agree that there were many factors that contributed to the eruption of violence.[123] Certainly the demobilization of World War I soldiers played a critical role. Washington was filled with veterans, both white and black, who were returning to their homes or headed elsewhere around the country. Many were still in military attire, as they were allowed to continue to wear their uniforms after being discharged from active-duty service. Many were also at loose ends; peak wartime employment had dropped off, creating tension and competition for scarce jobs. It was these veterans who were the primary participants in the rioting.

Black veterans, who had made as many sacrifices as whites and had fought just as heroically, were rightly proud of their service and expected to be treated with respect on their return home. Reality turned out to be very different. Although black veterans marched along with their white counterparts in the Welcome Home Parade on Pennsylvania Avenue in February, many whites were uneasy about African American participation in the war and did not want black citizens to have a continuing role in the military. In other parts of the country where race riots erupted in 1919, the sight of African Americans wearing military uniforms often provoked a white backlash. In fact, a white mob beat one African American to death in Blakeley, Georgia, for refusing to stop wearing his army uniform. Whites—particularly veterans and others throughout the South who had participated in civilian homeland defense leagues—were fearful of African Americans usurping their "place" in society and threatening the prevailing white-dominated order.

Against this backdrop of racial tension, a series of newspaper articles throughout the month of July inflamed passions in Washington and was the immediate cause of the violence. The articles recounted a half dozen cases in which women were attacked by black men. Although the *Washington Post* is often faulted for inciting the 1919 riots, all four daily D.C. papers—the *Post, Star, Herald* and *Times*—sensationalized these incidents, with the *Herald* and the *Times*, both in tabloid format, trumpeting the most alarming headlines.

The front page of the July 8, 1919 *Washington Times* displays one of the headlines that stirred up animosity toward African Americans in the weeks before the riots.

One African American man, who was never caught, apparently committed several attacks on women in upper Northwest Washington, beginning with an African American schoolteacher, Louise Simmons, who was dragged into the woods near Fessenden Street and Connecticut Avenue and assaulted on June 25. Subsequently, several more women, all of them white, were also attacked in upper Northwest, including secretary Mary Saunders, who was struck on the head with a rock and raped near the D.C. border. Although these crimes were obviously very serious, they did not represent a pattern of increasing aggression. The overall level of crime in the District had not increased. Nevertheless, intense press coverage of the assaults made it seem to edgy whites that African Americans as a group were rising up to attack them. "Woods Scoured in Hunt for Negro" ran a headline on the front page of the *Evening Star* on July 8. "Phone Girl Chased by 'Maniac' at Chevy Chase Gives New Clue" was the banner on the *Washington Times* that day. "Another Girl Is Attacked Here" the *Times* announced a week later. Some Northwest D.C. residents even formed a Klan-like "vigilance committee" to seek revenge. Nervous about the effect of all this fear mongering, the National Association for the Advancement of Colored People (NAACP) warned the newspapers that they were "sowing the seeds of a race riot." That is just what happened several days later.[124]

On the night of Friday, July 18, nineteen-year-old Elsie Stephnick, who had recently married a Navy Department employee, was supposedly accosted by two black men as she was walking home from her job at the Bureau of Engraving and Printing. She was not harmed, but Charles Ralls, an African American who lived in the Bloodfield neighborhood (west of the Navy Yard, roughly where the baseball stadium is now located), was questioned by police about the attack and later released. Hearing rumors that he was the one who attacked the wife of a fellow navy man, a mob of soldiers, sailors and marines formed to go after Ralls and his wife, who were both beaten near their home in Bloodfield. Other attacks broke out that night in Southwest as well, setting the stage for broader violence throughout Washington over the following four days.

The rioting mobs traveled largely on foot, scouring the streets for their victims, but occasionally they rode around in automobiles—called "terror cars"—and shot at bystanders. The mobs also often targeted streetcars. As African American journalist John Edward Bruce (1856–1924) pointed out, the "mixing of white and blacks on street railways" was one of the contributing factors that provoked whites to attack blacks.[125] Streetcars also were convenient. As roving gangs from both races looked for trouble, the captive operators and passengers aboard the cars, confined as they were to fixed routes and stops, proved to be easy marks.

The Pennsylvania Avenue cars suffered many attacks. "Two colored men were dragged from street cars near Pennsylvania avenue and 15th street during the night," the *Evening Star* reported on July 21. "Street car passengers were greatly alarmed by the incidents…Numerous other colored persons were at the street car transfer station when the trouble started, and several of them failed to get away in time to escape the assaults of the uniformed men."[126] According to the *Washington Times*, "At Fourteenth Street and Pennsylvania avenue an overseas soldier climbed through an open window of a street car and, grabbing a negro passenger by the coat collar, dragged him from the car. A woman passenger on the car became hysterical and was escorted from the scene by one of the soldiers."[127] In another case, the *New York Times* reported that "a band of soldiers and sailors dragged a young negro from a street car on G Street, Northwest, between Ninth and Tenth Streets. They beat him and chased him several blocks. His head was cut. He was taken home by the police."[128] Francis L. Thomas, a seventeen-year-old African American, was on the Seventh Street car headed home at about 11:15 on Sunday night when white sailors and soldiers stormed aboard and started beating him "unmercifully from head to foot" before throwing him out a window. In his subsequent statement to the NAACP, Thomas said that he had been so injured that it left him "in such a condition that I could hardly crawl back home."[129]

One of the striking features of the 1919 riots was that African Americans quickly responded by organizing their own defense and launching counterattacks on their white aggressors. As the white mobs grew on Sunday night and searched for new victims, they began heading north from Pennsylvania Avenue toward the Shaw/U Street neighborhood, then known as Uptown. They made it only to L Street, just north of Mount Vernon Square, where they clashed with hundreds of black residents and eventually retreated.

The next morning, some editions of the *Washington Post* carried an infamous (and entirely unfounded) call for the "mobilization of every available service man stationed in or near Washington" to participate in a "clean-up that will cause the events of the last two evenings to pale into insignificance."[130] While the effect on young white ex-servicemen, who were already engaged in the fight, is unknown, the ominous threat certainly mobilized more African Americans, who responded by buying up firearms and preparing for the race war to continue.

That evening, the newspapers reported attacks on streetcars by black residents that mirrored earlier white attacks. In Uptown, for example, the "trouble started at 7th and T streets about 1:15 o'clock in an attack upon Lewis C. Mueller, white, twenty-five years old, who was waiting for a street car. He was attacked by several colored men and severely beaten. His face and hands were cut and he was otherwise bruised and scarred, but he would not go to a hospital."[131] Across town, a "mob of between twenty-five and thirty negros, at 3 o'clock this afternoon, boarded a street car at Twenty-sixth and G streets northwest, in the vicinity of the U.S. Hospital, and beat the motorman and conductor. They then ran east to Twenty-fifth street, and scattered."[132] The aggression continued on both sides through Monday night and into Tuesday.

By Tuesday afternoon, however, the local and military authorities had finally taken control of the chaotic situation. Hundreds of active-duty troops under the command of Major General William G. Haan (1863–1924), a veteran of the fighting in Europe, were put on the streets with orders to arrest any and all persons causing disturbances. The massive official military presence suppressed renewed violence, and the riots of 1919 finally ended.

The short-lived race war did little to resolve tensions between whites and blacks. White racists continued to chafe at the progress that African Americans had made, something that was more evident in Washington than in other southern cities and included the non-segregated streetcar system. Southern congressmen continued to advocate for Jim Crow cars; William Lankford of Georgia pushed the idea again in 1923. But among the broader populace, the riots, if anything, were shocking and extreme, an embarrassment to

The front page of the July 23, 1919 *Washington Post* shows how coverage of the riots emphasized black violence, although whites were just as aggressive and had started the rioting.

the nation's capital and something to move beyond. The newspapers that had been the immediate instigators of the violence seem to have learned their lesson and didn't foment further racial disturbances. While the race "question" was still far from being resolved, the integration of the city's streetcars had survived unscathed, and African Americans who mixed with whites on those cars no longer needed to fear for their personal safety.

Chapter 8

YESTERDAY'S TECHNOLOGY

COMPETITION WITH AUTOMOBILES AND BUSES, 1920–1940

The period between the wars, from the 1920s through the 1930s, was an era of transition for streetcars in Washington and around the country. The clanking, thundering cars remained the preferred means of travel for hundreds of thousands of Washington-area residents; their efficiency in moving large numbers of people in and out of town was unrivaled. To observe the streams of cars, all packed to the gills at rush hour, shuffling along the major downtown routes, it must have seemed that they were the very bedrock of the city's transportation system, and in many ways they were. Yet streetcars were an endangered species, here and in almost every other major U.S. city. Urban planners and industry officials were quietly resigning themselves to dramatic reductions in a mode of transport that only a few decades earlier had been crucial to the growth and prosperity of the American city. How could such a reversal happen?

Automobiles and buses, of course, were the culprits. According to the *Washington Post*, the first "horseless carriage" rode the streets of the nation's capital on April 2, 1897, and was an immediate sensation, startling pedestrians and horses alike. Ironically, the strange vehicle was built and brought to Washington for William Schoepf, the court-appointed receiver of the bankrupt Eckington & Soldiers Home Railway. The particular machine in operation that day ran on compressed air (like the streetcars the Eckington line was experimenting with at the time), but gasoline-powered vehicles were not far off. The *Post* reporter who tagged along for the joyride in the new contraption was clearly thrilled with the cutting-edge technology and speculated about how motorized buses might soon be built:

> *This may be done by attaching a tractor, or powerful motor, to the front of the bus, and drawing it about the streets. The motor, in such a case, would be condensed to the exact space occupied by horses, and will take the sharpest curves even easier than did the flesh and blood tractors. If this is not desired, the motor may be attached directly to the wheels of the vehicle, and driven in the same way as a carriage.*[133]

The technological revolution came swiftly. In May 1900, just three years later, automobiles were beginning to appear around the city, and people were already talking about getting rid of streetcars. The *Post* reprinted a brief article from the *Chicago Record* making a prescient forecast:

> *There are those bold enough to predict that the car designed to run on rails laid in the streets will in time give way entirely to self-propelled vehicles, that require no other street foundation than the ordinary pavement.... It will only be necessary for the authorities to provide first-class pavements throughout the city, when all who desire to engage in the business of carrying passengers can do so. Thus cost and quality of service could be left to regulation by competition, which is now out of the question, because but a single corporation can be permitted to lay tracks and to operate cars in any given street.*[134]

While streetcar systems in Washington would continue to expand and grow in ridership for several more decades—and the entire system would continue to operate for another six—its ultimate fate was largely sealed at the very beginning of the twentieth century.

"Elegant, Comfortable, and Easy-Running Conveyances"

A certain rivalry between streetcars and buses had always existed. Although the Washington & Georgetown Railroad had bought Gilbert Vanderwerken's competing omnibus line in 1862 specifically to eliminate competition, its monopoly on mass transit was short-lived. In 1875, the Washington Chariot

Early Mass Transit in Washington, D.C.

A Washington Chariot Company bus. *D.C. Public Library, Star Collection,* © Washington Post.

Company was formed to reintroduce regularly scheduled horse-drawn coaches to compete with the cars. The new company deployed patented "Murch Chariot" omnibuses, which were enclosed carriages seating sixteen people on benches along the sides of their passenger compartments. These chariots looked a lot like streetcars, except for the large wheels; they even had straps hanging in the aisles for standees to grasp. The chariot was "an elegant, comfortable, and easy-running conveyance," according to the *National Republican*, and in time, the company kept nine of them running continually in each direction along Pennsylvania Avenue, with headway of just three or four minutes. At a fare of eight cents, the chariots pressured some of the competing street railways to lower their fares.

They lasted only a few years, however. The Washington Chariot Company folded in about 1880, and the Philadelphia-based Herdic Phaeton Company quickly stepped in to take its place. The company had been founded in 1879 by Peter H. Herdic (1824–1888), an energetic Pennsylvania entrepreneur who had patented his own omnibus design. The "herdic," similar in many ways to the Murch Chariot, featured a rear entrance (like a bobtail streetcar) and was lightly built but had better suspension. As with bobtail streetcars, passengers had to make their way to the front of the herdic to pay the driver. The five-cent fare was highly competitive.

Herdics would not die nearly as readily as the chariots. First deployed on the reliable Pennsylvania Avenue route, they were later extended to other major

A horse-drawn herdic stops on Capitol Hill. *D.C. Public Library, Star Collection,* © Washington Post.

thoroughfares. The first Herdic Phaeton Company went out of business in 1896, but within a year, it had been replaced by the Metropolitan Coach Company. The new company found that it could fill an important niche by providing service on major routes not served by streetcars, such as Sixteenth Street Northwest, a major north–south artery. Early twentieth-century Washingtonians grew to depend on herdics as an alternative to streetcars, but they were expensive to operate and service was often unreliable.

In time, the Metropolitan Coach Company struggled to earn a profit, just as with many suburban street railways. While expenses for the horse-drawn vehicles were high, fares had to be kept low and thus profits remained elusive. This proved true even after the company converted to primitive motorized buses in 1909. Service became erratic, and maintenance of the rickety vehicles declined, all the while that the company fought in court (to no avail) to get the streetcar companies to accept transfers from its vehicles. The motorized herdics eventually became notorious for their bad service. "Theoretically, the herdics are supposed to operate in the public interest and to carry passengers. But their real functions and activities are sealed in mystery. Mostly, they are used by Washingtonians to point out to visitors as one of the transportation jokes of the National Capital," the *Washington Times* reported in 1911.[135]

The joke finally ended in 1915, when the insolvent company ended its erratic service. That same year, the Public Utilities Commission authorized "jitney" bus service for the first time in the District. Jitneys, which had been

Early Mass Transit in Washington, D.C.

A horse-drawn streetcar encounters two herdics on a busy stretch of F Street in front of the Patent Office, circa 1890. *Author's collection.*

invented in Los Angeles just the preceding year, were cars or small trucks converted to passenger service that, like the herdics, offered rides for a nickel ("jitney" was a slang term for a nickel). They generally seated only a few passengers. The first applicant in D.C. was a certain Percy S. Wyerxa, who lived on Sixth Street downtown. He was informed that all he needed to go into the new business was a standard taxicab license.

Suddenly jitney buses were everywhere. They drew scorn and resentment from streetcar companies, which were constrained as much by elaborate regulations and high taxes (including fees to pay for traffic cops at major intersections) as by the rails that defined their routes. In contrast, the carefree jitneys had few overhead costs and could change routes on a whim. They were even known to "steal" passengers from streetcars by driving around them and picking people up from the car stops ahead.

Often unreliable and even unsafe, the unregulated jitneys did not last long. The Public Utilities Commission soon brought bus service under tight regulation, essentially driving jitneys out of business. Officially sanctioned buses were not allowed to compete directly with streetcars, which were recognized as more efficient for transporting large numbers of people along major commuter routes. Buses were permitted instead primarily on routes not served by streetcars. Early bus routes included Sixteenth Street, several cross-town lines and commuter routes connecting Northeast residential neighborhoods with downtown.

A sea change occurred in 1921, when local investors formed the Washington Rapid Transit Company to operate a new generation of modern buses on Sixteenth Street. For the first time, traditional streetcar service faced real competition. Among the features of the new buses were pneumatic tires, which significantly improved passenger comfort on paved roads, sharply contrasting with the hard metal wheels of streetcars screeching and grinding over their rails. The buses also had much more spacious and comfortable passenger compartments than their predecessors. In an advertisement in the *Evening Star*, the company boasted that its "[b]uses are of the latest type, well heated, lighted, and ventilated. Rattan seats, carrying two passengers each, with push buttons at each seat, with plenty of aisle room, and doors of sufficient width to permit comfortable exit and entrance."[136]

The new buses leapfrogged streetcars in efficiency as well as comfort. Since they could move to the curb for boarding and alighting, they eliminated the need for passengers to wait on narrow, crowded loading platforms in the middle of the street. They also were seen as helping to relieve traffic congestion because they could steer with the traffic around obstacles. Streetcars, in contrast, were wedded to fixed routes. All of the cars on a given line would quickly be brought to a stop if just one of them developed a problem and blocked the tracks. Given these advantages, few people questioned the idea that buses were technologically superior to streetcars.

The Washington Rapid Transit Company easily found patrons and grew quickly. It carried 750,000 passengers in its first six months of operation and frequently added new buses and routes thereafter. In September 1921, the *Washington Post* raved about the transit revolution:

> *The motor bus is rapidly coming into its own. This is an age of motor development. The past 20 years has brought into existence the motor car, the most useful and necessary invention of all time. The perfection of the automobile has brought rapid and safe transportation within the reach*

EARLY MASS TRANSIT IN WASHINGTON, D.C.

New buses of the Washington Rapid Transit Company are on display downtown on a rainy day in 1921. *Library of Congress.*

> *of rich and poor alike, and it can be truly said that the motor bus "has arrived." It occupies a secure place in urban passenger transit in the world's largest cities. Its popularity as a utility is attested by the throngs clamoring for seats, furnishing not only transportation, but the most inexpensive recreation in any city.*[137]

Rather than fight progress, streetcar companies embraced this futuristic new transit vehicle. Across the country, they began operating buses as a supplement to streetcar service. Bus lines could be inaugurated with little or no investment in infrastructure and were particularly useful on routes that were too sparsely patronized to be profitable as car lines. They might even improve streetcar profitability by bringing new customers to transfer points at the ends of existing routes.

Capital Traction and WRECo both started offering bus service in the early 1920s. They substituted buses on several less profitable streetcar routes, such as the extension of the Anacostia line to Randle Heights. In at least one case, bus service was added directly alongside an existing streetcar route when Capital Traction created a deluxe express bus service from Chevy Chase to downtown in 1925. The buses followed the same Connecticut Avenue route that had been graded and fitted with streetcar rails—at great expense—by the Rock Creek Railway in 1892. The elite new buses attracted customers willing to pay a premium to cut their commuting time and ride in comfort and style as they sped past the old-fashioned streetcars.

"A Consummation that Washington Has Desired for Years"

Merging the city's two streetcar companies—WRECo and Capital Traction—had been a goal for city officials for decades. One of the first moves toward consolidation had occurred in 1912, when an attempt was made to merge a raft of local street railway and electric utilities companies, including WRECo and several suburban streetcar lines and power companies, into what the *Sunday Star* called a "gigantic corporation," the Washington Utilities Company.[138] The ambitious scheme alarmed local officials and Congressional overseers, who feared the effects such a monopoly would have on the cost and quality of service. It is no coincidence that Congress created the Public Utilities Commission that same year. It also prohibited further consolidation of public utilities, including street railways, in the District of Columbia.[139]

This had left WRECo and Capital Traction frozen in place in the 1910s as competing companies. Much of the public saw them as very different entities. After WRECo's president, Clarence King, infamously crushed the transit union's attempt to win recognition in 1917, his company was seen as the city's "bad" streetcar company, offering inadequate service and treating its employees poorly. WRECo was responsible for many of the city's less-traveled streetcar routes, and it struggled to make money on them. Of the 160 miles of track it operated in 1916, over half were relatively lightly traveled suburban lines. With meager streetcar earnings, WRECo depended on income from its power company subsidiary, PEPCo, to stay profitable. In contrast, Capital Traction had the reputation of being the "good" streetcar company—well managed, profitable and offering excellent service. Capital Traction had a smaller system than WRECo, with more heavily patronized routes. Of the 57 miles of track it maintained in 1916, only 10 were "suburban" lines powered by overhead wires.[140] As a result, Capital Traction was consistently more profitable. Its management made a point of maintaining good relations both with its employees and the public.

EARLY MASS TRANSIT IN WASHINGTON, D.C.

A center-door streetcar waits at a platform on F Street in 1924. *Library of Congress.*

As long as it was profitable, Capital Traction had little incentive to merge with WRECo. It politely participated in merger talks with WRECo management, but little came of them. WRECo made a formal proposal for consolidation in 1918, but without active support from Capital Traction, nothing happened.

Circumstances changed, however, in the early 1920s. The end of World War I brought a renewed drop in patronage as government agencies downsized to peacetime levels. The rise of competition from automobiles and buses threatened both companies, making the protection of a larger holding company more desirable for Capital Traction. After the anti-merger law for street railways was repealed in 1925, efforts to combine Capital Traction and WRECo were redoubled.

The North American Company, a utilities holding company based in New Jersey, acquired the Washington Rapid Transit Company from its original D.C. investors that same year and also gained a controlling interest in WRECo. With these two properties in hand, it set its sights on adding

CAPITAL STREETCARS

A woman steps off a streetcar platform to avoid snow from a "sweeper" car cleaning the tracks on Pennsylvania Avenue in January 1923. *Library of Congress.*

Capital Traction to its transit empire. The company embarked on elaborate and complex negotiations over how the companies might be merged and what value should be placed on their assets. In 1928, a deal was hammered out that met the approval of the existing companies, their shareholders and the Public Utilities Commission; much to everyone's disappointment, however, it failed to win Congressional support.[141]

The onset of the Great Depression in 1929 added fresh urgency to the effort, and in early 1933, Congress finally approved the merger. All District of Columbia and suburban Maryland bus and streetcar companies were brought together as the new Capital Transit Company, and the North American Company retained a controlling interest in the firm. Everyone seemed relieved that the consolidation had finally taken place. "This is a consummation that Washington has desired for years," the *Washington Post* wrote.[142]

Thomas P. Littlepage, president of the Washington Chamber of Commerce, wrote to John Hanna, head of the new company, praising the merger: "The newly created Capital Transit Co. is launched at a most favorable time, and has a splendid opportunity to develop a coordinated mass transportation system which should be a model for other cities."[143]

Early Mass Transit in Washington, D.C.

In fact, the new company's outlook was not nearly so rosy. True, it had gained some valuable concessions—it would no longer have to pay for traffic cops to man all of the intersections traversed by streetcar lines or fund paving of sections of streets where its tracks lay—but it also faced formidable challenges.

While Washington was by no means the hardest-hit city in the nation, the Depression took a toll on area families and changed daily habits for many. Jobs dried up in the years before Franklin Roosevelt took office, reducing the commuter load on the streetcar lines. Housewives made fewer downtown shopping trips. The great movie palaces that had been built in the late 1920s—the Loew's Palace, the Earle and the stunning Fox (Capitol) Theater—still drew many patrons but faced increasing competition from radio, which kept people on a tight budget from venturing out for evening entertainment. Those who could afford to frequent the city's fancy Prohibition-era supper clubs—like Le Paradis on Thomas Circle, the Madrillon near the Treasury Department or the Lotus and Café Paree on Fourteenth Street—as often as not owned their own automobiles or rode in taxis.

Weak patronage meant that costs for the city's streetcar network continued to mount. In a vicious cycle, decreasing ridership meant that fares had to be

A Capital Traction streetcar is engulfed in automobile traffic at Seventeenth Street and Pennsylvania Avenue Northwest in this early 1920s photo. *Lee Rogers Collection, courtesy of the Maryland Rail Heritage Library.*

increased, which drove even more people away. In 1919, the traditional base fare of five cents per ride (extra for transfers), which had not changed for as long as anyone could remember, rose to seven cents, propelled by wartime inflation. Not long after, it went up again to eight cents. In 1929, after their first merger plan failed to win Congressional approval, Capital Traction and WRECo won approval to increase fares to ten cents, provoking outrage from a public that could little afford the increase and had long harbored resentment about the tyranny of the streetcar companies. When the new increase was first proposed in late 1928, the *Washington Herald* wrote that "[w]ith increased fares, the lines can continue independently gouging greater profits than ever out of the car-riders. Under a sane merger, the fare could be kept at 8 cents, overhead would be reduced, and perhaps some officials would lose their jobs."[144] The streetcar companies insisted that the increase was necessary. "We have practiced strict economy in operation," Capital Traction president John Hanna wrote in defense of the rise. "We have hoped and believed that the inroads of the private automobile would lessen. They have not."[145]

Automobiles—both private cars and taxicabs—were eating away at the streetcar business even more than buses. As the Depression deepened in the early 1930s, many workers who lost their jobs became taxi drivers. A price war among the glut of taxis in 1931 briefly drove taxi fares as low as ten cents—a private automobile ride for the same price as a crowded streetcar. The streetcar companies complained of the unfair competition but drew little sympathy from the public. "It is most pathetic the way they picture their so-called losses," one local resident wrote to the *Washington Post*. "It is time now for a showdown and it is up to the [street] car companies either to give the service to the public which they are charging for or to petition the [Public Utilities] commission for permission to return to the 5-cent fare, which is commensurate with the service they now give."[146]

Once established, the Capital Transit Company soon began consolidating lines. One of the first things it did in 1935 was to convert several major streetcar routes to bus service. One was the long Connecticut Avenue line that had been running express bus service alongside streetcars for ten years. There was surprisingly little contention about converting this line. Samuel C. Johnston, a city resident, was one outlier. In a letter to the editors of the *Post*, he warned that buses were no panacea. More of them were needed to handle the same number of passengers as streetcars, he argued, so congestion would actually be worsened, not improved. Further, buses polluted the air: "60 buses pouring out obnoxious fumes into the automobiles of those driving this route certainly is not going to add to the pleasure of driving nor to the health of those of us who have to take it."[147]

Others seemed less concerned about health risks. The *Post* reported that "residents along the new bus route were hailing the buses as a definite boon. Those who rode the 'cars' reported the trip downtown was much faster and

Motorman Tom Marshall peers at traffic from a streetcar on New York Avenue, circa 1936. *Library of Congress.*

smoother than before and those who don't ride said the buses were quieter than trolley cars." An avenue resident quipped that one of the old streetcars made more noise than a dozen of the new buses.[148] The verdict was in: people preferred buses.

Capital Transit likewise heard few complaints when it converted the six-mile-long Anacostia route—the same line that had been founded as the Anacostia & Potomac Railway and built up with such determination by Henry A. Griswold. Attorney William A. Roberts praised the conversion, stating that it would remove traffic hazards on the Anacostia Bridge and Nichols (Martin Luther King Jr.) Avenue, expand service in Congress Heights and achieve operational efficiencies.[149] Roberts served as the D.C. People's Counsel, a position created in 1926 to serve as advocate for the public before the Public Utilities Commission.

Other streetcar lines converted to bus operations in 1935 included a line serving Le Droit Park, which had begun as part of George Truesdell's Eckington & Soldiers Home Railway, as well as the suburban Maryland part of the Wisconsin Avenue line. After making numerous adjustments to other existing lines, Capital Transit announced in 1936 a comprehensive new system for designating streetcar and bus routes. The major streetcar lines were given numeric designations, such as the Route 40/42 series to Mount Pleasant, while bus lines were given a combination of alphabetic and numeric characters, such as the S2 service on Sixteenth Street. The same designation scheme remains in use today, although buses now serve all the routes.

"Quicker and Smoother than Most Automobiles"

Vehicle design evolved rapidly in the 1930s. Transportation designers began experimenting with stylish, Art Deco–inspired concepts that emphasized strong lines and sleek, fluid curves. "Streamlining," which celebrated industrial power and elegance, was the watchword of the day. Smooth finishes and sleek, bullet-like shapes were exhilarating and futuristic; everyone wanted them.

Streetcar industry executives hoped that a thoroughly modernized and streamlined vehicle might have a chance at winning back patrons who had concluded that the cars were transit dinosaurs. In 1929, the heads of twenty-nine streetcar companies from around the country agreed to form a committee, the Electric Railway Presidents' Conference Committee (PCC), to develop an all-new, technologically advanced streetcar that would be able to hold its own against competition from automobiles and buses and maybe even outdo them.

Engineers spent six years perfecting the new PCC design. Before it was finalized, early versions of the streamlined vehicle were produced in limited numbers. In 1935, Capital Transit acquired twenty of these prototypical cars for its main Pennsylvania Avenue line. They were advertised as "quicker and smoother than most automobiles" and featured "luxurious leather seats, improved lighting and ventilation."[150] Several were equipped with new wheels that contained a rubber lining insulating the metal outer rims from the inner wheels, making the ride significantly quieter and smoother. An *Evening Star* reporter tried out one of these "silent" streetcars and marveled that riders would be able to "carry on a normal-voice conversation, even while traveling over the roughest track or the bumpiest intersection."[151]

The first production version of the PCC car made its debut in New York in 1936. The *New York Times* admired its "sleek, boatlike exterior" and the "simplicity and cleanliness" of its interior.[152] In addition to the passenger comfort improvements, the cars featured other advances, including a set of four greatly improved fifty-horsepower motors that eliminated the

A new streamlined car takes on passengers in front of the Treasury Department on a summer day in 1935. *Library of Congress.*

sluggishness of older cars. New electromagnetic brakes improved stopping distances. Operators sat in seats and controlled the cars with their feet through pedal-mounted brakes and accelerators, just like buses and automobiles. This was a dramatic shift from the older streetcars, where motormen stood at the front and controlled the car entirely with hand-operated levers.

Capital Transit began introducing production PCC cars to its fleet in 1937, gradually bringing on large numbers of them through the early 1940s. The technologically advanced cars cost about $16,000 apiece—much more than previous models, which had run $5,000 in the 1920s. When they were introduced in August at the Peace Monument near the Capitol, the celebration recalled that of 1862, when the first streetcar rode on Pennsylvania Avenue. The *Evening Star* reported that the "$16,000 miracles" rolled proudly up the Fourteenth Street line, escorted by police motorcycles. Many dignitaries were on hand, including D.C. commissioner Melvin Hazen, who posed for the cameras at the controls of one of the cars. After reciting the advantages of the "sleek, silent creations," the *Star* reporter concluded that "best of all, a mere turn of a handle raises the window."[153]

The new cars required changes in operations to maximize their benefits. The performance advantages of the new cars would be lost if they were mixed in with older cars, so Capital Transit converted entire lines one at a time. The first line to shift to PCC service was the Fourteenth Street (Route

Capital Transit streetcar no. 1101, its first PCC car, sits parked outside the Navy Yard car barn in this 1937 photo. *National Capital Trolley Museum.*

50/54) line, followed by the popular Mount Pleasant line (Route 40/42) in 1938. Unlike older cars, PCC cars could only be operated from one end, so Capital Transit also had to install "loop" tracks at the end of its routes to allow the cars to turn around. Fitting out the electrical conduits for these loops was another expensive but unavoidable investment. As more cars were acquired and terminal loops constructed, additional routes were converted to PCC service. Eventually, all of Capital Transit's lines would use these cars.

In one sense, the PCC cars were a huge success. Capital Transit would ultimately acquire 489 of them, making for the third-largest fleet in the United States, after Chicago and Pittsburgh.[154] But this triumph of American engineering prowess was still just a streetcar, and it was unable to turn the tide away from buses and automobiles. A *Washington Post* editorial from 1935, just after the first streamlined cars hit D.C. streets, captured the prevailing sentiment:

> [T]*he new, pastel-green and slick-running street cars that have made their appearance in Washington…are vastly superior to their creaking predecessors, but still they do not seem to be the final solution to the District transportation problem. There is more hope of developing a modern transportation system in the pending plan to substitute buses on the northern reaches of Connecticut avenue.… [B]uses offer quiet, speed and comparative comfort.… It is some years now since the last "tram" was seen in the heart of either London or Paris. As well as in art galleries, we might seek to emulate the older capitals in transportation efficiency.*[155]

If the handwriting had not already been on the wall, it clearly was at this point, although not everyone was ready to consign streetcars to the scrap heap. They remained a highly efficient way to transport large numbers of people through densely traveled urban corridors. And they were soon to experience a sudden and dramatic—albeit brief—resurgence.

Chapter 9

WAR AND PEACE

THE WORLD WAR II YEARS AND AFTERWARD, 1940–1950

The World War II years and their aftermath were extraordinarily paradoxical for Capital Transit and other American streetcar companies. The war wreaked suffering and deprivation on many, but to Capital Transit it brought unprecedented patronage. As war workers swarmed into the city, ridership soared, reaching peaks that would never be equaled again. The decline that had pervaded the system since the 1920s completely vanished. And then, when the war ended, the reverse occurred. The nation at large experienced renewed growth and prosperity, while Capital Transit, like other streetcar companies, once again faced soaring costs and declining patronage. By 1949, when its parent company was compelled to sell out, the company was seized by corporate raiders and faced an uncertain future.

Ridership actually began increasing on Capital Transit in the late 1930s, when the Roosevelt administration dramatically increased government employment under the New Deal. An alphabet soup of government agencies set up shop around town, hiring thousands of new workers. The city's population grew 26 percent in the 1930s, from 486,869 in 1930 to 663,091 in 1940. Federal employment alone grew 22 percent in 1939 and another 27 percent in 1940, all before the influx of wartime workers.[156]

By 1940, Washington was preparing for a war it knew the country would eventually join. Thousands of men lined up at local elementary and high schools to register for the draft. After Pearl Harbor, gun emplacements were established on and around government buildings, and air raid sirens wailed

Early Mass Transit in Washington, D.C.

Streetcars compete with automobiles on Fifteenth Street alongside the Treasury Department in July 1936. *Library of Congress.*

across the city as drills were held. Blackout shades were fitted into windows in homes, businesses and public buildings alike, striving to make the city less of a target in the event of an attack. The already sprawling "temporary" Navy and Munitions Building near the Washington Monument, left over from World War I, was overwhelmed with new employees, and additional tempos were soon built lining the Mall. Ordinary people opened unused rooms in

Noted photographer Esther Bubley captured this scene in March 1943 of non-rush hour riders on the 40 line headed to Lincoln Park. *Library of Congress.*

their homes to newly arriving war workers, and everybody struggled with rationing, which drastically limited the consumption of gasoline, rubber, certain types of food and other commodities.

Capital Transit was swamped with riders, more than it could possibly accommodate. Private automobiles, dependent as they were on scarce gasoline and rubber tires, were no longer a viable option for most commuters, who turned back to streetcars. Because streetcar transportation was vital to the war effort, manufacturers were allowed to continue producing limited numbers of new PCC cars, despite the fact that virtually all other vehicle

Early Mass Transit in Washington, D.C.

A young boy rides on one of Capital Transit's new PCC cars in this April 1943 photo by Esther Bubley. *Library of Congress*.

manufacturing plants around the country were converted to strictly military use. Cities competed for the right to buy the cars, and Washington fared well. Although it had asked for even more, Capital Transit was allowed to acquire 66 new PCC cars in 1942, 141 in 1944 and another 50 in 1945.[157] The new cars helped, but even with all of them on the streets, most were overcrowded, especially in rush hour.

Buses offered little relief. In April 1942, the government ordered bus service reduced by up to 20 percent. Operating hours were staggered, stops eliminated and the use of charter and school buses sharply curtailed. Joseph B. Eastman, director of the Office of Defense Transportation, wrote that the new policy was "determined almost entirely by the stoppage of rubber imports and the desperate need of conserving all the rubber now in our possession. Waste of rubber tires under present conditions is little short of disloyalty to the national interest."[158]

"The Company Prefers Huskiness"

A greater wartime challenge for Capital Transit was in maintaining an adequate workforce. Large numbers of motormen and conductors left to join the military. Of the 2,881 motormen, conductors and streetcar operators on the rolls in January 1942, 1,172 left the company that year. While 980 replacements were found, more employees left in the coming two years, including 1,937 in 1944.[159]

Washington's streetcar operators and conductors had always been white males, and disrupting that racist and sexist tradition was not easy, even with wartime pressures. During World War I, some thought had been given to temporarily hiring women as conductors on streetcars—it had been done in other American cities—but Washington was too conservative in 1917 for such a bold leap. World War II, in contrast, finally gave women their chance.

The first female Capital Transit employee to operate a streetcar was Helen Blau, who quietly joined the company ranks in October 1942. "Shattering all precedents of the Capital Transit Co., a young lady has been seriously going through the processes of learning to operate streetcars in the District for the past 10 days," the *Evening Star* reported with astonishment.[160] At the time, company president Edward D. Merrill (1885–1984) assured reporters that the whole thing was just an experiment, that Blau was only operating empty streetcars during off hours and that there were positively no plans to have women operating in-service streetcars in the District.

Merrill's comments were disingenuous; just five days later, the company announced that it was indeed hiring women and that it planned to have them on the job within just a few months. As reported by the *Washington Post*, the company stressed that it wanted women of a certain physical type: "Strong-arm women who've done the family wash without muscle pain and who've driven trucks" were desired. "Physique is important. The company prefers huskiness: ages between 25 and 35 years are desirable. If the applicant is married her chances are better."

It was these strong recruits who formed the Women's Auxiliary Transit Service (WATS), Capital Transit's answer to the WACS and WAVES then

Early Mass Transit in Washington, D.C.

Hattie B. Sheehan, a WATS employee, gets training as a streetcar operator in this June 1943 photo by Esther Bubley. *Library of Congress*.

joining the military. Among the early recruits were Dorothy Berlett and Betty Whitehurst, who started training runs in January 1943 and became the public face of the new service. As they were introduced to the press, Berlett and Whitehurst endured a barrage of patronizing questions by journalists, who seemed much more interested in their supposed feminine frailties than their actual skills in handling the cars. Asked if she would be ready to respond to any "wise cracks" from passengers, Whitehurst cheerfully replied that she "didn't work as a waitress for 11 years for nothing."[161]

Woman-operated streetcars began appearing during rush hour in March 1943, and there were no indications that the women had to weather any

The versatile Hattie B. Sheehan is seen here working as a conductor. *Library of Congress.*

unusual harassment. Nor did any of them become flustered and break into tears, as some feared would happen. By July, thirty-five women were operating streetcars and buses, including the first husband-and-wife streetcar team of operator and conductor (the wife was the operator). "Some passengers, mostly nervous women, have gotten off buses and streetcars after discovering women were operating them but now, after a couple of months, they all stay and seem to be at ease," the *Star* observed.[162]

As many as 77 women worked streetcars and buses during the war years, but this represented only a fraction of the workforce of more than 1,700. Most left their jobs at the end of the war as male operators and conductors with greater seniority returned to Capital Transit. Just a handful—fewer than 10—stayed on through the 1950s into the early 1960s.[163]

Early Mass Transit in Washington, D.C.

"Domestic Fascism"

While women gained a toehold in the male-dominated Capital Transit Company, African Americans faced a much tougher battle. Blacks could ride with whites on streetcars, but none had ever served as motormen or conductors. Some lines—such as the 90/92 on U Street, the 60 on Eleventh Street and the 10/12 on Benning Road—served predominantly African American patrons, linking black residential and commercial areas with downtown, yet the cars were always driven by white men. Capital Transit employed hundreds of African Americans in menial positions, primarily maintenance and custodial work, but barred them from "platform" jobs—operating streetcars and buses. Black workers kept the cars in good working order and maintained the underground conduits that powered them but were denied the ability to operate them outside of maintenance yards.[164]

In 1941, labor leader A. Philip Randolph, working with Mary McLeod Bethune, president of the National Council of Negro Women, and NAACP secretary Walter White, planned a mass march on Washington to end job discrimination. The march of fifty thousand people down Pennsylvania Avenue was planned for July 1 but never took place. President Franklin Roosevelt was determined to keep the march from happening, and in exchange for calling it off, he issued an executive order at the end of June establishing the Fair Employment Practice Committee (FEPC) to investigate cases of discrimination in wartime hiring. The committee had little enforcement power, was poorly funded and was seen as largely ineffective, but for activists like Randolph, it could be a tool to raise awareness of discriminatory hiring and put pressure on companies to change their practices.

By the following year, the wartime manpower shortage had become acute, and the injustice of Capital Transit's refusal to hire African Americans to fill its pressing need for operators and conductors fueled renewed outrage. Local African American leaders formed a Committee on Jobs for Negros in Public Utilities, which petitioned President Merrill to change the company's policy. When he refused, the committee took the matter to the FEPC, which in November ordered Capital Transit to employ African Americans equitably in all positions within the company.

As a consummate technocrat, Merrill was perhaps not the kind of leader best suited to address this problem. Born in Des Moines, Iowa, he earned an engineering degree from the Massachusetts Institute of Technology and first worked as a civil engineer for the Union Pacific Railway. He served in streetcar companies in Seattle, Philadelphia and Chicago before coming to

CAPITAL TRANSIT CO.
NEEDS MEN

TOP PAY – PLENTY OF WORK

NO EXPERIENCE NECESSARY
TRAINING PAID FOR

★ STREETCAR –BUS OPERATORS

21-60 Years of Age
Draft Deferred

Must be in good health, have good vision and be free from color blindness; 5 feet 6 inches to 6 feet 2 inches in weight and weight in proportion (about 140 to 225 pounds); good moral character and a clear record of past employment essential. Motor vehicle operator's permit necessary.

PART-TIME WORK

★ STREETCAR –BUS OPERATORS

21-60 Years of Age
Draft Deferred

Must be able to report for work weekdays between 6 a. m. and 8 a. m. and then work for 2 or 3 hours.

Also need some men who are able to report for work between 3 p. m. and 4:30 p. m. and then work several hours. For other requirements see advertisement.

APPLY IN PERSON WEEKDAY MORNINGS

CAPITAL TRANSIT CO.

36th Street and Prospect Avenue N.W.

Take Route No. 20 "Cabin John" Streetcar

This Capital Transit advertisement appeared in the *Washington Post* in December 1942.

Early Mass Transit in Washington, D.C.

Washington in 1926 to head the Washington Rapid Transit Company. After taking over as president of Capital Transit in 1937, he had been widely admired as a prudent and capable leader.

But Merrill never complied with the FEPC order to end discrimination. Instead, he presided over a prolonged campaign of delays, excuses and intransigence. In asking for a postponement of the order, the company argued that compliance would be disastrous because white employees would refuse to work if African Americans were hired, crippling transit service in Washington. Then, at a large employee meeting in December, Merrill appeared to change his mind, stating that the company would follow the order and hire black motormen and bus drivers. Black newspapers around the country celebrated the news, but it turned out to be a mirage.[165] As predicted, white motormen and conductors bitterly opposed hiring of blacks, threatening to walk off the job. "We'll fight side by side with 'n……s' but we won't work side by side with them," one worker reportedly yelled during a contentious meeting of the Amalgamated Transit Union.[166] Merrill then backed away from his commitment.

Capital Transit's unwillingness to carry out the FEPC order, either because it did not want African Americans operating its vehicles or because it was incapable of standing up to the threats of its employees, increasingly made the company appear incapable of controlling its own workforce. The company made a feeble attempt to hire a few black workers in February 1943, when it brought on Bernard Simmons, an experienced chauffeur, as a motorman trainee. However, none of the instructors at the Benning Car Barn was willing to take Simmons as a student, and the company apparently never pushed any of them to do so. Simmons was told that the best the company could do was offer him a job as a janitor (he declined).

The push for equal opportunity at Capital Transit peaked in May 1943, when labor groups organized a large protest rally that was attended by civil rights leaders and several top D.C. government officials. A march of more than eight hundred protesters began in the heart of black Washington at Tenth and U Streets Northwest and proceeded to Franklin Park downtown, where rousing speeches were given. Major Edward J. Kelly, superintendent of police, joined the group, as did District Commissioner John Russell Young. Representative Vito Mercantonio of New York, a popular socialist firebrand, stirred up the crowd by declaring that race segregation and discrimination were "domestic Fascism" and must be stamped out.[167]

Despite the drama of the rally, it did little to change Capital Transit's policy. In January 1945, President Merrill testified that he was "embarrassed

Protestors marched in May 1943 to demand that African Americans be hired as streetcar and bus operators. *D.C. Public Library, Star Collection,* © Washington Post.

and humiliated" by his inability to comply with the FEPC order, fearing, as he claimed, the repercussions if white workers walked off the job en masse. Yet later that year, Capital Transit workers did just that, striking for higher wages and shutting the system down for more than a day until President Truman temporarily seized the company to get the streetcars and buses running again. The *Washington Post* commented wryly on the fact that Capital Transit had previously "asserted in highly moral tones" that it could not hire African American streetcar and bus operators "because to do so might precipitate a strike by white employees afflicted with race prejudice." And yet faced with demands for higher wages, the company "has shown no hesitation about challenging the intransigency of its employees." As a result, "the unthinkable interruption of public transportation is now in progress."[168] If anything was an embarrassment for Capital Transit, this should have been.

But bad press was nothing new, and it was certainly not enough to change the status quo. In fact, for nine more years, the company continued to refer to the 1943 Simmons incident as "proof" that hiring African Americans was impractical and that whites would walk off the job in droves if it were to occur. The intransigence was finally broken only after other racial barriers started to fall. "Discrimination has been broken down in theaters, restaurants and a host of other public activities," the *Post* wrote in February 1954. "The transit policy is lagging behind the community attitude, and there is every indication that the community would support a change and the improvements it would permit in transit operations."[169]

By January 1955, when Capital Transit was facing other serious problems (more on these in the next chapter), its management agreed to end the discrimination policy. Likewise under new leadership, the transit union also consented to the change. With little fanfare, the first handful of African Americans began operating streetcars and buses in March. There was no white backlash; not a single white employee walked off the job. A turning point had been reached, although the numbers of black transit operators would remain low for at least another decade.

Cutting the "Fat"

With the end of the war in 1945 came a gradual return to the city's peacetime norm, and the broader social trends that had been interrupted by the war soon returned. More than ever, the American dream was to have a spacious house in the suburbs and at least one automobile in the garage. As new home construction mushroomed in the late 1940s and early 1950s, more and more of it was unreachable by streetcar. For the first time since the Civil War, large numbers of Washingtonians didn't consider streetcar transportation essential to their daily lives.

Capital Transit spent much of 1946 restoring service that had been cut during the war due to manpower and materiel shortages, including non-rush hour streetcars and buses. Bringing service back to normal also meant addressing deferred upkeep on a sprawling network of tracks and underground conduits, which had always been difficult and expensive to maintain.

The conduit system had fulfilled its objective of keeping overhead wires out of downtown Washington, just as the *Evening Star*'s Crosby S. Noyes had so fervently advocated, but there had always been a substantial cost to pay for that luxury. In addition to the usual grinding and screeching of metal wheels on metal rails, Washington's streetcars were equipped with plows whose metal shoes clattered noisily as they rode over the iron conductor rails under the streets, especially at intersections, where they banged over gaps in the rails. Two cars approaching an intersection from opposite directions could make quite a racket.

All sorts of mishaps could result in a streetcar's plow being "pulled" from its fittings, causing the car to stall and block traffic on that line until the problem was resolved. Summer heat could cause the narrow slot in the middle of the tracks to pinch, which could pull the plow. So could an ice build-up in winter or even trash that worked its way into the slot. A loose plow would have to be freed from its jam and removed from the conduit, using the access panels that were positioned at frequent intervals along the tracks. Workers would attach a new plow to the car, or if it was in bad shape, the car might be towed to a car barn to have its plow reattached. The danger of such mishaps required a constant effort to clean and maintain the tracks and conduits, which posed endless headaches for service personnel.[170]

A classic example occurred one January day in 1948, when a broken fragment of automobile tire chain got caught in the slot of the streetcar tracks at the end of the Mount Pleasant line. The chain broke the plow off two streetcars as they reached the end of their rush hour run and turned around to return downtown. The *Evening Star* reported "shivering patrons, late for work, crowded the loading platforms" on Lamont Street, while workers struggled in the cold to replace the plows. They thought that they had things fixed when a third car's plow was also shorn off by a piece of the chain they hadn't noticed deep in the conduit. "It took an hour to straighten things out again," the *Star* reported.[171]

Pulled plows were nothing new, but the financial challenges of the postwar era were unprecedented. Inflation took a substantial toll on the company, which found itself exacerbating its problems by requesting multiple fare increases, the base fare rising from ten cents in 1947 to thirteen cents in 1948 and fifteen cents in 1950. The cycle of higher fares and fewer patrons inevitably led to significant service cuts. In January 1948, President Merrill put the best face on it he could, writing in the *Washington Post* that "in order to financially survive the 'squeeze' of higher wages and other costs which occurred in 1947, we have had to cut the 'fat' which existed in some operations and more nearly bring them in line with the traffic needs."[172]

The biggest of these service cuts was a plan to convert the 10/12 route, known as the Benning line, to buses. This was the former Columbia Railway on H Street Northeast, one of the oldest streetcar routes in the city and still the fourth-busiest line in 1946, when its partial elimination was first proposed. Although heavily traveled, the track on this route was old, not

EARLY MASS TRANSIT IN WASHINGTON, D.C.

A PCC car on route 92 travels along Eighth Street Northeast in 1949. *Author's collection.*

well configured to accommodate PCC cars and took up too much room on the narrow and congested road.[173]

The Public Utilities Commission at first denied Capital Transit's request to convert the Benning line, alarmed that such an important line would be slated for decommissioning. Like most city officials, the commissioners still saw streetcars as the "backbone" of mass transit and the best fit for the city's most densely traveled corridors. But Capital Transit's lawyers countered with a long list of reasons why the Benning line should be converted, and the Public Utilities Commission eventually relented. The cars finally stopped running on May 1, 1949. Despite notices in the mail and on buses and streetcars, some patrons still could be found standing on New York Avenue the following morning, patiently waiting—in vain—for the cars that had plied that route for more than seventy years.

Despite the declines in ridership and cutbacks in service, the city's streetcar system remained one of the best in the country. Thanks to the purchase of large numbers of PCC cars in the early 1940s, Capital Transit was well equipped with a modern fleet, and the company made prudent investments to improve their efficiency and reliability. Perhaps the most notable improvement, however, was not a Capital Transit initiative. It was the construction by the District government in the late 1940s of an elaborate underpass beneath Dupont Circle to streamline both automobile traffic and streetcar service along Connecticut Avenue.

With three major avenues (Connecticut, Massachusetts and New Hampshire) converging on two other cross streets (Nineteenth and P), Dupont Circle was a perennial traffic bottleneck. Matters were made worse by the fact that streetcar tracks ran around only the west side of the circle, resulting in northbound streetcars running disconcertingly against the flow of automobile traffic.[174] City highway officials sought to both ease traffic congestion and eliminate the dangerous streetcar routing by building an underpass to carry Connecticut Avenue beneath the circle.

The mammoth project was first proposed in 1937 but ran into opposition from area merchants and property owners. When the plan was revived in 1941, it still faced the opposition of one of the neighborhood's most powerful denizens, Eleanor "Cissy" Patterson (1884–1948), publisher of the *Washington Herald*. As the traffic problems mounted and the need for the underpass became more pressing, Patterson, whose mansion was on the quieter east side of the circle, dug in her heels. In 1947, when construction was imminent, she wrote an editorial for the *Herald* that criticized the planned underpass as "a regular rabbit warren of auto tunnels, street car

Progress of construction of the Dupont Circle underpass in July 1949, as seen from the south. *D.C. Department of Transportation.*

tunnels, pedestrian tunnels and underground as well as above-ground traffic experiments. We think that is bunk and expensive bunk as well."[175]

With Patterson's complaints drowned out by a chorus of local and federal officials supporting the project, construction began in the spring of 1948

An aerial view of the completed Dupont Circle underpass taken in 1958. At the bottom of the picture, two streetcars can be seen on the underpass's northern ramp. *D.C. Department of Transportation.*

(Patterson died from a heart attack that summer) and took almost two years to complete. The complex underpass consisted of two automobile tunnels in the center, surrounded by two separate tunnels for streetcars. The streetcar tunnels were constructed first, with temporary tracks running across the middle of the circle at street level. Once the streetcar tunnels were finished, the temporary tracks were removed and the automobile tunnels were built through the center and covered over. The enormous complex stretched five blocks, from N Street to S Street, and cost almost $5 million.

While the automobile tunnels weren't complete until early 1950, the streetcar tunnels had gone into service the previous fall. *Washington Post* reporter Mary Van Rensselaer Thayer was there to record the first run, when veteran operator Howard Norford was at the controls of PCC car no. 1550. As it stopped at the underground station for press photographers to take note, everyone tried to get Norford to smile. According to Thayer, he "unbent the tiniest fraction." Then, "with a triumphant ding-dang-ding-DANG he gave No. 1550 the gas and we whizzed along, the underground platform glittering with pearly tiles bordered in sapphire blue, station names lettered with handsome legibility in silver."[176] Patrons of the 40/42 line were universally pleased with the new tunnels. Streetcar trips through the circle were cut by several minutes, and congestion was significantly reduced.

Forced Listening

It was around this same time that Capital Transit embarked on a brief and ultimately unsuccessful experiment with FM radio broadcasts on its streetcars and buses. The odd venture was seen as a potential source of much-needed extra income for the company, but it turned out to inflame the emotions of streetcar riders much more than Capital Transit had bargained for.

It began in 1948, after "transit radio," as it was called, had been tried in several other American cities. In March, Ben Strouse, manager of local radio station WWDC, proposed installing FM radio receivers and loudspeakers in each of Capital Transit's buses and streetcars. To gain a new set of captive listeners, the radio station was willing to foot the $175 cost of fitting out each vehicle, as well as pay $6 per vehicle per month to Capital Transit. Strouse was optimistic that streetcar riders would enjoy the new service. "We'll give them something between jive and symphony—popular classical music," he told the *Evening Star*. "Commercials won't be more than 30 seconds long and we won't use more than one commercial every five minutes."[177]

Capital Transit approached the idea cautiously, trying it out on a bus on Connecticut Avenue and polling customers for their reactions. About 95 percent of riders liked the piped-in music, and subsequent surveys confirmed broad support for the "music as you ride" service. So the company decided to move forward with it in February 1949, when the first of several hundred Capital Transit buses and streetcars fitted with radio sets began serenading riders through the streets of the city. A *Washington Post* reporter confirmed that passengers were largely positive about the new service, although the enthusiasm was not unbridled. "This will make you forget your troubles," said Perry F. Scott, a Maryland businessman. District housewife Dorothy Hall said that she liked to listen to the music when she wasn't talking and suggested that "some hill-billy music twice a week" be featured. "It's cheerful and it makes the ride seem shorter," said Mary Rogers, a housewife from Southeast.[178]

Although opponents were supposedly fewer, they were far more vocal. *Evening Star* nightlife commentator Harry MacArthur voiced strong concerns as early as March 1948, when the first test bus hit the streets: "A pox on both of you, C.T.C. [Capital Transit Company] and WWDC-FM. This is an inhuman invasion of privacy. A man has every right to listen to the radio, all right, but a man also has a right to not listen to the radio, as your apartment house manager will tell you if your neighbor complains. Radios in the buses, indeed. Is there to be no right to life, liberty, and the pursuit of happiness around here?"[179]

Commercial advertising had been displayed in public transit vehicles since the nineteenth century with few complaints, but passengers weren't obliged to look up at the advertisements. As MacArthur's comments suggest, the outrage that ensued over "music as you ride" was based on the fact that riders had no way of keeping the audio barrage from entering their heads. Objectors felt that their rights were being violated, and they soon organized a Transit Riders Association to fight the "racket while you ride."[180] Based on their complaints, the PUC held a hearing on transit radio in October 1949 attended by dozens of opponents who aired a wide range of concerns. "What's to stop a bus company from conniving with the Democrats, the Republicans, the Socialists or the Communists to bombard us with propaganda all day and all night?" one rider asked.[181] The PUC, however, was not convinced. It ruled that transit radio posed no safety hazard and was "not inconsistent with" public convenience and comfort.

Opponents responded by redoubling their attacks. The renamed National Citizens Committee Against Forced Reading and Forced Listening brought suit against Capital Transit, arguing that "forced listening" was unconstitutional. The case eventually made its way to the Supreme Court, which ruled against the petitioners in May 1952, stating that due process had not been violated and that the music programs did not transgress free speech. The victory for transit radio proved to be short-lived, however, as WWDC and Capital Transit reached a mutual agreement a year later to end the service, which WWDC found unprofitable. Wary of the intense opposition that had developed while the court case was being heard, advertisers had been reluctant to take advantage of the service. "The experiment all in all proved to be a mistake from the standpoint of public relations as well as profit making," the *Evening Star* concluded. "The transit company and Radio Station WWDC-FM were wise in calling the whole business off."[182]

Kid Wolf

Meanwhile, 1949—the year the transit radio experiment began and the Dupont Circle underpass opened—marked the beginning of a profound and ultimately destructive change in how Capital Transit was managed. This happened when the company's owner, the North American Company, was forced to sell out. North American had been subsidizing the firm with income from its highly profitable PEPCo subsidiary, which supplied the streetcars' power. The symbiotic relationship of electric power and streetcar companies had been crucial to the viability of many of the country's privately owned streetcar systems, including Capital Transit. Nevertheless, in 1939, Congress put an end to all that by passing the Public Utility Holding Company Act, which prohibited holding companies from owning both power and transit companies. By the late 1940s, the North American Company could no longer put off divesting its holdings in one or the other firm, and it naturally chose to stick with the profitable electric company. This left Capital Transit in need of a new owner.

Although Capital Transit's operating expenses exceeded its income, it still had sizable cash reserves that had been accumulated during the war. Company management considered these reserves an important financial cushion, but to outsiders, they looked like ripe fruit when the company came up for sale. The company's board of directors was also aware of this vulnerability but inexplicably failed to take action. The directors considered using part of the cash reserves to buy back North American's stock. Their attorneys reviewed the scheme and assured them that it would be perfectly legal, yet they didn't act. A prominent local real estate investor, H. Grady Gore, then tried to buy the stock himself, but he couldn't line up the resources to purchase it all; North American refused to sell him only a part of its holdings.[183] With other local investors and banks declining to step forward because of the bleak long-term outlook for public transit, the stage was set for a wealthy Florida investor, Louis Elwood Wolfson (1912–2007), to step in and do what he did best.

Wolfson was yet another in the long line of entrepreneurs who has had an outsized influence on mass transportation in the nation's capital. He wasn't a native of Washington and lived in the city only briefly after he gained control of Capital Transit. He was a financial tycoon, one of the nation's first big-time corporate raiders. He ran the numbers on acquiring Capital Transit, noting the cash reserves of $7.5 million and the fact that he could gain control of the company for much less than that—about $2.2 million. He decided to pounce.

Wolfson had been born in St. Louis, Missouri, to Lithuanian immigrant parents. He grew up in Jacksonville, Florida, where his hardworking father ran a business collecting scrap metal and shipping it overseas at a profit. From an early age, Wolfson developed the personality of a fighter. He boxed under the name "Kid Wolf" as a teenager and was a star football player in high school, winning an athletic scholarship to the University of Georgia. He played varsity football and took courses in banking and finance but left after injuring his shoulder while making a tackle in the 1931 Yale Bowl. He returned to Jacksonville, borrowed $10,000 and, with one of his brothers, started the Florida Pipe & Supply Company, a construction supply firm.[184]

Wolfson was said to have gotten his first big break when he managed to buy plumbing fixtures from the son of department store magnate J.C. Penney for $275 and resold them piecemeal for $100,000. As his company prospered, Wolfson's talent for buying undervalued assets and selling them for big profits became his forte. His most notable early deal was the purchase from the federal government in 1946 of the St. John's River Shipbuilding Company, a facility no longer needed at the end of the war. Bidders on the facility all assumed that they had to continue operating it, as the Federal Maritime Commission had initially required, and their offers accordingly were low. But in a second round of bidding the requirement was inadvertently dropped, and Wolfson jumped in and placed the winning bid. He proceeded to dismantle the shipyard and sell its assets at a substantial profit. There were allegations of wrongdoing and a Congressional investigation, but Wolfson had not broken any law.

With his reputation as a corporate raider already established, Wolfson and a group of his associates offered in June 1949 to buy out North American's

The group that bought Capital Transit: Jack Surarky, E.B. Gerhert, Cecil Wolfson, Louis E. Wolfson and John A.B. Broadwater, photographed in September 1949. *D.C. Public Library, Star Collection,* © *Washington Post.*

controlling interest in Capital Transit for twenty dollars per share. Although there were no competing offers, Wolfson's bid still needed approval from both the Interstate Commerce Commission and the Securities and Exchange Commission. With an eye toward winning approval, Wolfson promised that he wouldn't make any major changes in the company's management. "We have no idea of changing the operating policy of the company," he declared in Jacksonville. "It has always been our ambition to participate in the interest of the company whose management renders such an efficient and useful service to the public."[185]

ICC examiner Vernon Baker held a hearing in July and subsequently recommended strongly that Wolfson and his cronies not be allowed to buy Capital Transit, arguing that they were not local (as the company's charter envisioned), had no experience in transit and that the sale would not be in the public interest. However, the ICC overruled his recommendation and approved the sale. Despite further protests from other shareholders, the SEC likewise approved the sale in September, and it was quickly closed before anyone else could mount serious opposition. The die had been cast.

Chapter 10

ENDGAME

WASHINGTON'S STREETCARS DISAPPEAR, 1950–1962

When Louis Wolfson and his associates took over Capital Transit in 1949, the city's streetcar system had just thirteen more years to live, although nobody knew it at the time. It would not have been shocking news. Streetcar systems had been contracting or shutting down altogether in cities across the country since the 1930s. From 1947 to 1949 alone, streetcar operations had ended in Atlanta, Memphis, Norfolk, Richmond, San Diego, Phoenix and Manhattan. Many more would close in the 1950s. Until this point, Washington's system had been considered one of the more modern and efficient, thanks in large part to Capital Transit's conservative business practices and its heavy investment in new PCC cars before and during the war years. But times were changing, and the company was in for a rough ride.

The vicious cycle of service cuts, fare increases and plummeting ridership continued in 1950, but with a new twist. The Public Utilities Commission allowed the company to raise its base fare from thirteen to fifteen cents and to make cuts in streetcar service on a variety of lines after it reported that net earnings had dropped 67 percent from the previous year. The need for the fare hike, which went into effect in July, was not unexpected, but what happened next was a surprise. In August, the Wolfson-controlled board of directors suddenly doubled the company's quarterly dividend from fifty cents to a dollar per share.[186] The move raised many eyebrows; if the company was in such desperate straits that it needed a fare hike, as it claimed, how could it also be distributing record dividends? "The July earnings statement of Capital Transit will be released next week. Local financial circles are

A posed publicity photo from the late 1940s shows riders boarding a Capital Transit streetcar at the Rosslyn loop on the Virginia side of Key Bridge. *D.C. Public Library, Washingtoniana Division.*

awaiting its figures to see how the transformation from rags to riches came about," the *Washington Post*'s S. Oliver Goodman wrote with dry sarcasm.[187] The July statement indeed showed a slight rebound due to the fare hike, but earnings were still down from the previous year and certainly didn't justify a doubling of dividends.

At the very least, it was bad form to extract higher fares from patrons and immediately deposit the new income in shareholders' pockets. And this was just the first of many actions the company's new management took that estranged regulators and the public alike. Wolfson's next move was to petition for a four-to-one stock split, angering both the PUC and the ICC. Stock splits, of course, are normally associated with rapidly growing, highly prosperous corporations, not declining transit firms. Yet the price of Capital Transit stock had been soaring, doubling in value from late 1949 to late 1950, as investors rushed to join Wolfson in draining Capital Transit of its cash reserves. In January 1951, ICC examiners wrote that Wolfson's proposed stock split was "unlawful, unreasonable, arbitrary, capricious and unsupported by substantial evidence." Rather than providing real value, the ICC saw it as "a speculative device to increase market prices temporarily and thereby enhance the opportunities of present stockholders to dispose of some or all of their holdings at a profit."[188] Unfortunately, closer study revealed that regulators had no legal basis to oppose the split, no matter how badly it sat with them. In late 1951, the stock split was approved.

By then, Wolfson and his associates had taken over all the top executive positions in the company, as well as almost all the seats on the board of directors, despite Wolfson's earlier pledge that he would stay on the sidelines. In April 1951, the company's longtime president and board chairman, Edward D. Merrill—an efficient technocrat who had persevered with the new owners for more than a year—finally stepped down. His replacement as president, John A.B. Broadwater, was one of Wolfson's closest associates but had no transit experience. Neither, of course, did Wolfson, who became board chair. Top executive salaries were also substantially hiked.

Wolfson moved his family to Washington in late 1950, settling into a spacious mansion in the well-to-do Forest Hills neighborhood. Having done so, he was able to claim in a January 1952 open letter that "[w]e are particularly proud of the fact that today, for the first time in many years, Capital Transit Company has become a predominantly Washington owned and managed enterprise."[189] It's unclear who, if anyone, was swayed by that disingenuous statement, but it soon didn't matter. Wolfson left the city later that same year, returning to Florida.

Meanwhile, the massive investor cash-out continued. On top of the higher regular dividends the company started paying in 1951, in January 1952 it declared an additional special dividend of $2.50 per share (the equivalent of $10.00 per share before the stock split), an extraordinary windfall for investors. While the splitting of this financial "melon" met with widespread dismay, the chairman of the PUC sheepishly explained to the public that it was all perfectly legal. The money being tapped for the dividends was in accounts that could legitimately be distributed to shareholders. As if to rub salt in the wounds of the public, just three days later the PUC agreed to another fare increase, this time affecting the widely used weekly passes.

With the PUC appearing unable or unwilling to harness the excesses of the Wolfson gang, outraged congressmen soon stepped into the fray, ordering their own investigations into the company's finances. Representative Fred L. Crawford (1888–1957) of Michigan fired off a letter to the chairman of the PUC demanding an explanation. "Information comes to me that the Florida interests which purchased CTC are milking the property at the expense of those citizens of the Metropolitan Area who are compelled to go about their business by means of CTC transportation."[190] He urged his

Gibson Crockett drew this cartoon that appeared on the front page of the *Evening Star* on March 2, 1952. *D.C. Public Library, Star Collection,* © *Washington Post.*

Senate colleagues to likewise investigate the "monkey business" at Capital Transit. His colleague, James C. Auchincloss (1885–1976) of New Jersey, called Capital Transit's actions "little short of ridiculous."[191]

Multiple investigations by the PUC and Congress were soon underway, but the company's management continued to drain its coffers. The handsome $1.00 regular quarterly dividend was bumped to $1.40 and then $1.60 over the next few years. Operating profits, when there were any, were never enough to cover these payouts. The money came from the cash reserves that had accumulated over the war years, accounts that Wolfson clearly had set his sights on from the beginning.

Given the Wolfson team's unapologetic profit taking, observers wondered if they were deliberately trying to alienate Capital Transit's overseers. Relentlessly pushing the PUC to grant ever more fare hikes—the base fare climbed to seventeen cents in 1952 and twenty cents in 1954—company officials nevertheless remained dissatisfied with the increases they received, complaining vociferously that they needed more and more. At the same time, they fought all attempts by the transit union to win higher wages for workers. Whenever the PUC granted wage increases for transit workers, the company demanded new fare hikes to cover the cost so that the profit stream would be untouched. The company's stranglehold on the PUC, its own workers and the riding public seemed unbreakable. An anonymous transit rider wrote to the *Evening Star* in April 1953, pleading, "Please, citizens of Washington and the Metropolitan Area, can't something be done to save us all and the Capital Transit Co. from the money-mad Wolfsons?"[192]

That same year, President John Broadwater testified that if the company weren't allowed to make a 7.5 percent profit, the entire operation would have to be turned over to the government. Most observers took this threat as a cue that Wolfson and his gang were getting ready to abandon ship. The *Washington Post* editorialized that "[t]he milking operations of the Capital Transit Co. took a spurt forward yesterday.... It is no longer possible to avoid the conclusion that the owners of CTC are stripping away its assets with the object of dumping an unprofitable wreckage on the city."[193]

The PUC, under pressure to stand up to the Wolfson group, retaliated in 1954 by obtaining a court injunction keeping Capital Transit from issuing another large dividend. At last, the investigations, court cases and other legal actions were finally catching up with the company. Its executives signed an agreement with the PUC in August whereby it would not ask for another fare hike before 1955 and would take steps to start hiring African Americans as operators. In return, it would be allowed to issue a modest dividend. The settlement seemed to ease tensions for the moment, but the city's transit system remained a ticking time bomb.

That bomb finally exploded in July 1955, when the annual contract with the transit union ran out. Negotiations for a new contract quickly reached an impasse. While the union wanted increases in both wages and pensions, management refused to agree to any raises that weren't fully covered by increases in fares or other gross receipts. Union president Walter J. Bierwagen (1911–1986) sharply criticized the company's intransigence: "We cannot consent to any contingencies at all. The company was purchased with the idea of certain risks and can't adopt the policy of profits for Wolfson and risk for the employes," he said.[194]

Cars park on streetcar tracks in the middle of Pennsylvania Avenue in July 1955. *Library of Congress.*

On July 1, a massive strike ensued, snarling city transportation and hardening opposition to the Wolfson regime. The *Evening Star* reported, "Downtown Washington staggered under its heaviest traffic flow in history today as thousands upon thousands of strike-thwarted transit riders added automobiles to the city street system." Long lines of cars "packed solidly in every lane from dozens of key intersections" choked traffic to a standstill.[195] Among the affected commuters was Vice President Richard Nixon, who was seen reading a newspaper in the back seat of his chauffeured car as it inched along Beach Drive in Rock Creek Park.[196]

District officials relaxed parking restrictions (metered parking spots were free during the strike) and allowed automobiles to park on the streetcar tracks that ran down the center of Pennsylvania Avenue and other major routes. The free parking spots likely enticed more commuters to drive to work, potentially exacerbating the problem. Garage owners reeled under a 20 percent drop in business as they "sadly watched their regular patrons park free."[197]

Everyone blamed Wolfson. "Mr. Wolfson has made almost every one in town mad at him—so mad that the striking workers find themselves in the novel position of looking like heroes to the rideless public," the *Star* observed. "I could tell you what I think about Wolfson and the company, but you couldn't print it," one striker told the *Washington Post*. Another remarked, "Some few of us laid a dollar or two away, expecting this to happen sometime. But for a lot of boys it's pretty tough. If Mr. Wolfson and his clique would have given his employees a little of the money they paid in dividends, there wouldn't have been a strike."[198]

District officials demanded that Wolfson come immediately to Washington to help resolve the crisis, but he remained in California, where he was "taking a few days off," according to his Jacksonville office.[199] Furious congressmen and senators immediately proposed legislation to wrest the Capital Transit franchise away from him if he wouldn't come to terms with the union. When Wolfson finally appeared before Congress on July 12, he was unrepentant. He complained of the "wild and irresponsible statements impugning my honor." "Apparently a scapegoat, on whom to vent the resentments of the community had to be found," he said, concluding, "The victim of the great amount of hate and bitterness engendered by this most unfortunate strike appears to be Louis E. Wolfson." He went on to attack the *Washington Post*, the city's "so-called morning newspaper," which "has got some young fellow as publisher who married the boss's daughter, and it keeps hammering away about slicing melons and dividends." After all this emotional talk, Wolfson made it clear that he would not budge from his position that any employee wage hike had to be directly funded from increased fares, and he dared Congress to take his franchise away, arguing that in the end it would cost taxpayers $40 million.[200] Having done nothing productive to help resolve the crisis, he then left town as quickly as he had come.

The strike dragged on into August, wearying local residents and damaging businesses that depended on transit riders. Under pressure to force a solution, Congress had no choice but to devise a takeover. By the end of the month, a plan was agreed upon that would revoke Capital Transit's charter after an additional year and give the D.C. commissioners broad authority to work out an interim transit arrangement. On August 14, noting that Capital Transit had "failed to measure up to its responsibilities as a public utility in the District of Columbia," President Eisenhower signed the measure into law. Within a week, the strike finally came to an end. Workers were granted part of the wage increases the union had sought, but fares were increased as

Workers clean and lubricate a switch on Pennsylvania Avenue on August 22, 1955, as the strike ended. *D.C. Public Library, Star Collection,* © Washington Post.

well. Capital Transit agreed to run the city's streetcars and buses for the rest of the year until its franchise ended.

The strike had lasted fifty-two days, making it the second-longest transit strike in U.S. history. So much time had passed that workmen had to take special actions to get the system back into operation, including lubricating rusting switches and cleaning out clogged conduits. Out on the Cabin John line in Maryland, tall grass choked the rails and had to be cleared away. When the cars finally began resuming their rounds, it was a tremendous relief to transit workers, who had lost a substantial amount of income, as well as riders who had struggled to find alternate modes of transportation. "I'm sure going to be glad to stand out there waiting to catch a streetcar," one commuter told the *Washington Post.* Even cabbies, who had made extra money during strike, were glad to see it end. One cabbie grumbled, "It will get some of these women drivers picking up their husbands off the street."[201]

Once the cars were running again and city life was back to normal, the PUC began wrestling with the question of how best to manage

Early Mass Transit in Washington, D.C.

Passengers are all smiles as they ride a bus from the Chevy Chase terminal the day transit service was restored. *D.C. Public Library, Star Collection,* © Washington Post.

the transition when Capital Transit's charter expired a year later. The commissioners were convinced that an all-bus system would be best for the city in the long term and that now was the time to make the switch. District Commissioner Thomas A. Lane, speaking on WWDC Radio's weekly *Report to the People*, argued that the strike had actually strengthened prospects for the next transit company because the new all-bus operation would be faster, less expensive and would increase the capacity of major traffic arteries without requiring costly street widening.[202] Further, with an all-bus operation coming, Capital Transit by law would be responsible for disposing of its old equipment and removing the streetcar tracks from the streets, saving taxpayers considerable expense.

At hearings in the fall, the PUC heard many witnesses endorse the idea that buses were the city's most forward-looking option. Capital Transit, faced with the expense of removing the streetcar tracks, found itself defending the much-maligned system and arguing that streetcars were more profitable than buses. In 1954, streetcars had earned $1.08 for every mile they traveled, whereas buses made only half that amount. In fact, Capital Transit's bus operations had actually lost money in the early 1950s. These figures were deceptive, however. The profitability of streetcars depended on the fact that they operated on the most densely traveled city routes, carrying large numbers of passengers, whereas many bus routes covered greater distances in the suburbs with considerably fewer passengers. When per-mile operating costs were factored in, streetcars were more expensive to operate than buses, at $0.946 per mile versus $0.663 per mile for buses.[203]

The most compelling defense of streetcars came from a New York engineering firm, W.C. Gilman & Company, which had conducted a study of the Washington mass transit system for Capital Transit and released its findings in October 1955. The Gilman report concluded that it would be a mistake to get rid of all the city's streetcars right away, arguing that streetcars moved as quickly as buses on congested downtown streets. The report noted that Capital Transit's modern PCC cars were in good condition, were more spacious than buses and offered a more comfortable ride, assuming the tracks were smooth and well maintained. The report then went on to argue that the massive public investment then underway to improve roads and highways was encouraging too many people to switch to driving automobiles instead of taking public transit.[204]

Jaunty and Flamboyant

After the report came out, the anti-streetcar sentiment seemed to shift. The PUC backed away from the all-at-once approach, favoring a phased conversion to buses. However, the question of who would ultimately take over the city's transit system remained unanswered. Several companies submitted proposals, but all were rejected. Finally, in June 1956, O. Roy Chalk (1907–1995), the owner of New York–based Trans Caribbean Airways, offered to buy Capital Transit for $13 million and oversee a gradual seven-year conversion to all-bus operations. Chalk held marathon meetings with officials from both Capital Transit and the PUC to iron out the details of the agreement. Company shareholders delightedly approved the deal, which was highly favorable to investors, as did Congress, which passed a bill incorporating the main tenets of the deal. President Eisenhower signed it into law in July, and Chalk took ownership in August. Under Chalk, the name of the company was changed from Capital Transit to the D.C. Transit System.

EARLY MASS TRANSIT IN WASHINGTON, D.C.

John A.B. Broadwater of Capital Transit receives a check from O. Roy Chalk for the purchase of the city's transit system as attorney Edward F. Colladay looks on. *D.C. Public Library, Star Collection,* © Washington Post.

The last of the city's powerful transit moguls, Chalk was among the most colorful. Impeccably dressed, full of energy and ever attentive to appearances and public relations, the "jaunty and flamboyant" Chalk, as the *Post* described him,[205] contrasted sharply with the dour Louis Wolfson. Chalk had been born in London, the son of a Russian father and Polish mother, who brought him to the United States when he was three years old. The family settled in the Bronx, and Chalk later attended New York University Law School. He learned the New York real estate business through family connections and made money during the Depression by buying real estate at depressed prices. He was a consultant on military air transport during the war, spending time in Washington, and afterward bought a surplus military transport plane to start Trans Caribbean Airways, a charter airline that he would later sell to American Airlines. By the time he bought Capital Transit, he was a millionaire.

While Wolfson seemed to think only about money, Chalk had an obvious zest for streetcars and buses, which he wanted to modernize and make glamorous for the jet age. He issued his transit operators new dark-green uniforms that featured gold sleeve bands and looked like pilots' uniforms. He also adopted a distinctive two-toned bright green-and-white paint scheme highlighted with orange striping (supposedly his wife liked this color combination), making D.C. Transit's PCC cars and buses look as much as possible like streamlined, Mid-Century Modern airliners.

Although D.C. Transit was required to phase out streetcars within seven years, once Chalk took over, he began pushing to keep them as long as possible. Like Capital Transit's consultants, he realized that the PCC cars, most still in very good condition, were a valuable asset and that it would be costly to remove them and their conduit-based tracks. It would also be costly to purchase large quantities of new buses to replace them.

To demonstrate how modern and comfortable its streetcars could be, D.C. Transit overhauled one of them into a luxurious "super" streetcar. Designated the Silver Sightseer, the car's main attraction was that it was air-conditioned; it was said to be the first air-conditioned streetcar in the world. The exterior was dolled up with chrome trim and little metal flags, and the interior featured pale-pink fluorescent lighting and seats with armrests and footrests. To complete the jet age transformation, the car was staffed by a flight attendant–like hostess, although she didn't serve refreshments. The Silver Sightseer entered service in 1957, traveling the city's original streetcar route between the Capitol and the White House and charging the same twenty-cent fare as a regular streetcar.

Encouraged by the public's approval of the new car, D.C. Transit petitioned the PUC to add air conditioning to more of its streetcars. The commission, however, rebuffed this initiative, arguing that company funds shouldn't be invested in vehicles that were soon to be decommissioned. The *Washington Post* gave Chalk an "A for effort" and lauded the fact that

EARLY MASS TRANSIT IN WASHINGTON, D.C.

The Silver Sightseer was a specially modified PCC car that featured air conditioning and was meant to show how comfortable streetcars could be. *Author's collection.*

"someone is seriously attempting to make transit service in Washington more attractive," but like the PUC, the newspaper's editors doubted the wisdom of investing in streetcars. "[U]nfortunately streetcars are an anachronism in modern traffic and the remedies that would permit their retention are all extremely expensive," the *Post* concluded.[206]

The first major conversion in the D.C. Transit era occurred in September 1958, when Route 80 and 82 lines switched to buses. The two lines, remnants of the old Eckington & Soldiers Home Railway, had served the Eckington, Brookland and upper Rhode Island Avenue communities in Northeast and were heavily traveled by the city's African American population. The changeover reduced the streetcar network by 15 percent. Earley W. Bryant, operating one of the last cars on the line, summed up a common view: "I hate to see the streetcar go, but I've got to agree that the buses do their job better."[207]

With the end of the city's legacy transit system drawing ever closer, the debate over the wisdom of eliminating streetcars in Washington intensified.

As much as the venerable old cars had been vilified through the years, they were still the core of the city's mass transit system, and thousands of Washingtonians used them on a daily basis. Unwilling to accept their demise without a fight, supporters began organizing and lobbying to save them. In October 1957, a coalition of some twenty-five local civic organizations formed an Emergency Committee to Save the Streetcars. Its president was seventy-six-year-old Gover M. Koockogey, a former Government Printing Office employee and president of the Kalorama Citizens Association. "To junk cars and rails with 15 to 20 years or more of useful life is nothing short of criminal waste," Koockogey wrote. His committee urged Congress to rescind the law mandating conversion to buses.

Although the PUC consistently supported conversion, views in Congress were decidedly mixed. In 1958, Representative John L. McMillan (1898–1979), chair of the House District Committee, expressed support for continued streetcar operations, questioning the PUC's calculations about the benefits of conversion and stating that an all-bus system "would prove to be a disaster and a calamity." He noted that "if it had not been for the streetcars, mass transportation would have been almost impossible during World War II."[208] Similarly, in 1960 Senator Wayne L. Morse (1900–1974), noting that the 1956 law establishing D.C. Transit had been rushed to enactment, called for PUC hearings to reexamine the conversion policy and offered to introduce a "save the trolleys" bill in the next session of Congress. However, despite these misgivings, there was little the dissenters were willing to do, as ostensibly powerful as they were. By that point, too many streetcar lines had been shut down to turn back without causing lots of disruption and incurring significant expense. No one on Capitol Hill was willing to spend the political capital to reverse the course of events, and no legislation revoking the conversion mandate ever passed the House or Senate.

On January 3, 1960, the same day that Senator John F. Kennedy kicked off his campaign for the presidency, nearly half of Washington's remaining streetcar system was junked. Three major lines—the 20, 30 and 70/72/74 routes—were converted to bus operations. Route 20 had been the highly popular scenic line to Glen Echo Park and Cabin John, Maryland, the only remaining streetcar line in 1960 that extended into Maryland. Route 30 was the Pennsylvania Avenue line, the original Washington & Georgetown Railroad route that had been in existence since 1862. And the 70/72/74 was the workhorse Seventh Street line, also dating in part from 1862, that extended up Georgia Avenue to Brightwood. The wholesale abandonment of routes that had been a part of Washington life for so long was cause for much nostalgia and angst. "There are those who will feel for a long while hereafter that the streetcars of the three lines were sacrificed to mere administrative caprice," reporter John McKelway observed in the *Sunday Star*. "They will take it as a personal loss and see not the slightest communal gain." Many of these folks, McKelway wrote, "are just plain in love with the Cabin John line and always will be."[209]

McKelway joined about forty diehard streetcar patrons at 12:10 a.m. on January 3 for a final raucous ride on the Cabin John line. "They chattered all the way out and back. They jeered at the motorman. They made cracks about O. Roy Chalk. They pulled the trolley [pole] off [the overhead wire] once. They rang bells when they didn't want to get off." Sitting in the back of the car, the revelers sang "Auld Lang Syne" "raucously and without sentiment." All the mischief was apparently too much for the exhausted motorman, who at one point stopped the car and got up to address the motley assembly: "Look you guys. I've been hearing that bell for eight hours. If you want to get off, get off. But stop ringing that bell unless you want to get off."[210] Such was the unceremonious finale for the Cabin John line and a large part of Washington streetcar history.

With these three major routes gone, just four lines remained in service: the 40/42 to Mount Pleasant, the 50/54 on Fourteenth Street, the 60 on Eleventh Street and the 90/92 line on U Street and Florida Avenue. Even with just this bare-bones system left in operation, the city's streetcar backers were not yet ready to admit defeat. As late as April 1961, several of them testified to the PUC about the merits of retaining streetcars. The *Washington Post* reported that a group of "several never-say-die trolley partisans, applauded by a small group of supporters" argued that giving up on streetcars would, among other things, forfeit an opportunity to take an evolutionary approach to building a subway for the city. They also argued that "a primary cause of conversion to buses here and elsewhere in the Nation is an alliance between bus manufacturers, equipment and fuel suppliers and road builders," a conspiracy theory that would persist for decades to come. To make the case more personal, several transit patrons added their own perspectives. Mrs. Edward B. Morris complained that "reading on 'the jerky buses' gives her a headache, or even nausea," while Mrs. Thorn P. Starkey warned that "if we keep covering over vacant lands and destroying vegetation to accommodate the private automobile, Washingtonians will have to carry oxygen tanks on their backs."[211]

The PUC was not won over by any of these desperate arguments. After much consideration and revision by D.C. Transit and the PUC, the target for final conversion of the last streetcar lines was set for early 1962. By that

CAPITAL STREETCARS

A line of streetcars stands immobilized by snow clogging the conduit slot on Independence Avenue near New Jersey Avenue in January 1961. According to the *Evening Star*, the entire streetcar fleet was paralyzed by the storm. *D.C. Public Library, Star Collection,* © *Washington Post.*

point, most Washingtonians were looking forward to a streetcar-free future. The performance of the streetcar network during a disastrous fourteen-inch snowfall in February 1958 had convinced many that the system simply no longer could function properly. Because maintenance of the conduits had dropped off so much, tie-ups caused by the snow could not be quickly resolved. Snow, ice and broken automobile tire chains jammed many of the conduits and sometimes shorted out power, stranding many cars on downtown streets and interrupting service when customers needed it most. In some cases, D.C. road crews salted streets where conduits lay (they were supposed to avoid them), invariably shorting the power. The 20, 50 and 90/92 lines were out of commission for several days, their cars virtually abandoned on the tracks. Parts of the 40/42 routes were inoperable for as long as five days. Buses, meanwhile, fared much better. More than ever, frustrated customers yearned for the day when the balky streetcars would be gone forever.[212] Severe snowstorms returned in early 1961, creating similar problems and cementing the antipathy for streetcars.

Next to convert, in December 1961, were the 40/42 and 60 lines. In late November, the Mount Pleasant community held a mock funeral for its streetcars. The date for the end of streetcars coincided with the 100th anniversary of the founding of the community, which predated streetcar service but was nevertheless known as one of the city's preeminent streetcar suburbs. A vintage 1918 streetcar that had been preserved for special events led an elaborate hour-long parade of twenty-five marching bands that brought dancing to the streets of Mount Pleasant. A week later, the cars were gone.

That left just the 50/54 and 90/92 routes, which were shut down on January 28, 1962, the final day of streetcar service in the District of Columbia. By the time they were finally converted to bus operations, they were in very poor condition, having suffered from many years of neglect. U Street residents complained in December 1961 that the 90/92 streetcars were so noisy and poorly maintained that the racket kept them up at night and the vibration damaged their houses. D.C. Transit's track maintenance chief admitted that the company had not been maintaining its tracks: "It's like owning an automobile. You wouldn't buy a new motor if you knew you were going to sell the car next year."[213]

The end came with a mixture of nostalgia, emotion and relief. The date had been moved up for fear that the system wouldn't be able to survive another late winter snowstorm. Many commuters were relieved that the streetcars were finally out of the way and the streets could be freely salted if a storm came. Others had trouble letting go. *Washington Post* reporter Jack Eisen summed up the mood: "Some will cheer. Most will ask, 'So what?' More than a few will see [streetcars] go with a passing twinge of nostalgia, recognizing that a piece of their lives has faded away."[214]

Over the last days of service, ridership surged as sentimentalists took extra trips. Streetcar fans from around the country converged on Washington to ride the doomed cars and snap countless photographs as souvenirs. D.C. Transit allowed children to ride for free so that they could experience streetcars one last time with their parents. On the final day of service, the same vintage 1918 car that had led the Mount Pleasant parade took a ceremonial farewell trip, creaking its way around the entire remaining network of tracks. It was appropriately packed to standing room only, as so many cars had been over the system's hundred-year history. A massive "Last Day of Streetcars" banner was draped across its side, and a funeral wreath and black crepe festooned its lone headlight.[215] When it completed its run and returned to the Navy Yard car barn at 4:45 a.m., an era in Washington history came to a quiet close.

An eloquent editorial in the *Washington Post*, reflecting the automobile-centric attitude so common at the time, served as the streetcars' epitaph:

Historic PCC car no. 1101 passes the Peace Monument on Pennsylvania Avenue on the last day of streetcars, January 28, 1962. *National Capital Trolley Museum.*

Yes, we know that streetcars are a hopeless anachronism and there is no need to tell us that times have changed, that progress must be served, etc. We freely concede that the trolley was a nuisance to motorists as it clanked along at a matronly gait, clogging traffic and fraying nerves. And those islands [the loading platforms] *were a menace—the little poultices of concrete wedged on the street so that they practically invited motorists to scar up fenders.*

And what about the rails? Horrible things. In wet weather, it was a menace for drivers to glide down the streetcar tracks, wobbling like a waterbug whenever tires touched slippery steel. We also remember the discomfort of riding along inside those teetering boxcars, so warm in summer and so draughty in winter.

Were the sounds pleasant? Emphatically not. There was the annoying ding-ding-ding whenever the streetcar encountered an uncooperative obstacle. Moreover, the clacking sound of the trolleys as they traversed switches and turnoffs was in that peculiar range of decibels that affects the spine unpleasantly. Indeed, there is not a single redeeming thing that can be said about streetcars—they were bumpy, balky and as uselessly old-fashioned as the bustles of Victorian days.

As of Sunday, the streetcars of Washington clunked their last. We miss them.[216]

Chapter 11

Lost and Found

NOSTALGIA FOR THE STREETCAR ERA, 1962–2015

The demise of streetcars in Washington, D.C., marked a turning point in the city's transit history; the long love/hate relationship that had evolved over one hundred years between Washingtonians and their traditional mass transit system came to an abrupt end. Psychologically speaking, the slate was wiped clean. The struggles over cost, service and fairness receded into the past as the public shifted its attention, and complaints, to the bus system that was supposed to be such a technological advance. Plans for a new subway system—the ultimate solution in many commuters' eyes—drew attention further away from the streetcar past. Yet reminders of that past were all around. Vestiges of the elaborate network of rails, conduits, cars and buildings still linger to this day, and the thriving National Capital Trolley Museum in suburban Maryland keeps the city's streetcar legacy from being forgotten.

Louis Wolfson may have left the city on bad terms, but he was never found guilty of any wrongdoing in connection with Capital Transit. He continued to acquire and trade in companies, some proving more profitable than others. Half a century after his departure from the District, it was still possible to find at least one economist arguing that what he did for Washington's streetcar company was a good thing.[217] When he died in 2008, he was remembered chiefly for events that happened long after the D.C. episode. He was convicted of federal securities violations in 1967 and 1968 and served nine months in prison. Payments by his charitable foundation gave the impression that he tried to buy influence with Supreme Court justice Abe Fortas (1910–1982) to help clear him of these charges. Tainted by the scandal, Fortas resigned from the court in 1969. Meanwhile, Wolfson put his legal troubles behind him and continued to indulge a lifelong passion for racehorses. He is perhaps best remembered as the owner of Affirmed, the horse that won the Triple Crown in 1978.

As for O. Roy Chalk, he fared little better in D.C.'s court of public opinion. Buses did not prove to be any speedier than streetcars on congested downtown streets, nor more pleasant to ride. Although they were less costly to operate than streetcars, they were certainly not inexpensive. Ridership levels stabilized temporarily when Chalk took over but soon resumed their long-term decline. Chalk found that, like Wolfson, his costs continued to climb, and he, too, petitioned the PUC for numerous fare increases. By the late 1960s, D.C. Transit had developed a reputation for high costs and poor service. Fares went up three times in 1968 alone. In 1970, the standard fare rose to forty cents, twice what it was when Chalk took over.[218]

In 1973, the Washington Metropolitan Area Transit Authority, a public entity chartered to develop the city's new subway system, seized the buses from Chalk, paying him $45 million. Chalk remained in Washington, running the remains of the D.C. Transit System (chiefly real estate), as well as his other various business assets, from his ornate office suite in the former Capital Traction Car Barn at the foot of Key Bridge in Georgetown. Regarding losing the buses, Chalk told *Washington Post* reporter Jack Eisen in 1978, "I'm not an unhappy man. I've got a load off my shoulders."[219] As late as the early 1990s, shortly before his death, Chalk was still wheeling and dealing from his car barn office, attempting to broker trade agreements between Russia and the United States.

THE BARGAIN OF THE WEEK

Even before the last D.C. streetcar pulled into the Navy Yard car barn in January 1962, excess PCC cars had been piling up in storage as streetcar lines were discontinued. D.C. Transit tried to sell the cars to other transit systems, but most North American cities were busy getting rid of their own streetcars, and the market was glutted. In addition, the D.C. cars were slightly shorter than standard PCC cars, making them less attractive to most North American buyers. Nevertheless, D.C. Transit was eventually able to sell 190 of its cars to other transit systems, representing more than one-third of the

Decommissioned streetcars lined up at the Benning Car Barn in 1963. *D.C. Public Library, Star Collection,* © *Washington Post.*

489 PCC cars it had originally acquired. Their short length turned out to suit European systems well, and 74 of D.C.'s cars eventually went to Sarajevo, Yugoslavia, while another 101 were put in service in Barcelona, Spain. And 15 were sold to a department store in Fort Worth, Texas, which used them

for a shuttle service between an outlying five-thousand-car parking lot and its sprawling downtown store.[220]

Most of the cars never saw active service again. Many sat moldering for years in several D.C. Transit yards and car barns. In widely varying conditions, the cars waited for buyers. In January 1962, the *Evening Star* reported that used streetcars were "the bargain of the week." "Anyone can have one for a couple hundred dollars," D.C. Transit vice-president James H. Flanagan proclaimed, noting that buyers were responsible for hauling them away.[221] While a few were converted to diners, country cottages and chicken coops—one was even repurposed as a church—most were sold for scrap. All except for a few historic museum pieces were gone by 1967.

Removing the vast network of tracks and conduits that snaked through D.C. streets proved to be a much slower and more expensive task. In 1962, the D.C government projected that it would take four years to remove them all, but it actually took much longer. In the meantime, motorists sued D.C. Transit for injuries and damages caused by the tracks, which could be hazardous when slippery and likely contributed to many front-end misalignments. One man sued after his auto bumped over a hole in the street where one of the thousands of conduit access covers should have been in place. The bus company fought all such claims, arguing that they were the city's responsibility.

Congress had specified that D.C. Transit and the city jointly fund track removal and align it with the city's existing schedule for street repaving. While some of the track and conduits were physically removed, many were simply paved over. D.C. officials argued that the steel and concrete conduit structure actually made the streets stronger and that it was better to keep them in place, at least in the short term. In the first few years after streetcars, the city made rapid progress, with about ninety miles of track (three-fifths of the system) being removed or paved over at a cost of $4 million.

But work began to slow after 1965. The city adopted a policy of only removing track when major reconstruction was planned for the street, leaving much of the remaining rails untouched for years. In 1969, when the *Washington Daily News* asked D.C. Highway and Traffic director Thomas F. Airis when the track would all be gone, the response was "eventually."[222] Ultimately, U.S. District Court judge Gerhard A. Gesell ruled that the District's "leisurely, indefinite schedule" for track removal was intolerable in light of the continuing public nuisance the tracks posed. He ordered all remaining track removed or paved over by 1976.

Capital Streetcars

Old streetcar tracks on Florida Avenue at North Capitol Street are partially paved over in this 1963 photo. *D.C. Department of Transportation.*

Cobblestone-paved sections of O and P Streets in Georgetown, which local citizen groups lobbied to save, were the only exception to the judge's order. These segments remained virtually unaltered for several more decades, and the street gradually settled around them, making them increasingly dangerous. In 2011, the District Department of Transportation undertook a painstaking project to restore these segments as reminders of the city's once extensive network of street railways. The rails, hatch covers and cobblestones were all removed, cleaned, repaired and replaced in thoroughly reconstructed streets. Completed in 2012, the restored track segments are the only remaining examples of Washington's unique underground conduit system.[223]

Generally considered less of a nuisance than the tracks were the many car barns that graced the ends of former streetcar routes. Some were demolished, including the large car house at the foot of Seventh Street on the Southwest Waterfront, which was torn down as part of the draconian "urban renewal" of that neighborhood. Among the surviving barns are some that are easily overlooked. The humble Eckington car barn at Fifth and T Streets Northeast, dating to 1899, now serves as a U.S. Postal Service vehicle maintenance facility, while the car barn and stable at Fourteenth and Boundary Streets Northwest, built in 1877 and now vacant, served for decades as a commercial laundry.

Several car barns stand out as distinguished landmarks. One of the best known is the elegant Capital Traction building on M Street in Georgetown. Designed by noted Washington architect Waddy B. Wood (1869–1944), the massive structure was built from 1895 to 1897 and originally intended to be a union station where four privately owned car lines would converge. Walls thirteen feet thick at their base supported loading and unloading of streetcars on several different levels. Yet within months of opening, its function changed, after Capital Traction's previous headquarters on Pennsylvania Avenue was destroyed in the great cable powerhouse fire of 1897. The company soon moved its main offices into the Georgetown station, leaving streetcars and office workers to share the same building for half a century, until the Rosslyn line finally closed in 1949. While vehicle entrances are still plainly visible at street level, the building has housed only offices since 1950. An ornamental pediment over the central bay includes rope-and-pulley motifs recalling the brief cable era when the building was constructed.

Across town, the Navy Yard car barn at Eighth and M Streets Southeast is another prominent survivor. Designed by Kansas City architect Walter C. Root (1859–1925) and built in 1891, the building's fanciful, castle-like design reflects the Romanesque Revival style that enlivens many public buildings of that era. It marked the eastern terminus of the original Pennsylvania Avenue line of the Washington & Georgetown Railroad and was also the end point of the last streetcar ride in 1962. At some point after the streetcar era, the structure was painted a bright blue and came to be known as the "Blue Castle." The Richard Wright Public Charter School is currently its major tenant.

Some ten blocks north of the Navy Yard car barn on Capitol Hill stands the former Metropolitan Railroad car house at Fourteenth and East Capitol Streets Northeast. Also designed by Waddy B. Wood, architect of the Georgetown barn, the facility on East Capitol Street was built in 1896, when the Metropolitan was converting to underground electrical conduit power. The East Capitol Street building became the company's headquarters and continued as the headquarters of WRECo until it merged with Capital Traction. After streetcar service ended, the sprawling complex sat empty and decaying for nearly two decades until it was remodeled and reopened as the Car Barn Condominium in 1981.

A fourth car barn is less well known but just as distinguished. The Capital Traction car barn at Fourteenth and Decatur Streets Northwest was completed

A contemporary view of the Capital Traction Car Barn at Fourteenth and Decatur Streets. *Photo by the author.*

in 1906, the year after the company extended its popular Fourteenth Street line, which had previously ended at Park Road in Columbia Heights, north to Decatur Street. The elegant building, designed by the prestigious firm of Wood, Dunn and Deming, could accommodate more than 250 streetcars. Considered one of the most attractive car barns in the city, it comes closest of all the remaining car barns to its original purpose: it is now used to house city buses.

Large as these barns are, the most massive surviving remnant of Washington's streetcar era is not a building at all and has remained largely hidden from public view for decades. It is the elaborate Dupont Circle underpass, which cost millions of dollars and left its neighborhood a mess of construction debris for three years while it was under construction. In the end, the tunnels saw service for a mere eleven years, perhaps vindicating Cissy Patterson's claim that the "blunderpass" was a waste of time and money. D.C. Transit tried to use the tunnels for buses, but they were not big enough. For about a year or two beginning in 1963, the complex was designated as a fallout shelter, but that quickly came to an end. Many other ideas for reusing the tunnels were proposed over the years, including as an underground mall, a health club and a produce market. Then in 1995, the west-side tunnel reopened as a food court dubbed "Dupont Down Under." *Washington Post* architecture critic Benjamin Forgey thought the reopening of the tunnel "a delightful occurrence, way overdue,"[224] but few customers were willing to venture down into the subterranean cavern, and the food court was shuttered the following year. Most recently, in 2014, the Arts Coalition for the Dupont Underground signed a lease with the city to reuse parts of the tunnels as a performing arts space. The group aimed to hold its first event in 2015.

"Quite a Miraculous Improvement"

Like sports teams, most streetcar systems in the United States had their diehard fans, and D.C. streetcars were no exception. The desire to preserve and celebrate the country's streetcar heritage first took form in the 1930s, when the cars were still alive but already endangered. The Electric Railroaders' Association was founded in New York in 1934 by Edwin J. Quinby (1895–1981) with the goal of celebrating streetcars and lobbying on their behalf wherever they were threatened. A local chapter was established in 1938 to champion Washington's street railways. It organized special charter excursions and was instrumental in getting Capital Transit to save several vintage cars that otherwise likely would have been scrapped. The venerable 1918 car that would run special last-day excursions on each of the D.C. routes was preserved in 1950 at the group's urging.

These well-organized fans were the driving force behind the founding of the National Capital Trolley Museum (under a slightly different name) in 1959. Using money out of their own pockets, the museum's supporters began acquiring old streetcars, and in 1965, they broke ground on a museum site in a scenic park near the Northwest Branch of the Anacostia River in Montgomery County, Maryland. Over the next five years, a car barn and museum building were constructed and a meandering track laid out for historic streetcar rides. The trolley museum officially opened in October 1969. Senator Charles McC. Mathias was one of the dignitaries who joined in hammering a golden spike into the tracks at the opening-day ceremonies. Starting with a small collection of mostly European trolleys, the museum's holdings were greatly augmented in 1970 when O. Roy Chalk was persuaded to dispose of D.C. Transit's small remaining collection of historic streetcars. Four of the company's six cars, including the 1918 "last day" car as well as Capital Transit's first PCC car, were given to the museum. The other two, dating from the 1890s, were donated to the Smithsonian; one is now on permanent display at the National Museum of American History.

Tragically, one of the cars donated to the trolley museum, the Silver Sightseer, was destroyed by fire as it sat on the track outside the museum's car barn in late 1970. Arson was suspected. The museum experienced a much bigger fire many years later, in 2003, when one of its car barns went up in smoke along with eight cars (purely an accident this time). Despite these setbacks, the museum has remained a major attraction for streetcar fans and children of all ages for more than four decades, interpreting the streetcar era with rides on its demonstration railway, displaying artifacts and educational exhibits, supporting local schools with classroom lessons and preserving streetcars dating from 1898 to 1972. One old PCC car from the lot that D.C. Transit sold to a Fort Worth department store wound up in the Ozark Mountains. The trolley museum brokered a deal to return it to Washington in 1987. The museum's collection now includes seven historic cars from the District, two from other American cities and eight from Canada and Europe.

Montgomery County councilwoman Avis Birely addresses attendees at the groundbreaking for the National Capital Trolley Museum in November 1965. *National Capital Trolley Museum.*

Early Mass Transit in Washington, D.C.

A museum is all well and good, but for many local fans the ultimate prize was bringing the cars back to the streets of Washington. Almost as soon as streetcars disappeared, supporters began lobbying for their return. Quickly forgotten were the formidable challenges of operating the streetcar system, including the expense and difficulty of maintaining the District's unique underground electrical conduits. In their place, the romance of the trolleys flourished as it never had in real life. Like martyred heroes, streetcars gained exaggerated virtues and suffered few if any faults. They were attractive, spacious, comfortable to ride in, quiet, efficient and ran on clean electric energy. Why would anyone not want these marvelous conveyances gliding down their streets?

But if trolleys were so great, how did it happen that so many cities let them go? For many of the romantics, it was simply too difficult to accept that streetcars, in Washington or any other city, had died a natural death. The only explanation was deliberate, premeditated murder. Powerful interests—namely the nation's big automobile, oil and tire companies—must have been behind this perfidy. Ever greedy for greater profits and mindless of the long-term damage they were inflicting, these companies were accused of engaging in a diabolical plot to eradicate the humble streetcar and replace it with gas-guzzling, tire-burning, private automobiles.

Primary evidence of this conspiracy was a suit brought by the Justice Department in 1947 against National City Lines, a transit holding company (which never had any Washington area assets) controlled by General Motors, Standard Oil of California, Phillips Petroleum and Firestone Tire and Rubber. GM and its partners were found guilty of antitrust law violations, chiefly conspiring to monopolize sales of buses, fuel and tires to the transit companies held by National City Lines. As early as the 1950s, streetcar boosters imagined this crime to be a conspiracy to shut down profitable streetcar systems in American cities against the wishes of the public and replace them with buses. According to the theory, the clunky and unsatisfactory buses would ultimately drive people away from public transit altogether and into their private automobiles. As time went by, the enticing theory gained many adherents. It was the basis for the plot of the 1988 Hollywood film *Who Framed Roger Rabbit*, as well as a documentary, *Taken for a Ride*, that aired on public television in 1996.

History shows that no such conspiracy ever existed. Perhaps the best explanation is simply that none was needed. General Motors certainly took every opportunity to promote its products and even conspired to corner the market for them in cities where National City Lines operated. But it had no need to foist automobiles on an already adoring public. Most postwar Americans were fervent believers in the joy of owning automobiles and the freedom they brought to drive wherever their owners pleased whenever they wanted. Few had any fondness for the hassles and limitations of public transportation. Public policy mirrored this sentiment, with the federal government investing vast sums in the 1950s and 1960s to support ubiquitous automobile travel with better roads and highways. Streetcars, by contrast, were a quaint relic of the past, a nuisance to be done away with as expeditiously as possible.

In fact, in the 1970s, the primary legacy of streetcars in the District seemed to be urban blight. A study conducted for the D.C. Office of Planning in 1974 noted that most of the city's former trolley routes were in steep decline. Business strips like Fourteenth Street, Eleventh Street, Georgia Avenue, U Street and H Street Northeast historically had been built up on the assumption that people would travel to them on streetcars. With the advent of automobiles, these ribbon-like commercial corridors failed because they offered little parking and couldn't compete with suburban shopping malls. The disappearance of streetcars thus had seemingly left behind swaths of economic ruin.[225]

But perhaps the streetcars themselves weren't really to blame. In 1975, the *Washington Post*'s architecture critic, Wolf von Eckardt (1918-1995), observed, "It would be quite a miraculous improvement…if we could just get back to the old-fashioned trolley cars that were efficient and fun to ride. They not only got us from one point to another, but they also let us see and enjoy what was in between. Their only sin was that they got in the way of impatient motorists, which was why they were banned in America." Eckardt supported a "citizens' proposal" to start running streetcars again on the tracks that still remained downtown as a supplement to the new Metro subway system. According to Eckardt, the citizens' proposal stated that streetcars were cheaper to run than buses and wouldn't bunch up as buses did. They would be less noisy, offer a smoother ride and wouldn't pollute the air.[226]

In 1976, the Georgetown Citizens Association made its own proposal to revive streetcars, advocating that the tracks that still ran down the center of M Street in Georgetown be brought back to life with a trolley that would run from the Key Bridge to the planned subway station in Foggy Bottom. The group thought that paving over the surviving tracks would be a "regressive step in seeking a solution to Georgetown's traffic problems, destroying what remains of [M Street's] character." Reviving streetcars would be a far better alternative. The study concluded that "the facilities are available, the need is more than evident, and the cost would not be prohibitive."[227] But others were not as convinced. The D.C government shrugged off the proposal. Deeming the remaining M Street tracks a safety hazard, the city paved them over in 1977.

But talk of bringing back the trolleys persisted. Urban planners across the country were taking a fresh look at how streetcars might actually reverse the decline of inner cities. The new buzzword was "light rail," which sounded more modern and efficient than "trolley" or "streetcar" but usually meant something similar. The first modern light rail system opened in San Diego in 1981. Light rail systems were eventually built in several North American cities, including Sacramento, Buffalo, Baltimore and Portland, Oregon.

In 1997, D.C.'s Department of Public Works issued a transportation plan that called for a network of light rail lines to be built across the District. The goal was to facilitate crosstown travel, which was largely overlooked by the commuter-oriented Metro subway. The city proposed three light rail lines, including one from Georgetown to the Navy Yard that would have partially mirrored the city's original Washington & Georgetown railway. The other two lines would run from Adams Morgan to Minnesota Avenue and from Georgia Avenue to Barney Circle. The total cost for these three lines was estimated at $425 million.[228] Although no action was taken directly as a result of the plan, it laid the groundwork for future developments.

In 2002, with light rail systems being proposed both in nearby Maryland (the "Purple Line") and Virginia (a streetcar line along Columbia Pike in Arlington), D.C. officials began actively promoting streetcars for the District. In addition to improving crosstown transit, streetcars were touted as stimulating economic development and relieving capacity issues on the subway and bus systems. D.C. government officials took their cue from Portland, Oregon, which in 2001 had started a downtown streetcar loop that was drawing rave reviews. Just as Charles Glover and Henry Hurt had toured western cities in 1887 to reassure themselves that cable was the right technology choice for the Washington & Georgetown Railroad, so D.C. officials visited Portland in 2002 and came away convinced that a modern streetcar system would do wonders for the District. Excited by what they found, they began planning new streetcar lines that would target underdeveloped and isolated areas of the city that seemed ripe for regrowth.

Anacostia and other "east of the river" communities were first on their list. In November 2004, Mayor Anthony A. Williams thrust a shovel in the ground across the street from the Anacostia Metro station where the first new streetcar tracks in almost half a century were to be laid. The planned "demonstration" line was to run south to Bolling Air Force Base, connecting the underserved community of Barry Farms and aiming to spur economic development in southeast D.C. But just as the original Anacostia & Potomac Railway was delayed for years after it first won construction approval, so the new Anacostia line likewise faced delays. Track construction did not begin until 2009, five years after the ceremonial groundbreaking, and then stopped the following year as plans continued to change.

Perhaps the most striking parallel with the past was the controversy that erupted over the use of overhead wires. Just as the city's first mechanized streetcar line—the Eckington & Soldiers' Home Railway—used overhead electric wires in 1888, so would the new streetcars. Despite all the advances in technology over 120 years, this was still the most practical method for powering streetcars and was used by virtually all other modern systems. Yet the 1889 law banning overhead wires in downtown Washington was still on the books, so a new overhead wire system presumably would be illegal.

By 2010, attention had shifted from Anacostia to a 2.2-mile stretch of H Street Northeast that was within the downtown boundaries established in the 1889 federal law. The city council ducked the problem by passing a new city law allowing overhead wires on this segment. Whether the city had the authority to overturn a federal law was argued by critics but never challenged in court. However, a longer-term solution to the problem remained unclear. If the streetcar network were to be built across the city, the problem would come up again, and no easy solution was at hand. One idea was to adopt a hybrid system using batteries to power the cars over track segments where overhead wires couldn't be used. Battery-powered streetcars had been tried unsuccessfully in the 1890s. Modern batteries would certainly be more reliable, but would they be good enough? At the time this book was written, the question had not been answered.

It was fitting that the new streetcars were destined to make their debut on H Street Northeast, a thoroughfare that once hosted the Columbia Railway, one of the city's earliest streetcar lines. H Street was a rising commercial corridor that had been devastated in the riots of 1968 but was beginning to rapidly redevelop. Streetcar installation began in 2009, when tracks were laid as part of road reconstruction. The first cars were set on these rails in December 2013. The city purchased three streetcars from a manufacturer in the Czech Republic in 2007 and three more in 2012 from Oregon-based United Streetcar LLC. Testing of these cars began on H Street in 2014.

Challenges and setbacks, both technical and political, abounded. While some city officials were highly enthusiastic, others were skeptical. Budget cuts

Early Mass Transit in Washington, D.C.

In early 2015, the tracks on H Street Northeast stood empty, awaiting the much-delayed arrival of streetcar service. *Photo by the author.*

kept the project scrambling and ultimately quashed hopes for an extensive thirty-seven-mile citywide network. A 2012 opening date, announced in 2010, proved wildly unrealistic. More delays were experienced getting approval to build a car barn at the end of the track. Also, a method for collecting fares on the cars, which have multiple entrances and exits, had not been worked out. Once cars began making test runs on H Street, further issues developed. Washingtonians rediscovered the fact that streetcars move slowly and inevitably tie up traffic behind them. In addition, because the tracks were laid close to parking lanes on H Street, improperly parked vehicles could bring the cars to a complete stop. Several minor accidents ensued in the tight quarters. To skeptical observers, the project had a helter-skelter quality to it. "It was ill-planned, ill-thought-out, ill-engineered, ill-everything," council member and former mayor Marion Barry (1936–2014) told the *Washington Post*.[229]

In early 2015, after the project had missed several promised opening dates, newly inaugurated mayor Muriel Bowser called for a thorough review, throwing into question whether the cars would ever go into public service.

While Bowser subsequently pledged to open the H Street line, it remained unclear how extensive D.C.'s streetcar network ultimately would be.

There can be no going back to the days when streetcars were the transit glue that held the capital together, but much of the psychology of modern streetcar investment—the hopes for connecting and energizing isolated neighborhoods and spurring economic development—remains remarkably similar to the aspirations of past streetcar promoters. Henry A. Griswold, George Truesdell and Francis G. Newlands all had faith in the transformative power of streetcars, envisioning economic prosperity blossoming along their routes. They all achieved some measure of success, but none of their streetcar investments was as profitable as people expected it to be. Perhaps the fate of the modern D.C. streetcar will be similar, and history will yet again repeat itself.

Notes

Chapter 1

1. A detailed discussion of the L'Enfant Plan and L'Enfant's thinking is in Gutheim and Lee's *Worthy of the Nation*.
2. Hunt, *Writings of James Madison*, vol. 8, 394, n.2.
3. Dickens, *American Notes for General Circulation*, chapter 8.
4. *Daily National Intelligencer*, March 10, 1830.
5. Quoted in Muller, *Mark Twain in Washington, D.C.*, 23.
6. *Evening Star*, "Atrocious Conduct," June 7, 1855.
7. Ibid., "Beef's Blood and Mutton Tallow vs. Italian Silks and Valencia Laces," October 29, 1855.
8. *Daily National Intelligencer*, March 14, 1853.
9. James Goode stated that the horse used as a model was Clark Mills's own Thoroughbred, named Olympus. However, Mills may have obtained Olympus from Vanderwerken's Arlington farm. Goode, "Four Salutes to the Nation."
10. *Evening Star*, "The New City Railroad," February 1, 1854.
11. *Daily National Intelligencer*, "The City Railroad," February 9, 1854.
12. *Evening Star*, "The City Railroad," February 9, 1854.

Chapter 2

13. *Washington Post*, "Street Railway Stock," May 10, 1890, 9.
14. The aqueduct project, carried out under the direction of Captain Montgomery C. Meigs (1816–1892) in the 1850s, brought running water for the first time to Georgetown and Washington.
15. *Daily National Intelligencer*, "City Railroad," July 14, 1862.
16. *Evening Star*, "Cars for the Passenger Railroad," July 12, 1862.
17. Ibid., "The Passenger Railway," July 29, 1862.
18. Scott and Webb, *Who Is Markie?*
19. *Daily National Intelligencer*, "The City Railroad on Seventh Street," July 21, 1863.
20. King, *100 Years of Capital Traction*, 5.
21. *Capital Transit Company Records, 1862–1956*, MS 442, Box 108, collection of the Historical Society of Washington, D.C.
22. *Evening Star*, "The Metropolitan Railroad Company," November 28, 1864.
23. Ibid., "Old Horse Car Days," November 3, 1906.
24. Ibid., "The Heat and Street Railways," July 3, 1868.
25. Ibid., December 31, 1864.
26. "A Little Girl's Experience of the War," manuscript in the special collections of the Gelman Library, George Washington University, presumed to have been written by Anna Sherman. I became aware of the manuscript reading part of this excerpt in Furgurson, *Freedom Rising*.
27. McShane and Tarr, *Horse in the City*, 11.
28. *Evening Star*, "The Old-Time Hill-Horse Boys," June 18, 1911.
29. Ibid., "Fined for Cruelty to Horses," April 25, 1893.
30. *Washington Post*, "Reveries of the Horsecar, Dreams of Atom Trolleys," September 11, 1949.

Chapter 3

31. Carpenter, *Carp's Washington*, 7.
32. *Evening Star*, "Old-Time Hill-Horse Boys," June 18, 1911.
33. Peck, *Walt Whitman in Washington, D.C.*, 102.
34. *Calamus*, 23.
35. Brooks, *Washington in Lincoln's Time*, 191.
36. *Evening Star*, "Street Car Abuses," January 3, 1885.
37. *Washington Post*, "A Petition and a Pledge," July 23, 1888.

38. Masur, *Example for All the Land*, 44.
39. Ibid., 100. Masur's detailed and scholarly assessment of the streetcar issue in Washington is highly recommended.
40. *Evening Star*, "War Meeting of the Colored People," June 10, 1863.
41. Ibid., "Cars for the Colored," November 28, 1863.
42. For example, *National Republican*, "An Outrage," February 10, 1864.
43. *Congressional Globe*, February 10, 1864, 553.
44. *Evening Star*, February 23, 1865.
45. Ibid., "Freedmen's Affairs in the District," September 2, 1865.
46. Painter, *Narrative of Sojourner Truth*, 124–26.
47. *National Republican*, "Alleged Assault Upon Sojourner Truth," September 22, 1865.
48. Masur, *Example for All the Land*, 108.

CHAPTER 4

49. *National Leader*, "The Crowded Street Car," reprinted, March 2, 1889.
50. *Evening Star*, "Underground Wires Again," August 17, 1888.
51. *Washington Post*, "Bad Streetcar Service," January 24, 1889.
52. *Evening Star*, editorial, August 10, 1888.
53. Griffin, *Motive Power for Street Cars*.
54. *Washington Post*, "The Overhead Wires," August 17, 1888.
55. D.C. appropriations acts for 1890 and 1891, reprinted in *Laws Relating to Street Railway Franchises in the District of Columbia*, U.S. Congress, 1896, 192–94.
56. *Washington Post*, "President Hurt Returns," May 15, 1887.
57. *Evening Star*, "The New Cable Road," August 6, 1892.
58. *Washington Post*, "Cable Cars and Accidents," September 7, 1893.
59. *Evening Star*, "Rapid Transit," October 22, 1892.
60. Ibid., "Trolley Logic," July 25, 1893.
61. Ibid., "A Successful Trip," July 26, 1895.
62. Ibid., "Running Regularly," July 29, 1895.

CHAPTER 5

63. *Evening Star*, "Street Railroads," March 19, 1892.
64. Ibid., "Street Railway Projects," April 23, 1890.
65. *Washington Post*, "Tribute to Henry A. Griswold," April 27, 1909.

66. *Evening Star*, "The Anacostia Railway Company," July 3, 1876.
67. King, *100 Years of Capital Traction*, 14.
68. Muller and Levinn, "H.A. Griswold and Anacostia's Streetcar Story."
69. *Evening Star*, "A Complaint Against the Anacostia Railway," February 10, 1892.
70. King, *100 Years of Capital Traction*, 14.
71. *Evening Star*, "Anacostia Street Cars," May 14, 1896.
72. *Washington Post*, "Strike Declared Off," July 20, 1895.
73. King, *100 Years of Capital Traction*, 56.
74. *Washington Post*, "Rose by Magic's Wand," December 7, 1890,
75. Ibid., "The Eckington Railroad," October 19, 1888.
76. In 1895, the Capital Railway, chartered as a rapid transit alternative to the Anacostia & Potomac Railroad, also briefly experimented with a surface contact system on a portion of its line on Capitol Hill. Its results were equally disappointing.
77. *Washington Post*, "Easy Riding on the Cars," December 14, 1890.
78. Ibid., "Brookland's Complaint," February 4, 1892.
79. Ibid., "Back to Horse Cars," September 12, 1895
80. Ibid., "Ride by Easy Stages," September 30, 1895.
81. Ibid., "Their Burden of Debt," October 3, 1896.
82. Ibid., "Air Motors Now in Use," March 21, 1897.
83. Ibid., "New Car Line Opened," April 25, 1890.
84. *Evening Star*, "The District in Congress," February 28, 1888.
85. French, "Chevy Chase Village," 322.
86. *Washington Post*, "Rock Creek Road Is Ready," September 17, 1892.
87. Bolles, "Rock Creek Electric Railway," 24.
88. *Washington Post*, "Both Lines Combined," September 22, 1895.
89. Ibid., "Massive Building in Ruins," September 30, 1897.
90. Cunningham, "Cable Cars in the Nation's Capital," 49.
91. Atwood, *Francis G. Newlands*, 38–39.
92. *Washington Post*, "Francis G. Newlands," December 26, 1917.

Chapter 6

93. *Evening Star*, "The End Seat Question," July 28, 1899.
94. Clarence L. Cullen, "Open Car Etiquette," *Evening Star*, April 13, 1907.
95. *Evening Star*, "The 'End Seat Hog,'" June 17, 1898.
96. *Washington Post*, "The Hog in the Street Car," August 12, 1898.

Notes to Pages 114–138

97. Jack Eisen, "Trolley Runs Out of Juice After 99 Years," *Washington Post*, January 28, 1962.
98. King, *100 Years of Capital Traction*, 206, 216.
99. *Evening Star*, "Citizens Complain of Noise," July 18, 1900.
100. *Washington Post*, "Seek Wreck Blame," August 2, 1919.
101. *Washington Times*, "Car Steps Too High, Women Protest," August 6, 1908.
102. *Washington Post*, "Ask New Type of Car," January 4, 1912.
103. *Evening Star*, "The Street Railway Service," July 28, 1900.
104. Ibid., "Street Car Facilities," December 9, 1902.
105. Ingham, *Biographical Dictionary of American Business Leaders*, 1,685.
106. *Washington Times*, "No Seat, No Nickel Exponent in Cell," February 14, 1911.
107. *Washington Post*, "Tied Up the Entire Line," June 14, 1901.
108. *Streetcar and Bus Resources of Washington, D.C.*, 64.
109. *History of the Amalgamated Transit Union*, 11.
110. *Washington Post*, "Trolley Pole Struck Him," September 21, 1903.
111. *Washington Times*, "Man in the Electric Pit—Washington's Oddest Occupation," April 10, 1904.
112. *Washington Post*, "Agreement Reached," December 15, 1894.
113. Ibid., "Strikebreakers Quit," March 19, 1917.
114. *Washington Post*, "Stirs Union Carmen," March 27, 1917.
115. *Evening Star*, "For Public Ownership or Absolute Control of Capital Car Lines," October 6, 1917.
116. *Street Railways in the District of Columbia*, 32.

Chapter 7

117. *Washington Post*, "Burned in a Conduit," June 27, 1900.
118. *Evening Star*, "Burned by Electric Wire," June 27, 1900.
119. *Washington Post*, "Sat in Negroes' Seat," June 14, 1902.
120. Ibid., "Jim Crow Street Cars," November 7, 1902.
121. *Chicago Defender*, "No 'Jim-Crow' Street Cars in Washington," December 21, 1912.
122. *Evening Star*, "Plans 40 Days' Prayer Against Jim Crow Bill," February 16, 1915.
123. One of the best analyses of the 1919 riots in Washington is Krugler, "A Mob in Uniform." See also McWhirter, *Red Summer*.

124. Krugler, "Mob in Uniform," 56.
125. Gilbert, *Selected Writings of John Edward Bruce*, 149.
126. *Evening Star*, "Colored Men Shoot at Patients and Sentry," July 21, 1919.
127. *Washington Times*, "Negros in Automobile Fire at Group of Sailors; Escape," July 21, 1919.
128. *New York Times*, "Service Men Beat Negroes in Race Riot at Capital," July 21, 1919.
129. Krugler, "Mob in Uniform," 59.
130. *Washington Post*, "Mobilization for Tonight," July 21, 1919.
131. *Evening Star*, "Colored Men Shoot at Patients and Sentry," July 21, 1919.
132. *Washington Times*, "Negros in Automobile Fire at Group of Sailors; Escape," July 21, 1919.

Chapter 8

133. *Washington Post*, "Motor Carriage Here: The Horseless Vehicle Caused a Street Sensation," April 3, 1897.
134. Ibid., "The Street Car of the Future," May 2, 1900.
135. *Washington Times*, "Muck Raking for Old Herdic Line," April 23, 1911.
136. *Evening Star*, advertisement, February 27, 1921.
137. *Washington Post*, "Buses in Capital Will Be Increased," September 25, 1921.
138. *Evening Star*, "Plans and Scope of Local Merger," September 29, 1912.
139. Kohler, *Capital Transit*, 9.
140. See Kohler, *Capital Transit*.
141. Ibid., 9–12.
142. *Washington Post*, "The Traction Merger," December 23, 1932.
143. Ibid., "Merger of Car Services Praised," October 1, 1933.
144. *Washington Herald*, "Is the Capital Traction Trying to Kill Merger?," October 20, 1928.
145. *Washington Daily News*, "To Washington Street Car Patrons," June 14, 1929.
146. *Washington Post*, "Street Car Companies Are Advised to Lower Their Fares to Compete with Taxi Service," July 31, 1931.
147. Ibid., "Favors Try-Outs for New Buses," August 3, 1935.
148. Ibid., "62 Buses Replacing Trolleys Set New Pace to Chevy Chase," September 16, 1935.
149. Ibid., "Bus Service Wins Praise of Roberts," April 13, 1935.
150. *Evening Star*, "New Street Cars in Service Today," June 2, 1935.
151. Ibid., "Silent Street Car Put into Service," July 27, 1935.

152. *New York Times*, "Streamlined Trolley Built," December 13, 1936.
153. *Evening Star*, "'Toonerville' Motorman Sees Newest Car," August 28, 1937.
154. Kohler, *Capital Transit*, 45.
155. *Washington Post*, "Outmoded Street Cars," June 21, 1935.

Chapter 9

156. Kohler, *Capital Transit*, 53.
157. Ibid., 261–64.
158. Quoted in a Capital Transit Company memorandum to "Our Patrons and Friends," January 20, 1943.
159. The numbers are for all "platform" employees (those who worked directly on service vehicles) leaving the company in 1942 and 1944, not just employees leaving for military service. See Rucker, "CTCo Goes to War."
160. *Evening Star*, "Woman Given Trial as Operator of Capital Streetcar," October 23, 1942.
161. *Washington Post*, "2 Women Open Training Today Aboard Capital Transit Vehicles," January 6, 1943.
162. *Evening Star*, "Open House Held by WATS in New Recreation Room," July 12, 1943.
163. Kohler, *Capital Transit*, 78
164. Ibid., 71.
165. *Washington Post*, "Capital Transit Agrees to Open Trolley, Bus Jobs to Negroes," December 16, 1942; *Atlanta Daily World*, "Capital Transit Gives In; Hires Negroes," December 20, 1942; *Chicago Defender*, "Capital Bus Official Bows; Hires Negros," December 26, 1942.
166. *Chicago Defender*, "Capital Bus Official Bows; Hires Negros," December 26, 1942.
167. *Baltimore Sun*, "Capital Transit Jobs for Negros Demanded," May 8, 1943.
168. *Washington Post*, "Transit Tie-Up," November 7, 1945.
169. Ibid., "Negro Transit Operators," February 8, 1954.
170. Deiter, *Story of METRO*, 12.
171. *Evening Star*, "Mt. Pleasant Line Streetcars Tied Up Nearly Hour," January 28, 1948.
172. *Washington Post*, "Capital Transit Tightens Belt as Costs Soar," January 3, 1948.
173. Kohler, *Capital Transit*, 95.

174. This was a legacy of the days of horse-drawn streetcars. Tracks were originally laid only on the western side of the circle to make for a shorter connection with the O and P Street loop to Georgetown. Kohler, *Capital Transit*, 108.
175. Quoted in Kohler, *Capital Transit*, 109.
176. Mary Van Rensselaer Thayer, "Ol' No. 1550 Nonchalantly Makes First Run in Newly Opened Tube Under Dupont Circle," *Washington Post*, November 3, 1949.
177. *Evening Star*, "Bus Passengers Voting Selves into Non-Stop Radio Programs," March 16, 1948.
178. *Washington Post*, "Yes, You Still Can Stop the Bus but You Can't Stop the Music," February 6, 1949.
179. Harry MacArthur, "After Dark: Let Radio Invade His Privacy and a Columnist Will Howl," *Evening Star*, March 18, 1948.
180. Kohler, *Capital Transit*, 101–4.
181. *Evening Star*, "Capital Transit Plans to Put 7 Times as Many Radios in Use," October 28, 1949.
182. Ibid., "Exit Transit Music," June 7, 1953.
183. Henriques, *White Sharks of Wall Street*, 76–77.
184. Weinberger, "What's in a Name?," 4–5.
185. *Evening Star*, "SEC Action Due in Transit Stock Sale Next Week," June 11, 1949.

Chapter 10

186. *Evening Star*, "Transit Firm Doubles Dividends; Financial District Is Surprised," August 24, 1950.
187. S. Oliver Goodman, "Capital Transit Pays Record $1 Dividend," *Washington Post*, August 25, 1950.
188. Kohler, *Capital Transit*, 130.
189. *Evening Star*, "A New Year's Message and a Report," January 3, 1952.
190. Ibid., "Transit Passes to Cost $2.10," January 4, 1952.
191. Ibid., "Demand Grows Louder for Transit Probe," January 5, 1952.
192. Ibid., "Letters to the Star," April 9, 1953.
193. *Washington Post*, "CTC's Reckless Course," February 26, 1954.
194. Herman F. Schaden, "Transit Yields Point, Strike Threat Remains," *Evening Star*, June 30, 1955.
195. *Evening Star*, "D.C. Heads Call Wolfson in Strike," July 1, 1955.

196. Ibid., "Traffic Jams Showed No Respect for Rank," July 1, 1955.
197. Ibid.
198. *Washington Post*, "Strikers Are Grim, Bitter at Wolfson," July 5, 1955.
199. *Evening Star*, "Transit Sickness Now in Acute Stage," July 3, 1955.
200. Edward F. Ryan, "Hopes of Transit Peace Are Dashed by Wolfson; He Testifies, Disappears," *Washington Post*, July 13, 1955.
201. Jean White, "Driver, Rider, Policeman Hail End of Transit Strike," *Washington Post*, August 22, 1955.
202. Wes Barthelmes, "Strike Aid to Transit of Future, Says Lane," *Washington Post*, August 28, 1955.
203. Kohler, *Capital Transit*, 146.
204. *Evening Star*, "Streetcar Retention Is Urged in Report," October 5, 1955.
205. *Washington Post*, "O. Roy Chalk, D.C. Transit Owner Before Metro System, Dies at Age 88," December 2, 1995.
206. Ibid., "Cool Transit," July 24, 1957.
207. Ibid., "Buses Supplant Two Trolley Lines," September 7, 1958.
208. Ibid., "Plea to Keep Streetcars Gets Support," August 24, 1958.
209. John McKelway, "More of DC Transit's Pleasant Familiar Noises Are Stilled Forever," *Evening Star*, January 3, 1960.
210. Ibid., "40 Make Final Trip on Cabin John Trolley," *Evening Star*, January 4, 1960.
211. Morton Mintz, "PUC Hears Trolley Backers Plead for Continued Service," *Washington Post*, April 11, 1961.
212. Kohler, *Capital Transit*, 163.
213. *Washington Post*, "Streetcars Mar Sleep on U St.," December 12, 1961.
214. Jack Eisen, "Trolley Runs Out of Juice After 99 Years," *Washington Post*, January 28, 1962.
215. *New York Times*, "Capital Trolleys Reach End of Line," January 28, 1962.
216. *Washington Post*, "Ring Out the Old," January 31, 1962.

Chapter 11

217. Henry G. Manne, "The Original Corporate Raider," *Wall Street Journal*, January 18, 2008.
218. Schrag, *Great Society Subway*, 175–79.
219. Jack Eisen, "His Empire Is Smaller, but He's Not Unhappy," *Washington Post*, February 8, 1978.
220. Kohler, *Capital Transit*, 301–8.

221. *Evening Star*, "Bargain of the Week: 414 Used Streetcars," January 21, 1962.
222. Jonathan Cottin, "'Eventually' the Trolley Tracks Will Be Gone," *Daily News*, November 24, 1969.
223. Cherkasky and Rice, *Remembering Georgetown's Streetcar Era*.
224. Benjamin Forgey, "Dupont Down Under: Trolley Good," *Washington Post*, March 11, 1995.
225. *Washington Post*, "Blight Followed Trolley Lines," September 15, 1974.
226. Wolf von Eckardt, "Trolley, Please Come Back," *Washington Post*, May 31, 1975.
227. Citizens Association of Georgetown, *Report on Restoration of Streetcars and Cobblestones*.
228. *Transportation Vision, Strategy, and Action Plan*, 28–29.
229. Michael Laris, "Key Questions Still Surround Planned Opening of D.C. Streetcar Line," *Washington Post*, October 22, 2014.

Selected Bibliography

Amalgamated Transit Union Local 689. *The Fight to Desegregate the Washington D.C. Transit System.* Parts I and II, undated video.

Atwood, Albert W. *Francis G. Newlands: A Builder of the Nation.* N.p.: Newlands Company, 1969.

Bolles, F.G. "The Rock Creek Electric Railway, Washington, D.C." *Electrical World* 21, no. 2 (January 14, 1893).

Brooks, Noah. *Washington in Lincoln's Time.* Reprint, New York: Rinehart & Company, 1958.

Calamus: A Series of Letters Written During the Years 1868–1880 by Walt Whitman to a Young Friend (Peter Doyle). Boston, MA: Laurens Maynard, 1897.

Capital Transit Company Records, 1862–1956. Call no. MS 442. Historical Society of Washington, D.C.

Carpenter, Frank G. *Carp's Washington.* New York: McGraw-Hill Book Company, 1960.

Cherkasky, Mara. *Mount Pleasant.* Charleston, SC: Arcadia Publishing, 2007.

Cherkasky, Mara, and Bill Rice. *Remembering Georgetown's Streetcar Era: The O and P Streets Rehabilitation Project.* Washington, D.C.: District Department of Transportation, 2013.

Citizens Association of Georgetown, Subcommittee on M Street. *Report on Restoration of Streetcars and Cobblestones.* Washington, D.C., September 9, 1976.

Cudahy, Brian J. *Cash Tokens and Transfers: A History of Urban Mass Transit in North America.* New York: Fordham University Press, 1990.

Selected Bibliography

Cunningham, G.F. "Cable Cars in the Nation's Capital." *The Turnout* (April 1953).

D.C. Transit System Inc. *100 Years of Rail Transportation in the Metropolitan Washington Area 1862–1962*. Washington, D.C.: self-published, 1967.

Deiter, Ronald H. *The Story of METRO: Transportation and Politics in the Nation's Capital*. Glendale, CA: Interurban Press, 1985.

Dickens, Charles. *American Notes for General Circulation*. London: Chapman & Hall, 1842.

Feeley, John J., Jr., and Rosie Dempsey. *Brookland*. Charleston, SC: Arcadia Publishing, 2011.

French, Roderick S. "Chevy Chase Village in the Context of the National Suburban Movement, 1870–1900." *Records of the Columbia Historical Society* 49 (1974). Columbia Historical Society, Washington, D.C.

Furgurson, Ernest B. *Freedom Rising: Washington in the Civil War*. New York: Alfred A. Knopf, 2004.

Gilbert, Peter, ed. *The Selected Writings of John Edward Bruce: Militant Black Journalist*. New York: Arno Press, 1971.

Goode, James M. *Capital Losses: A Cultural History of Washington's Destroyed Buildings*. 2nd ed. Washington, D.C.: Smithsonian Books, 2003.

Goode, James M. "Four Salutes to the Nation: The Equestrian Statues of General Andrew Jackson." *White House History*, no. 27 (2010). White House Historical Association, Washington, D.C.

Green, Constance McLaughlin. *The Secret City: A History of Race Relations in the Nation's Capital*. Princeton, NJ: Princeton University Press, 1967.

———. *Washington: A History of the Capital, 1800–1950*. Princeton, NJ: Princeton University Press, 1962.

Griffin, Eugene, Captain, U.S. Army Corps of Engineers. *Motive Power for Street Cars*. U.S. Senate Misc. Doc. No. 84, March 20, 1888.

Gutheim, Frederick, and Antoinette J. Lee. *Worthy of the Nation: Washington, DC, from L'Enfant to the National Capital Planning Commission*. 2nd ed. Baltimore, MD: Johns Hopkins University Press, 2006.

Hansen, Stephen A. *Kalorama Triangle: The History of a Capital Neighborhood*. Charleston, SC: The History Press, 2011.

Henriques, Diana B. *The White Sharks of Wall Street: Thomas Mellon Evans and the Original Corporate Raiders*. New York: Scribner, 2000.

Hilton, George W. *The Cable Car in America*. Berkeley, CA: Howell-North Books, 1971.

A History of the Amalgamated Transit Union. Washington, D.C.: Amalgamated Transit Union, 1992.

Selected Bibliography

Hunt, Gaillard, ed. *The Writings of James Madison.* Vol. 8, *1808–1819.* New York: Knickerbocker Press, 1908.

Ingham, John N. *Biographical Dictionary of American Business Leaders.* Vol. 4. Westport, CT: Greenwood Press, 1983.

Junior League of Washington. *The City of Washington: An Illustrated History.* Reprint, New York: Wings Books, 1992. Originally published in Washington, D.C., 1977.

King, Leroy O., Jr. *100 Years of Capital Traction: The Story of Streetcars in the Nation's Capital.* N.p.: Taylor Publishing Company, 1972.

Kohler, Peter C. *Capital Transit: Washington's Street Cars: The Final Era, 1933–1962.* Colesville, MD: National Capital Trolley Museum, 2001.

Krugler, David F. "A Mob in Uniform: Soldiers and Civilians in Washington's Red Summer, 1919." *Washington History* 21 (2009). Historical Society of Washington, D.C.

Kukulski, Ray, and Bill Gallagher. *Washington's Trolley System: The Forces that Shaped It, the Benefits that Were Created and the Elements that Caused Its Demise.* N.p.: self-published, March 7, 2009. Available at http://static.wamu.org/d/links/11080.pdf.

Lampl, Elizabeth Jo, and Kimberly Prothro Williams. *Chevy Chase: A Home Suburb for the Nation's Capital.* Silver Spring: Maryland-National Capital Park and Planning Commission, 1998.

Leon William Guinand Papers, 1865–84. Call no. MS 518. Historical Society of Washington, D.C.

Lessoff, Alan. *The Nation and Its City: Politics, "Corruption" and Progress in Washington, D.C., 1861–1902.* Baltimore, MD: Johns Hopkins University Press, 1994.

Levey, Bob, and Jane Freundel Levey. *Washington Album: A Pictorial History of the Nation's Capital.* Washington, D.C.: Washington Post Books, 2000.

Masur, Kate. *An Example for All the Land: Emancipation and the Struggle Over Equality in Washington, D.C.* Chapel Hill: University of North Carolina Press, 2010.

McShane, Clay, and Joel A. Tarr. *The Horse in the City: Living Machines in the Nineteenth Century.* Baltimore, MD: Johns Hopkins University Press, 2007.

McWhirter, Cameron. *Red Summer: The Summer of 1919 and the Awakening of Black America.* New York: Henry Holt and Company, 2011.

Merrill, E.D. "Changing Fashions in Transportation." *Records of the Columbia Historical Society* 48–49 (1949). Columbia Historical Society, Washington, D.C.

Middleton, William D. *The Time of the Trolley: The Street Railway from Horsecar to Light Rail* Vol. 1. San Marino, CA: Golden West Books, 1987.

Selected Bibliography

Miller, John Anderson. *Fares, Please! A Popular History of Trolleys, Horsecars, Streetcars, Buses, Elevateds and Subways*. New York: Dover Publications Inc., 1960.

Muller, John, and Jason Levinn. "H.A. Griswold and Anacostia's Streetcar Story." "Greater Greater Washington" blog, March 6, 2013.

Muller, John. *Mark Twain in Washington, D.C.: The Adventures of a Capital Correspondent*. Charleston, SC: The History Press, 2013.

Norton, Peter D. *Fighting Traffic: The Dawn of the Motor Age in the American City*. Cambridge, MA: MIT Press, 2008.

Painter, Nell Irvin, ed. *Narrative of Sojourner Truth: A Bondswoman of Olden Time, with a History of Her Labors and Correspondence Drawn from Her "Book of Life."* New York: Penguin Books, 1998.

Peck, Garrett. *Walt Whitman in Washington, D.C.* Charleston, SC: The History Press, 2015.

Post, Robert C. *Urban Mass Transit: The Life Story of a Technology*. Westport, CT: Greenwood Press, 2007.

Rucker, Ken. "CTCo Goes to War." *NCTM* 1, no. 1 (Spring 1994).

Schrag, Zachary M. *The Great Society Subway: A History of the Washington Metro*. Baltimore, MD: Johns Hopkins University Press, 2006.

Scott, Frances, and Anne Cipriani Webb. *Who Is Markie?: The Life of Martha Custis Williams Carter, Cousin and Confidante of Robert E. Lee*. Berwyn Heights, MD: Heritage Books, 2007.

Slater, Cliff. "General Motors and the Demise of Streetcars." *Transportation Quarterly* 51, no. 3 (Summer 1997). Eno Transportation Foundation.

Smith, Kathryn Schneider. *Washington at Home: An Illustrated History of Neighborhoods in the Nation's Capital*. 2nd ed. Baltimore, MD: Johns Hopkins University Press, 2010.

Streetcar and Bus Resources of Washington, D.C., 1862–1962. National Register of Historic Places Multiple Property Documentation Form. National Park Service, 2006.

Street Railways in the District of Columbia. Letter from the Public Utilities Commission of the District of Columbia. Washington, D.C.: Government Printing Office, 1918.

Templeman, Eleanor Lee. *Arlington Heritage: Vignettes of a Virginia County*. New York: Avenal Books, 1959.

Tindall, William. "Beginnings of Street Railways in the National Capital." *Records of the Columbia Historical Society* 21 (1918). Columbia Historical Society, Washington, D.C.

A Transportation Vision, Strategy, and Action Plan for the Nation's Capital. Washington, D.C.: Government of the District of Columbia, 1997.

Selected Bibliography

Weinberger, Alan M. "What's in a Name? The Tale of Louis Wolfson's Affirmed." *Hofstra Law Review* 39, no. 3 (2011).

White, John H., Jr. "Public Transport in Washington before the Great Consolidation of 1902." *Records of the Columbia Historical Society* 66–68 (1968). Columbia Historical Society, Washington, D.C.

Williams, Paul K. *Washington, D.C.: The World War II Years*. Charleston, SC: Arcadia Publishing, 2004.

INDEX

A

Affirmed (racehorse) 201
African Americans 51, 133, 167, 185
Altamont (apartment house) 114
Amalgamated Transit Union 127, 169, 185
Anacostia 15, 77, 211
Anacostia & Potomac Railway 78, 156
Arlington, Virginia 27
Armes, Colonel George Augustus 96
Augusta, Dr. Alexander T. 53
automobiles 143

B

Baltimore & Ohio Railroad 26
Baltzley, Edmund and Edwin 96
Barcelona, Spain 202
Barry Farms 212
Barry, Marion 213
battery propulsion 73, 91
Beeler, John A. 130
Belt Railway 36
Benning Car Barn 169
Benning Road 123, 167
Bethune, Mary McLeod 167
Bierwagen, Walter J. 185
Black, Alexander C. 119
Blau, Helen (streetcar operator) 164
Bloodfield 140
bobtail cars 47
Bolling Air Force Base 212
Bowser, Muriel 213
Brightwood 115, 194
Brightwood Railway 94
Broadwater, John A.B. 183, 185
Brookland 89, 91
Brooks, Noah 46, 52
Brooks, Representative Preston 54
Brower, Abraham 17
Bruce, John Edward (journalist) 140
Bryant, Earley W. (operator) 193
Budapest, Austria-Hungary 72, 74
Burroughs, John 45
buses 143, 154, 163, 189
Byrne, John 34

C

Cabin John, Maryland 96
cable propulsion 65, 105
Capital Railway 83
Capital Traction Car Barn 201, 205

INDEX

Capital Traction Company 103, 105, 110, 114, 127, 130, 149
Capital Transit Company 152, 154, 158, 159, 160, 181
Capitol, North O Street and South Washington Railway 36
Carpenter, Frank G. 44
Catholic University of America 89
center-door cars 118
Center Market 79
Chalk, O. Roy 190, 201, 207
Chesapeake Junction 123
Chevy Chase 96, 149
Chevy Chase Land Company 97, 107
Clark, Florence L. 41
Clark, Representative Champ 136
Clemons, Samuel L. 19
Cochran, Joseph 40
Columbia Railway 36, 49, 50, 111, 172, 212
Committee on Jobs for Negros in Public Utilities 167
compressed air propulsion 92
conduits 203
Congress 24, 25, 27, 44, 50, 54, 59, 62, 64, 74, 76, 78, 92, 100, 120, 123, 129, 136, 152, 178, 183, 187, 190, 194, 203
Congress Heights 83, 156
Congressional Cemetery 79
Connecticut Avenue & Park Railway 35
conspiracy 209
Correia da Serra, José 16
Crawford, Representative Fred L. 183
Crosby, Oscar T. 93, 110

D

Davis, Montgomery 43
D.C. Transit System 190, 201
Decatur Street Car Barn 205
Dickens, Charles 17
District Department of Transportation 204

Doyle, Peter 45
Drew, Reverend Simon P.W. 137
Drum, General Richard C. 95
Dupont Circle underpass 173, 206

E

East Capitol Street Car Barn 205
East Potomac Park 130
Eckington 84, 115, 126, 204
Eckington & Soldiers' Home Railway 62, 88, 143, 156, 193
Edmunds, Senator George F. 63
Edson, John Joy 75
Eisenhower, Dwight D. 187, 190
Electric Railroaders' Association 207
Emergency Hospital 133
end-seat hogs 110

F

Fair Employment Practice Committee (FEPC) 167
Falls Grove 27
fares 121, 154
Fortas, Justice Abe 201
Fort Worth, Texas 202
Freedmen's Hospital 53, 58
French, B.B. 25

G

Gales, Joseph, Jr. 84
General Motors Corporation 209
Georgetown 17, 204, 210
Georgetown & Tenallytown Railway 94
Glen Echo, Maryland 96, 110, 114
Glen Echo Park 194
Glover, Charles C. 65, 103
Goad, Isaac B. 114
Gore, H. Grady 179
Grant, Ulysses S. 45
Great Depression 153, 154
Great Epizootic of 1872 41
gripman 67, 70
Griswold, Henry Adams 78

Index

Griswold's Addition 79
Guinand, Leon William 78

H

Haan, General William G. 141
Hale, Senator Eugene 77
Hallidie, Andrew S. 66
Hanna, John 154
Haviland, Laura Smith 58
Hazen, Melvin 158
Heflin, Representative James Thomas "Cotton Tom" 134
Henderson, Representative David B. 100
Herdic, Peter H. 145
Herdic Phaeton Company 145
hill horse boys 40
Hill, Major George 26
Hoadley, Joseph H. 92
hobble skirts 117
horsecars 36, 91
horses 37, 62, 92, 105
Horton, Draper F. 120
H Street Northeast 172, 212
Hurt, Henry 65

I

Ingalls, Senator John James 76
Interstate Commerce Commission 120, 180, 182

J

Jim Crow segregation laws 134
jitneys 146
Jones, Mary "Mother" 129

K

Kennedy, John F. 194
King, Clarence P. 127, 150
Koockogey, Gover M. 194

L

Lane, Thomas A. (commissioner) 189
Le Droit Park 156

Lee, Mary Custis 134
L'Enfant, Peter Charles 15, 226
Libby Prison 84
light rail 211
Love Conduit system 102

M

Managasset 113
Mathias, Senator Charles McC. 207
McKelway, John (reporter) 195
McMillan Commission 63
McMillan, Representative John L. 194
Mercantonio, Representative Vito 169
Merrill, Edward D. 164, 167, 172, 183
Metropolitan Coach Company 146
Metropolitan Railroad 33, 37, 41, 43, 50, 55, 73, 78, 101, 126, 205
Mills, Clark 23
Morse, Senator Wayne L. 194
Mount Pleasant 156, 159, 172, 196
movie palaces 153
Murch Chariot 145

N

National Association for the Advancement of Colored People (NAACP) 139, 140, 167
National Capital Trolley Museum 207
National City Lines 209
National Hotel 29
Navy Yard Bridge 78, 83
Navy Yard Car Barn 197, 201, 205
Newlands, Senator Francis G. 96, 106
Norford, Howard (streetcar operator) 176
North American Company 151, 178
Noyes, Crosby S. 63
Noyes, Theodore W. 72

O

Ody, Lawrence 67
Office of Defense Transportation 163
Office of Planning 210
omnibuses 17, 26, 31, 33, 51, 145
open cars 108, 123

INDEX

Orr, Rezin 127
overhead wires 62, 71, 73, 212

P

Parks, Rosa 51
Pascal, Blaise 17
Patterson, Eleanor "Cissy" 174, 206
"Pay as You Enter" 121
PCC cars 157, 162, 173, 192, 201, 208
Peace Monument 45
Penney, J.C. 179
Percherons 38
Phillips, Samuel 126
pitmen 124
plow pits 102, 124
population 16, 62, 130, 160
Portland, Oregon 211
Potomac Electric Power Company (PEPCo) 93, 111, 150, 178
powerhouse 67
Presidents' Conference Committee (PCC) 157
Public Utilities Commission 121, 129, 146, 150, 152, 173, 181, 183, 188, 190, 192
Public Utility Holding Company Act 178
pulled plows 172
Purple Line 211

Q

Quinby, Edwin J. 207

R

radio broadcasts on buses and streetcars 176
Ralls, Charles 139
Randle, Arthur E. 83
Randle Heights 137, 149
Randolph, A. Philip 167
Ransom, Mrs. Frederick L. 116
rapid transit 62, 69
Reeside, John E. 22
Reilly, James (motorman) 115
riots of 1919 137

Roberts, William A. 156
Robinson electric cars 91
Rock Creek Railway 96, 150
Roddenbery, Representative Seaborn A. 136
Roosevelt, Franklin D. 153, 167
Root, Walter C. 68, 205
rush hour 130

S

Sarajevo, Yugoslavia 202
Schoepf, William Kesley 92, 100, 143
Securities and Exchange Commission 180
Sharon, William 96
Sherman, Anna 37
Silver Sightseer 192, 208
Simmons, Bernard 169
Smallwood, William (conductor) 123
Smith, Joseph (laborer) 133
Society for the Prevention of Cruelty to Animals (SPCA) 43
Sprague, Frank J. 71
stables 23
Stephenson, John 17, 24
Stevens, Representative Thaddeus 55
Stewart, Senator William M. 100
St. John's River Shipbuilding Company 179
strikes 82, 126, 186
Strouse, Ben 176
Sumner, Senator Charles 54
surface contact electric propulsion 90

T

taxis 154
Tenallytown (Tenleytown) 94, 137
Thomas, Francis L. 140
Thomson-Houston Electric Company 88
track removal 203
trailers 67
Trans Caribbean Airways 190
Transit Riders Association 177

Index

trolley 62, 72
Truesdell, Colonel George 84, 100, 113
Truman, Harry S 170
Truth, Sojourner 56
Tune, Steptoe T. 32
Tunnicliff's Tavern 17

U

underground conduit electric propulsion 74, 101, 106, 111, 171
Union Railroad 35
unions 126
U.S. Colored Troops 52, 53

V

Vanderwerken, Gilbert 22, 26, 144
Vest, Senator George Graham 62
veterans 138
Von Eckardt, Wolf 210

W

Waite, Morrison R. 45, 50
Walter Reed Army Hospital 115
Washington and Great Falls Electric Railway 95
Washington Asylum 82
Washington Chariot Company 145
Washington, George 15
Washington & Georgetown Railroad 26, 27, 29, 33, 40, 41, 47, 50, 52, 55, 65, 67, 69, 102, 144, 194
Washington Metropolitan Area Transit Authority 201
Washington Railway & Electric Company (WRECo) 113, 114, 127, 149, 205
Washington Rapid Transit Company 148
Washington Traction and Electric Company 93, 112, 133
Washington Utilities Company 150
W.C. Gilman & Company 190
Weeden, John C. 58

Whitehurst, Betty (streetcar operator) 165
Whitman, Walt 45
Williams, Anthony A. 211
Williams, Martha Custis 31
Wolfson, Louis E. 178, 181, 200
Woman's Christian Temperance Union (WCTU) 123
women operators 164
Women's Auxiliary Transit Service (WATS) 164
women's suffrage 116
Wood, Dunn and Deming 206
Wood, Waddy B. 205
workers 83, 122, 164, 185
World War I 130, 138
World War II 160
WWDC (radio station) 176
Wyerxa, Percy S. 147

Y

Yerby, George W. 24
Yerkes, Charles Tyson 119

About the Author

John DeFerrari, a native Washingtonian with a lifelong passion for local history, pens the "Streets of Washington" blog and is the author of *Lost Washington, D.C.* (The History Press, 2011) and *Historic Restaurants of Washington, D.C.: Capital Eats* (The History Press, 2013). He has a master's degree in English literature from Harvard University and works for the federal government.

Visit us at
www.historypress.net

This title is also available as an e-book

CPSIA information can be obtained
at www.ICGtesting.com
Printed in the USA
LVHW061703080321
680885LV00001B/10